ALSO BY KAREEM ABDUL-JABBAR

BROTHERS IN ARMS
A SEASON ON THE RESERVATION
BLACK PROFILES IN COURAGE
KAREEM
GIANT STEPS

KAREEM ABDUL-JABBAR

WITH RAYMOND OBSTFELD

ON THE SHOULDERS OF GIANTS

My Journey

Through the

Harlem Renaissance

SIMON & SCHUSTER
NEW YORK LONDON
TORONTO SYDNEY

🏃 SIMON & SCHUSTER
Rockefeller Center
1230 Avenue of the Americas
New York, NY 10020

For information about special discounts for bulk purchases,
please contact Simon & Schuster Special Sales at
1-800-456-6798 or business@simonandschuster.com.

Designed by Karolina Harris

Manufactured in the United States of America

10 9 8 7 6 5 4 3 2 1

Library of Congress Cataloging-in-Publication Data is available.

ISBN 978-1-4165-3489-1

This book is dedicated to those who had the courage and resolve to participate in the great migration of black people to the cities of North America. The oppressive and often brutal atmosphere of the southern United States and the Caribbean basin motivated these brave Americans to find a place in the world where they could thrive. The promise of America's founding fathers—to allow people to enjoy "life, liberty, and the pursuit of happiness"—was profoundly challenged by their ambition. Their presence determined whether or not the goals of the founding fathers would ever apply to all Americans. Starting in the 1920s, blacks brought their lives and hopes to the cities of America's northern tier in their quest to achieve the American dream. It is to these pioneers that this book is dedicated. Their sacrifices have borne fruit. All black Americans owe them in so many ways; and our nation would have been so much less without them. Their spirit marches on.

KAREEM ABDUL-JABBAR

To my wife, Loretta, a brilliant writer and teacher, whose insights and suggestions make me a better writer. And to my children, Max and Harper, who made me want to write this book with the hope that it would provide more shoulders to stand on so they could see farther than I have.

RAYMOND OBSTFELD

CONTENTS

FOREWORD:
C'MON, GET HAPPY

BY QUINCY JONES

Most people get it wrong. History isn't about showcasing the differences between us and those who lived before us so that we can feel superior; it's about revealing the similarities so we can feel gratitude and humility. Look around. See that guy with the earbuds and iPod jogging by? See that woman driving next to you, her head bobbing to the radio? How about those children on the playground gleefully dancing to the CD their teacher is playing on the boom box? What they have in common with the generations of people who came before them—before there were iPods, or radios, or CDs—is a passion for music.

Russian writer Leo Tolstoy (*War and Peace*) said, "Music is the shorthand of emotion." I'd go Leo one better and say, "Music is the shortcut to happiness." A recent poll of Americans about happiness asked what actions they took when trying to improve their mood. In other words, what did they do to get happier? Most said they sought the company of family and friends. But surprisingly, nearly as many said they played music in order to cheer up. In third place was prayer or some form of communication with God. From this we can see that people rely on music for more than just background wallpaper, it is a source of happiness—perhaps even spiritual fulfillment. This happiness isn't the result of eardrum-busting volume or finger-snapping beats; it's the articulation of emotions that express clearly what a person is feeling but is unable to put into words. Having those emotions expressed is liberating for a person and therefore makes him or her happier. That desire to be able to express our feelings, and the sense of fulfillment we feel when a song helps us do that, is what we share with the cave-dwellers who pounded on animal hides and danced around a fire, with the bejeweled audiences listening to the swelling sounds of a symphony, and the kid on the stoop improvising a little dance as he listens to the latest tune he downloaded. Music is the only thing on the planet that affects the right and left side of the brain simultane-ously—the emotion and intellect.

In *On the Shoulders of Giants*, Kareem Abdul-Jabbar does some-thing no other book of the Harlem Renaissance has done before. He makes the connection between an enormously important time in America, and especially African-American history, and our lives today. He shows how black-faced minstrel shows resulted in the stand-up comedy of Redd Foxx, Eddie Murphy, and Chris Rock. He shows how the political activism of W. E. B. Du Bois, James Weldon Johnson, and Marcus Garvey inspired Malcolm X, Dr. Martin Luther King Jr., and U.S. Supreme Court Justice Thur-good Marshall. He shows how the innovative and daring artistry of Louis Armstrong, Cab Calloway, and Ma Rainey made possible the music of Prince, Alicia Keys, and Bob Dylan.

Beyond the history lesson, though, Kareem offers an intimate account of how the Harlem Renaissance affected him personally and helped shape the kind of man he has become. He details how the values, accomplishments, and dreams of those giants of the Harlem Renaissance influenced his own values, motivated his own accomplishments, and still guide his dreams for his future and the future of his community.

In other words, Kareem shows us why we should feel gratitude and humility.

Introduction:
Our Future
or Our Fate

■ Our youth can be our fate or our future. If young people embrace Black culture, ground themselves in it, and feel compelled to continue the legacy, then they are our future. But if they turn their backs on their Blackness, if they have contempt for their fathers and mothers, if they do nothing but engage in self-congratulatory narratives and music about themselves and imagine that they are actually any threat to this society or that they have any future in it simply by talking negative, then they are not our future; they are our fate.

scholar, co-organizer of the Million Man March,
and Kwanzaa founder RON KARENGA
(quoted in BAKARI KITWANA'S The Hip Hop Generation)

A reporter once asked me, "If you hadn't become a professional basketball player, what other profession would you have chosen?" I'll never forget the shocked look on his face when I answered, "A history teacher."

Yes, you read right. A history teacher.

My interest in history isn't idle curiosity about who inflicted what bloody atrocity on whom; that's merely sordid gossip about the dead. To me, history is a living road map that allows us to see where others have been, what mistakes they've made, and how we can avoid those same mistakes ourselves. Even better, we also see what others have done well and can embrace their triumphs. We can let their accomplishments inspire us to be greater. We do that same thing with members of our family—avoiding mistakes our parents made, following in professions in which they've been successful—so for me, history is like my extended family. Aunt Harriet Tubman. Uncle Frederick Douglass. Cousin Miles Davis.

Sir Isaac Newton, one of history's most significant scientists, put his own world-changing accomplishments in a modest perspective when he wrote, "If I have seen further [than other men], it is by standing upon the shoulders of giants." Now, because I stand seven feet two inches, most people probably think I can see just fine without standing on anyone's shoulders.

They'd be wrong.

My height is a matter of genetics. Can't take any credit there. But who I am, how I see the world, and what impact I want to have on others in my community—that all comes from my heart and brain. And what my heart feels and my brain thinks have been shaped by the many "giants" in my life. Most people can point to the important giants who helped influence their development. Usually it's parents, grandparents, teachers, and religious leaders. Same thing holds true for me. My father taught me to have passion for jazz and basketball, and my mother taught me to have compassion for others. And, because I've always had a keen interest in history, I've had the additional advantage of a whole range of giants from the past. Their thoughts, their accomplishments, and even their mistakes have helped me choose the paths I've walked in my life.

Dr. Carter Godwin Woodson, known as the Father of Black History, once said, "Those who have no record of what their forebears have accomplished lose the inspiration which comes from the teaching of biography and history." One time and place in history provided a powerful inspiration to me. Between 1920 and 1940, in the Harlem section of New York City, some of this country's greatest artists, musicians, writers, actors, and athletes were engaged in a cultural revolution that would change America forever. This time was called the Harlem Renaissance because, like the sixteenth-century Italian Renaissance of Michelangelo and Raphael, it redefined an entire culture. These men and women were determined to change how white America viewed people of color, and as a result of their dedication and raw talent, they produced some of the most influential works and accomplishments in American history. The Harlem Renaissance was like a tidal wave washing through history, especially African-American history, and as a teenager, I was caught up in that massive wave. It swept me along, as it did many other black men and women, and made us what we are today: proud and successful African-Americans who, because we know exactly where we came from, also know exactly where we want to go. We proudly and humbly acknowledge the shoulders we have stood upon to see our future road, and we now stand ready to be those same strong shoulders for others. Hopefully, this book will act as a set of tall and mighty shoulders.

American philosopher George Santayana once said, "Those who cannot remember the past are condemned to repeat it." True enough. But the corollary to that is that those who don't know their own history will never see the *potential* for what they could be. Plenty of people will tell you what you can't do, what you should never hope to accomplish, and why you shouldn't even try. If people listened to such naysayers, nothing would ever get accomplished. Before 1954, conventional wisdom held that it was impossible for a human to run the mile faster than four minutes. Then Britain's Roger Bannister ran it in 3:59.4. A month later, Australian John Landy ran it in 3:57.9. The current record is held by Moroccan Hicham El Guerrouj, who ran it in 3:43.13. Every time someone does something remarkable like that, we all have to acknowledge that we have the same spark within us. Maybe it won't be a four-minute mile, maybe it'll be a poem or painting or a hook shot you never thought you were capable of doing. Until you saw others do it.

The Harlem Renaissance contributed to the man I am today—and the man I hope to be tomorrow. Opening the door to that period of history opened many subsequent doors to guide me. The Harlem Rens basketball team helped me see the kind of athlete I could become. Jazz musicians like Duke Ellington and Bessie Smith helped me enjoy the pleasures of uniquely black music and use that as a sound track to celebrate my place in the black community. Writers like Langston Hughes and Zora Neale Hurston encouraged me to love the written word and inspired me to write books of my own. Such as this one.

So, how did I come up with the idea for this book and its unique structure? Aside from my family, I have four major passions that define who I am. First, I was born in Harlem, which has been the capital city of the African-American community since the start of the Harlem Renaissance back in the 1920s. More important to me than anything else I do, or have ever done (yes, including basketball), is my active participation in improving the lives of and opportunities for all members of the black community. Second, I love basketball. I love the camaraderie and sense of communal purpose I get from working with dedicated teammates toward a common goal. Equally important, basketball provided me and other black athletes with a national and international stage from which to shatter racial stereotypes. Third, jazz is an original African-American art form, so my passion for it is both because of the intensity and playfulness of the music, as well as its importance in black history. I like the idea that all my fondest memories will be orchestrated by a music that links my personal history with the history of my ancestors. Fourth, part of my participation in both the African-American and American cultures is to communicate what I've learned from my unique perspective of interacting with some of the most influential members of both. To use words to create a giant set of shoulders that any reader could climb aboard.

This book focuses on those passions by tracing their origins in the Harlem Renaissance that so inspired me. " 'Some Technicolor Bazaar': How Harlem Became the Center of the Universe" details the rise of Harlem as the Black Mecca. Millions of blacks migrated from the South and West Indies to live in what they saw as a new and attainable Promised Land. " 'Master Intellects and Creative Giants': The 'Talented Tenth' Paint the World Black" presents the brilliant minds behind the Harlem Renaissance, from the intellects that formulated its philosophy to the writers who embodied its spirit. Through their works of literature, they made white America see black Americans in a whole new light. " 'Fairness Creeps out of the Soul': Basketball Comes to Harlem" recounts the exploits of one of the greatest basketball teams ever to play, the Renaissance Big Five, commonly known as the Rens. Despite relentless racism, they defeated the best black and white teams in the country, amassing one of the most astounding records in the history of the game. There is no doubt that they made it possible for me to be as successful as I was. " 'Musical Fireworks': Jazz Lights Up the Heavens of Harlem" follows the evolution of jazz from its modest birth in the slave songs of the South to its adoption as the music of choice of the Jazz Age.

The unique structure of *On the Shoulders of Giants* is an acknowledgment of and homage to African-American history. The chapters are arranged in a call-and-response format, traditional to West African cultures, where it was used in public gatherings to discuss local politics and in religious rituals. African music would use the same call-and-response as a way to mimic human voices and vocal interaction. Slaves brought this means of expression to the Americas, where it became a staple in their community gatherings as well as in their religion and music. Gospel music, the blues, and jazz all use call-and-response, in which one musician will play a melodic phrase and a second musician will respond to that phrase, as if they were having a dialogue. When a preacher makes a statement and the congregation shouts back, that's call-and-response. When a dramatic scene takes place in a movie and the audience hollers at the screen, that's call-and-response. In this book, each chapter describes one particular aspect of the Harlem Renaissance that was significant in influencing me—then I respond

"SOME TECHNICOLOR BAZAAR"

How Harlem Became

the Center of the Universe

■ Harlem! . . . Its brutality, gang rowdyism, promiscuous thickness. Its hot desires. But, oh, the rich blood-red color of it! The warm accent of its composite voice, the fruitiness of its laughter, the trailing rhythm of its "blues" and the improvised surprises of its jazz.

poet and novelist CLAUDE MCKAY

■ It's Harlem—and anything goes. Harlem, the new playground of New York! Harlem—the colored city in the greatest metropolis of the white man! Harlem—the capital of miscegenation! Harlem—the gay musical, the Parisian home of vice!

author EDWARD DOHERTY

■ I'd rather be a lamppost in Harlem than governor of Georgia.

FOLK SAYING

WHEN BLACK WAS IN VOGUE

Once upon a time there was an enchanted land called . . . Harlem. Considering all the transcendent things that have been said about the Harlem of the twenties and thirties, it would be easy to romanticize the place as an elaborate set of a movie musical-comedy extravaganza, filled with bubbly jazz melodies and populated by a happy cast of all-singing, all-dancing cockeyed optimists. But to do so would simplify the complexities of the history-making, life-and-death struggle that was really going on in Harlem. And it would reduce the residents to convenient one-dimensional stereotypes—the same indignities that the Harlem Renaissance fought so hard to erase.

Since the beginning of the twentieth century, Harlem has been considered the unofficial capital of an unofficial country: Black America. Because of that, in the minds of most white Americans, Harlem has symbolized *all* African-Americans—educated or illiterate, urban or rural, cop or criminal. One size fits all.

And that is the problem that Harlem, as a symbol of Black America, has faced from the beginning: there have always been *two* Harlems.

First, there was the idealized Harlem that white people imagined because of its portrayal in white films and in white literature. In the beginning of the Jazz Age, whites concocted "Oz" Harlem, the Technicolor home of sassy black women and musically inclined black men, eager to burst into song or dance at any opportunity. Sure, times were tough and they had plenty of nothin', but, hey, by their own admission (or at least by the admission of black characters created by white writers), nothin' was plenty for them. Whites admired how Harlemites had learned to accept their miserable lot in life with a Christian smile and without pointing any angry fingers of blame. "We could all learn a lesson in humility from them," whites said approvingly. In Oz Harlem, white folk were welcome, particularly in high-class nightclubs such as the Cotton Club, which featured black jazz performers, black dancing girls, and a deferential black staff—but allowed only white patrons. In Oz Harlem, blacks entertained and served, but didn't mingle with whites. Oz Harlem was a white fantasy of perfect race relations, a racist's Disneyland ("the honkiest place on earth"). And thousands of whites visited this Harlem weekly, seeing only what they wanted to see. Like people visiting a zoo who marvel at the animals but ignore the cages.

But behind the velvet curtain of Oz Harlem was the other Harlem—"Daily" Harlem—the one that black people wrote about, sang about, painted and sculpted. The one where black people actually lived, worked, cooked, went to church, gossiped about neighbors, and buried loved ones. This was the Harlem where they raised families, raised rent, and, on occasion, raised the roof. During the Harlem Renaissance of the 1920s and 1930s, those two Harlems—Oz Harlem and Daily Harlem—came to represent the two different ways all African-Americans throughout the country were viewed, not just by whites, but by other blacks as well.

In the end, these two radically different visions couldn't peacefully coexist. For those who were part of the Harlem Renaissance, white America's romanticized ideal of happy black folk singing away their worries and cares only encouraged the poverty and injustice to flourish. It allowed the real problems to be ignored. Especially by white politicians who had the power to change things. Ignoring Harlem, and African-Americans throughout the country, was business as usual for most politicians. As police detective Coffin Ed Johnson says in the film *Cotton Comes to Harlem* (1970), "What the hell do the attorney general, the State Department, or even the president of the United States know about one goddamn thing that's going on up here in Harlem?"

But Harlem would not be ignored.

Jazz legend Miles Davis said, "Jazz is the big brother of revolution. Revolution follows it around." What was going on in Harlem in the 1920s and 1930s was nothing short of a cultural and political revolution. Certainly jazz provided the backbeat, but the revolution itself was orchestrated by a group of confident, educated, and talented young men and women undeterred by the perceptions and injustices of the past, their eyes firmly fixed on the prize: a future filled with limitless opportunities for blacks.

And most of these cultural warriors would live and work and create, even if only for a short while, in Harlem.

HOW HARLEM GOT ITS BLACK

At the beginning of the twentieth century, Harlem seemed an unlikely location for a capital of Black America—or the Mecca of anybody but moneyed whites. Located just north of Central Park, Harlem was where upper-middle-class whites resided in fancy apartments and magnificent brownstone houses. If you wanted to find the majority of New York City's black population, you'd have to travel south of Central Park to the West Side, particularly to an area called the Tenderloin. This was where most of the city's sixty thousand African-Americans were crammed. And living around them, like an army laying siege to a castle, were various groups of whites, mostly Irish immigrants, dedicated to driving the blacks away.

Central Park was a physical border beyond which blacks were not welcome; but money was the practical barrier keeping blacks from living in upscale Harlem. Without equal education or job opportunities, movin' on up to Harlem didn't seem possible. Yet, we know it happened, or this book would be about the Tenderloin Renaissance. But how? Ironically, it was Harlem's desirability among the well-off whites that eventually resulted in Harlem's evolving from ritzy white enclave to the destination for blacks from all over the country, and even from outside the country.

The section of the Tenderloin between Twenty-seventh Street and Fifty-third Street was called Black Bohemia. Black Bohemia sounds almost cheerful, like a lively jazz club or a tropical Jamaican resort. But, in fact, it was a squalid ghetto where black families strove to raise their children amidst brothels, gambling dens, nightclubs, pool halls, and unbearable poverty. In 1911, the average black laborer earned $28 a month; the average rent for a small four-room apartment in Black Bohemia was $20 a month ($2 to $5 more per month than in white neighborhoods). That left only $8 a month to survive. In 1900, *Harper's Weekly* condemned the housing situation:

Property is not rented to negroes in New York until white people will no longer have it. Then the rents are put up from thirty to fifty per cent, and negroes are permitted to take a street or sometimes a neighborhood. There are really not many negro sections, and all that exist are fearfully crowded. . . . Moreover, [the landlords] make no repairs, and the property usually goes to rack and ruin. . . . As a rule . . . negroes in New York are not beholden to property owners for anything except discomfort and extortion.

The rents weren't the most serious problem. Hostility toward blacks reached explosive proportions in August of 1900 during the Tenderloin riots. The spark that lit the fuse occurred on August 12, on Forty-first Street and Eighth Avenue when a white undercover police officer dressed as a civilian attempted to arrest a black woman whom he thought was a prostitute soliciting. When the husband, not knowing the man was a police officer, attempted to defend his wife, the officer clubbed him. The husband then stabbed the officer with a penknife, killing him. Though the husband, because of the circumstances, was exonerated a couple days after the stabbing, police and white gangs roamed black neighborhoods in the Tenderloin looking for vengeance. Innocent pedestrians who ran to the police for protection were shoved into the crowd of rioters by angry officers. Frank Moss, who compiled the affidavits of black victims, said in his account, *The Story of a Riot:*

The unanimous testimony of the newspaper reports was that the mob could have been broken and destroyed immediately and with little difficulty . . . [but that] policemen stood by and made no effort to protect the Negroes who were assailed. They ran with the crowds in pursuit of their prey; they took defenseless men who ran to them for protection and threw them to the rioters, and in many cases they beat and clubbed men and women more brutally than the mob did.

An official investigation not only cleared the police of wrongdoing, but praised them for keeping the situation under control. Yet, "the situation" was anything but under control for black residents, who lived under the constant threat of violence. Realizing that geography was destiny, the residents of Black Bohemia began looking around for someplace else to live—someplace where their children would have a better life than they did. As one Tenderloin resident observed, "Every day was moving day."

Harlem, by contrast, has heaven. White heaven. Thick, healthy trees lined the wide streets and avenues, which were newly paved and bracketed by luxurious apartments and houses. In a way, this was the paradise that public transportation had built. Named Nieuw Haarlem (New Harlem) in 1658 by the Dutch settlers after a Dutch city, and renamed Harlem when the English took control in 1664, the area quickly became a haven for wealthy farmers, who built expansive estates overlooking the Hudson River. Passage to New York City proper required a ninety-minute steamboat ride. That kept Harlem isolated and virtually undeveloped until 1880, when the city constructed an elevated railroad along Eighth Avenue. This access to the west side of Harlem encouraged developers to turn the agricultural fields of Harlem into what they envisioned as a refuge for upper-middle-class whites from the turmoil of downtown Manhattan. Then came even more good news: a subway would be built under Lenox Avenue, making the east side of Harlem a mere eight-minute ride to downtown rather than the hours it used to take by streetcar. In anticipation of the subway, which was scheduled to be completed in 1904, developers began constructing many new apartment buildings. However, so many speculators had the same idea that too many buildings were constructed. By 1902, with two more years until the subway would reach Harlem, and brand-new buildings standing around unoccupied, many of those speculators faced bankruptcy.

In Harlem, necessity was the mother of integration.

Enter twenty-four-year-old real estate agent Philip A. Payton, later known as the Father of Colored Harlem. If anyone was the quintessential example of a Harlem Renaissance man, it was Payton. Despite being a college graduate, the only jobs he could get were as a barber, a slot-machine attendant, and a porter in an apartment building. Payton later recounted the early struggle:

The hardships that my wife and I went through before things broke for us would fill a book. If I have gained any success, to my wife belongs the major portion of the credit. . . . My customary amount of cash to leave the house with was fifteen cents; five cents to ride downtown, five cents for luncheon and five cents to ride back up town at night. . . . I just simply was not making any money. My wife was doing sewing, a day's work or anything else she could get to do to help me along. . . . All of my friends discouraged me. All of them told me how I couldn't make it, but none of them, how I could. They tried to convince me that there was no show for a colored man in such a business in New York.

Opportunities just weren't there, so he made his own and became one of the first black real estate agents in New York. "I was a real estate agent, making a specialty in management of colored tenement property for nearly a year before I actually succeeded in getting a colored tenement to manage," Payton said in an interview. "My first opportunity came as a result of a dispute between two landlords in West 134th Street. To 'get even' one of them turned his house over to me to fill with colored tenants." Though blacks got their first opportunity to move to Harlem to spite another landlord, Payton took full advantage of the chink in the wall. His success was such that he convinced several other desperate white landlords to allow him to fill their vacant apartment houses, not with the white residents they'd hoped for, but with blacks anxious for decent housing and a safe neighborhood. And come they did. It was as if the great sea that was Central Park had parted, and African-Americans fled toward what many considered the New Jerusalem.

Despite the growing African-American population, white landlords refused to give up without a fight. They saw the incoming blacks as invaders and were determined to drive them right back to the Tenderloin. The *Harlem Home News* articulated white fears in 1911: "We must warn owners of property . . . that the invaders are clamoring for admission right at their doors and that they must wake up and get busy before it is too late to repel the black hordes that stand ready to destroy the homes and scatter the fortunes of the whites." Whites responded to the call to arms and counterattacked by forming realty companies for the express purpose of buying any houses in which blacks lived and evicting them. The real estate publication the *New York Indicator* chided that blacks should live "in some colony in the outskirts of the city, where their transportation and other problems will not inflict injustices and disgust on worthy citizens." John G. Taylor, the president of the Property Owners Protective Association, suggested that a "dead line" be built to mark the border between whites and blacks; this demarcation would be in the form of a twenty-four-foot fence (not unlike the one proposed in 2006 between the United States and Mexico).

In 1904, Payton responded by founding the Afro-American Realty Company to buy and lease residences in Harlem that would then be rented to blacks. But aggressive pressure from white real estate agents, including the Property Owners Protective Association, made it difficult for Payton to procure mortgages, or even keep the ones he had. His Afro-American Realty Company was soon forced out of business. But Payton wasn't. Fueled by his failure, he quickly partnered with a wealthy undertaker, bought two five-story apartment houses, evicted the white tenants, and rented to blacks. Two of his salesmen from the defunct Afro-American Realty Company also started buying buildings, evicting whites, and renting to blacks. They convinced other African-Americans to invest in Harlem real estate, including the wealthy St. Philips Protestant Episcopal Church, which bought thirteen apartment houses and replaced the white tenants with black ones. Eventually, white landlords abandoned Harlem. In 1905, only about 4,000 blacks lived north of 125th Street; by 1920, 84,000 blacks lived there; by 1930, 200,000 blacks lived there, which was 60 percent of the population of Harlem. Payton, and the blacks of the Tenderloin, had their revenge: Payton became the most successful black real estate agent in New York City, and the black families of the Tenderloin had a new home—and new hope.

But the black residents of the Tenderloin weren't the only ones in search of hope.

MOVIN' ON UP: JIM CROW AND THE GREAT BLACK MIGRATION

In 1910, while Harlem was developing into a popular black neighborhood among New York City's African-Americans, 90 percent of the black population of the United States still lived in the South, most of them in rural areas. In fact, three out of four black Americans lived on farms. If blacks in the Tenderloin thought they had it bad trying to migrate to Harlem, the Southern blacks had it even worse, contending with severe poverty, discriminatory Jim Crow laws, and frequent lynchings. These harsh living conditions, combined with the onset of World War I, and severe blows to the cotton crop, convinced many to leave the South. Between 1915 and 1930, *2 million* Southern blacks migrated to the North, mostly to New York City, Detroit, Cleveland, and Chicago. In 1910, New York City's black population was 91,709; by 1930, the population had more than tripled to 328,000. Because of this Great Black Migration, the Harlem Renaissance would not only be possible, but necessary.

One major cause of the Great Black Migration was the Jim Crow laws, named after a popular character in minstrel shows, a demeaning caricature portraying Southern blacks as dumb and lazy (see the chapter " 'Musical Fireworks': Jazz Lights Up the Heavens of Harlem"). Certainly many Southern laws reflected the attitude that blacks were more like cartoon characters than human beings. These restrictive laws were a direct reaction to civil rights laws that white Southerners felt were forced upon them by meddling Northern politicians. Immediately after the Civil War ended in 1865, the Republican-run federal government began actively protecting black rights through the policy of Reconstruction. As a result, they pushed passage of the Civil Rights Act of 1866 and the Civil Rights Act of 1875. However, in 1883, the U.S. Supreme Court struck down most of the Civil Rights Act of 1875, ruling that Congress did not have the constitutional power to regulate the conduct of individuals. The Democrat-run Southern legislatures took advantage by passing laws meant to chip away at any federally mandated civil rights.

The first Jim Crow law was probably the 1890 law that required segregation of all railroad cars in New Orleans. This was quickly followed throughout the South by laws restricting blacks from voting through poll taxes and literacy tests, which were not required of whites. Other laws made interracial marriage or cohabitation illegal and forced segregation of schools, restaurants, drinking fountains, and libraries. Mississippi even threatened a $500 fine or six months' imprisonment for anyone who printed or circulated written material that argued "in favor of social equality or of intermarriage between whites and Negroes." Blacks were also sent to prison more often than whites for petty crimes, where, through a convict-lease system, they were forced to labor for no pay. Slavery by another name. In 1863, President Lincoln had issued his Emancipation Proclamation, resulting in the eventual freeing of 4 million slaves. Fifty years later, Jim Crow laws had virtually wiped out most gains Southern black Americans had earned.

Though the Jim Crow laws were harsh, Southern blacks had even more to fear from those acting outside the law. Black farmers were sometimes driven from their land by "white-capping," in which white riders (traditionally wearing white caps to disguise themselves) threatened or attacked blacks. Hundreds of cases of white-capping were recorded, especially in Mississippi. The white-cap fashion statement became an icon of the Ku Klux Klan, which was founded in 1866, as much to fight Northern businessmen as to harass freed blacks. President Ulysses S. Grant used the Civil Rights Act of 1871 (also known as the Ku Klux Klan Act) to shatter the Klan, but it returned again in full force in 1915, inspired in part by D. W. Griffith's classic film *Birth of a Nation*, which portrayed Klansmen as romantic heroes. This time around, the Klan went national, with millions of Americans eager to join their ranks. By 1920, the same year that the Harlem Renaissance was hitting its stride and black music and literature were being noticed on an international level, KKK membership had risen to include a massive 15 percent of eligible Americans. As African-Americans began to achieve more rights, opportunities, and success, a white backlash arose like a giant tidal wave to attempt to stop the progress.

Lynching was one popular method of stopping this progress. Between 1889 and 1918, 2,522 blacks were lynched, 79 percent in Southern communities. Causes for being lynched included everything from homicide to theft to "insult to a white person." In 1906, Atlanta, Georgia, was the site of one of the most violent race riots in history. The local press had begun publishing unsubstantiated accounts of black men assaulting white women (the one charge that seemed to have the most effect in inspiring white violence) and urging the formation of a local Ku Klux Klan. White mobs responded by roaming through black neighborhoods beating and killing blacks and destroying their homes and businesses. The black president of a theological society was pistol-whipped by the police officer he'd run to for help. The violence continued for days, forcing the militia to march in to restore peace. In the end, twenty-five to forty blacks were murdered through beatings, bullets, and lynching. Two whites died, one of them a woman who suffered a heart attack when she saw the mobs roaming outside. Walter White, in his book *A Man Called White*, recounted his experience as a thirteen-year-old black boy facing a white mob:

Father told Mother to take my sisters, the youngest of them only six, to the rear of the house, which offered more protection from stones and bullets. . . . In a very few minutes the vanguard of the mob, some of them bearing torches, appeared. A voice which we recognized as that of the son of the grocer with whom we had traded for many years yelled, "That's where that nigger mail carrier lives! Let's burn it down! It's too nice for a nigger to live in!" In the eerie light Father turned his drawn face toward me. In a voice as quiet as though he were asking me to pass him the sugar at the breakfast table, he said, "Son, don't shoot until the first man puts his foot on the lawn and then—don't you miss!"

A volley of shots from family friends sent the mob scurrying away. Young Walter White came away from that night of terror a changed person: "I was sick with loathing for the hatred which had flared before me that night and come so close to making me a killer; but I was glad I was not one of those who hated; I was glad I was not one of those made sick and murderous by pride."

The effect of the riot spread beyond the confines of Atlanta. African-Americans across the country were reevaluating their approach to civil rights. They began to question the approach of the de facto leader of the civil rights movement, Booker T. Washington, who advocated a passive approach of not doing anything to anger the white masses. Clearly, the escalation and sheer savagery of the violence against blacks argued against it. Black America was searching for new, more aggressive leadership. One leader who would emerge, and be the guiding intellect of the Harlem Renaissance, was W. E. B. Du Bois, who, while on his way to the *Atlanta Constitution* newspaper to protest a lynching, passed a butcher shop. Displayed in the window along with the freshly butchered meat were the severed knees of a black lynching victim. Overcome with emotion, Du Bois returned to his home. Sometime later he would express his outrage at the violence of the Atlanta riots in a poem, "Litany of Atlanta (Done at Atlanta, in the Day of Death, 1906)." But more effectively, he would express his outrage at the *causes* of the Atlanta riots by helping to create the Harlem Renaissance.

Meantime, the violence continued; the lynchings continued. In 1901, George Henry White, a former slave and the only African-American in the House of Representatives, introduced a bill that would make lynching a federal crime. He argued that lynching was a form of terrorism and those who used it should be convicted of treason. As evidence, he showed that of the 109 people lynched in 1899, 87 were black. The bill was defeated. Until 1918, not one person in the South was punished for participating in a lynching. The effect of this situation was clear: "Every time a lynching takes place in a community down South," said Chicago's Urban League president T. Arnold Hall, "you can depend on it that colored people will arrive in Chicago within two weeks." Perhaps one measure of the success of the Harlem Renaissance's efforts to reinvent the image of the African-American is that lynchings became rare after the Harlem Renaissance. Still, black Americans had endured this kind of treatment for so long that many saw it as part of the cost of living. It would take a lot more pressure to finally mobilize 2 million people to leave.

FLIGHT OF THE BOLL WEEVIL, FLIGHT OF THE BLACK FARMER

One major source of pressure was a small invader from Mexico. It can be said that some of the weight of the Renaissance was carried into Harlem on the fragile wings of a tiny insect: the boll weevil. In 1892, the boll weevil traveled up from Mexico into Texas and by 1922 had made its way to Virginia. In its wake, this tenacious beetle was destroying 8 percent of the annual cotton crop in the United States. With cotton as the mainstay of Southern agriculture, the effects on the local economy were devastating, especially to blacks, most of whose livelihoods were directly tied to agriculture. Thousands of farmers lost their livelihood and were forced to find some other way to support their families. The boll weevil invasion inspired several blues songs that became mainstays of Harlem Renaissance musicians such as Bessie Smith. Modern variations of boll weevil songs have been recorded by singers from Harry Belafonte and Teresa Brewer to the rock duo White Stripes.

Whoever recorded it, the basic sentiment of catastrophic loss was the same:

The Boll Weevil knocked on my front door,
He said I've come to eat,
I'm gonna starve you plum to death
And get the shoes right off yo feet.

Some historians attribute the enduring popularity of boll weevil songs not just as a testament to disaster, but as a divine retribution visited upon the heads of the wealthy white plantation owners. God was punishing them for their long dishonorable history of mistreating African-Americans.

WORLD WAR I: FIGHT, NOT FLIGHT

The final, and some believe the most significant, cause of the Great Black Migration was World War I (1914–18). America's entry into the war in 1917 had a twofold effect: first, it created an enormous demand for manufactured war material; second, it cut off industrial America's chief source of cheap labor: European immigrants. In 1914, 1,218,480 European immigrants arrived willing to work for little pay; by 1918, the war had choked off that supply to 110,618. In addition, 4 million young, able-bodied men were removed from the American workplace and sent to fight, thereby creating an even larger labor shortage. Industrial America, mostly located in the North, had to look elsewhere for laborers who met their two major criteria: able-bodied and cheap. They looked to the South.

The Great Black Migration wasn't caused just by people escaping, some were being actively recruited. Representatives from Northern companies came South to extol the virtues of moving North. The average wage for black workers in the South was far below what was being offered in the North. Southern black steelworkers made only $2.50 per day, while in the North they made $4.50 a day. And if that wasn't enough incentive, recruiters were helped in this task by black newspapers, particularly the *Chicago Defender*, the largest and most influential black-owned newspaper in the country (for whom Harlem Renaissance poet Langston Hughes was a columnist). The weekly's subscription was 125,000, but two-thirds of the readers lived outside Chicago. The paper relentlessly portrayed the North as a Promised Land of true freedom. Acclaimed Harlem Renaissance writer Richard Wright (1908–60), whose novel *Native Son* (1940) explores the issues of racism he faced while growing up in Mississippi, recalled the siren song of the North that wafted from the pages of newspapers like the *Defender*: "The North symbolized to me all that I had not felt or seen; it had no relation to what actually existed. Yet by imagining a place where everything is possible, it kept hope alive inside of me."

So effective was the *Defender*'s campaign of hope in siphoning off black workers from the South that the paper was banned in many Southern towns. Desperate white employers sometimes actually boarded trains carrying black workers to the North and attempted to violently drag them off. But what these workers were leaving behind was much worse than a beating, and the trains rolled north, one after another, day after day.

The war had inadvertently provided an economic opportunity for Southern blacks at a time when they had run out of options. But there was another, more personal, effect of World War I. Black soldiers came back expecting more from their country. Four hundred thousand of them had just fought a war for democracy, and they wanted to experience the full fruits of that democracy themselves. Certainly they were owed it. After all, they had distinguished themselves as heroes on the battlefields of France, returning with an inordinate amount of honors. The 370th Infantry won 21 American Distinguished Service Crosses and 68 French War Crosses; the 369th Infantry, called the Hell Fighters by the French, were given the Croix de Guerre for gallantry; 171 black soldiers were awarded the French Legion of Honor. Also, the first American soldier awarded the French Croix de Guerre with star and palm was black sergeant Henry Johnson.

While World War I nudged into motion the Great Black Migration, it gave an angry shove to the Harlem Renaissance, providing it with passionate momentum. That momentum came not just from the pride of what black soldiers had proven to white America, but outrage at how white America responded to those accomplishments. At first, most black leaders had supported the war. W. E. B. Du Bois advocated a "close ranks" policy, suggesting that once the common enemy abroad was defeated, blacks could return to the task at hand: improving life for blacks in this country: "This is a crisis of the world. . . . We of the colored race have no ordinary interest in the outcome. That which the German power represents today spells death to the aspirations of Negroes and all the darker races for equality, freedom, and democracy. . . . Let us, while this war lasts, forget our special grievances and close our ranks shoulder to shoulder with our white fellow citizens."

But many white Americans did not want a black shoulder standing with theirs. While the South was pleased to draft blacks into the army, they didn't want them at the local training camps. Black soldiers were routinely discriminated against or outright attacked in Southern towns near boot camps. The discrimination continued even in battle. The French admiration for African-American soldiers was vigorously discouraged by the American military, which, in 1918, sent a memo to the French military titled "Secret Information Concerning the Black American Troops." The memo warned the French not to praise black soldiers too highly because that would "deeply wound" white American soldiers. It also suggested that French officers "not eat with [black soldiers], must not shake hands with them or seek to talk with them or meet with them outside the requirements of military service." This attitude ignored that black troops were killed at a higher rate than white soldiers: 14.4 percent for blacks; 6.3 percent for whites. This had a devastating effect on the morale of the black soldiers fighting so hard in Europe. During one particularly brutal battle in 1918, one Harlem soldier contemplated the irony of his situation, writing in his diary:

I seem to feel that the Germans (who have done so much to destroy the high ideals for which we have fought so hard and were willing to sacrifice so much), after the coming peace, will enjoy more privileges and will have the door of opportunity opened to [them] more heartily than to the American Negro, whose patriotism is above question, and who has given his life's blood on every field of honor, in order to keep the flag which stands for such noble ideals from touching the ground.

Many blacks saw the return of their soldiers from war as a new beginning for African-Americans everywhere. The glorious victories and conspicuous bravery of black soldiers had proved that blacks were equals, and certainly white America would embrace this irrefutable evidence. Du Bois, in an editorial in the *Crisis*, waxed poetic about the new road ahead: "But by the God of heaven, we are cowards and jackasses if now that the war is over we do not marshal every ounce of our brain and brawn to fight a sterner, longer, more unbending battle against the forces of hell in our own land. . . . Make way for democracy! We saved it in France, and by the Great Jehovah, we will save it in the United States of America, or know the reason why."

"RED SUMMER": THE WAR BROUGHT HOME

Yet, during the summer of 1919, when black soldiers were returning from the war, many blacks, including W. E. B. Du Bois, had cause to question their original patriotic "close ranks" stance as well as their optimism about the road ahead. A series of twenty-five major race riots broke out across the country resulting in eighty-three blacks being lynched, and many more being beaten, shot, or burned out of their homes. So bloody were the riots that Harlem Renaissance writer James Weldon Johnson referred to that summer as Red Summer. There had been race riots before, but not this many and not with such widespread devastation. Certainly something was different. Partly, it was the result of blacks returning from war, trained in combat, and less willing to accept insult or injury. The *New York Times* complained about this new black attitude: "There had been no trouble with the Negro before the war when most admitted the superiority of the white race." But blacks had a different take on the events, as expressed by the Southern black woman who wrote to the *Crisis,* the official magazine of the National Association for the Advancement of Colored People (NAACP), edited by W. E. B. Du Bois: "The Washington riot gave me a thrill that comes once in a life time . . . at last our men had stood up like men. . . . I stood up alone in my room . . . and exclaimed aloud, 'Oh I thank God, thank God.' The pent up horror, grief and humiliation of a life time—half a century—was being stripped from me."

World War I had changed the face of Europe, reshaping enemy countries into more manageable chunks. But the Great War had also changed the face of America, reshaping the way blacks felt about themselves, making them more actively resistant to being reshaped into manageable chunks by white America. Red Summer was the war brought home, and every black community was a country under siege, with whites attempting to send the clear message "Now that the war is over, everything goes back to the way it was." Harlem was one such country, and on this point, the Harlem Renaissance might just as easily have been called the Harlem Resistance. Harlem Renaissance writer Claude McKay responded to Red Summer with the poem "If We Must Die," a call to action to every African-American:

If we must die, let it not be like hogs
Hunted and penned in the inglorious spot,
While round us bark the mad and hungry dogs,

Making their mock at our accursed lot.
If we must die, O let us nobly die,
So that our precious blood may not be shed
In Vain; then even the monsters we defy
Shall be constrained to honor us though dead!
O kinsmen! We must meet the common foe!
Though far outnumbered let us show us brave,
And for their thousand blows deal one deathblow!
What though before us lies the open grave?
Like men we'll face the murderous, cowardly pack,
Pressed to the wall, dying, but fighting back.

Ironically, the Great Black Migration did more to better black-white relations in the South than anything else. Finally aware at just how valuable and necessary blacks were to the Southern economy, many whites decided that the best way to stem the migration was by changing the way blacks were treated. Whites began talking to blacks and, more astounding, listening to them and their grievances. White merchants were more solicitous to their black customers, and the custom of arresting blacks for petty offenses dwindled.

Still, the migration continued. One Alabama minister's prayer suggested the migration had biblical origins: "We feel and believe that this great Exodus is God's hand and plan. In a mysterious way God is moving upon the hearts of our people to go where He has prepared for them." Northern cities swelled with Southern immigrants, who had to adapt to the ways of big-city life as well as the ways of the North, often with just as much difficulty as immigrants from foreign countries. So vast was the movement that many people got lost or separated. In 1938, Jack L. Cooper, black radio personality and the country's first African-American DJ, started a radio show called *Search for Missing Persons*, dedicated to bringing together black migrants with their lost family and friends. During the next twelve years, because of his show, twenty thousand people were reunited.

True, there was a hefty cost to the people who, through an enormous leap of faith, uprooted their families to move to a place they'd only heard about. But the possible rewards were well worth it. In 1925 Alain Locke, Howard University philosophy professor and leading voice of the Harlem Renaissance, wrote in his essay "The New Negro" that the causes of the migration to Harlem were more deliberately political than the traditional causes attributed to the mass movement:

The tide of Negro migration, northward and city-ward, is not to be fully explained as a blind flood started by the demands of war industry coupled with the shutting off of foreign migration, or by the pressure of poor crops coupled with increased social terrorism in certain sections of the South and Southwest. Neither labor demand, the boll-weevil nor the Ku Klux Klan is a basic factor, however contributory any or all of them have been. The wash and rush of this human tide on the beach line of the Northern city centers is to be explained primarily in terms of a new vision of opportunity, of social and economic freedom, of a spirit to seize, even in the face of an extortionate and heavy toll, a chance for the improvement of conditions. With each successive wave of it, the movement of the Negro becomes more and more a mass movement toward the larger and the more democratic chance—in the Negro's case a deliberate flight not only from countryside to city, but from medieval America to modern.

Harlem was to be the model of this "modern" America, where blacks arrived daily to get a taste of the life they had rarely dared to demand, but only to imagine. Blacks didn't come to Harlem just to get away from something bad, they were actually choosing to rush toward something good: a place where they would form a "common consciousness," as Locke put it, adding, "In Harlem, Negro life is seizing upon its first chances for group expression and self-determination. It is—or promises at least to be—a race capital. ... Without pretense to their political significance, Harlem has the same role to play for the New Negro as Dublin has had for the New Ireland or Prague for the New Czechoslovakia."

THE REAL HARLEM:
LIFE IN THE BLACK LANE

When migrant the Reverend Betty Neal arrived in Harlem, she thought her dreams had come true: "[When we first arrived,] Bubba and me thought Harlem was Heaven, all the lights and the sights. I asked my aunt, 'Where do all the white people live?' " Statistically, Harlem was only 30 percent black in the 1920s, but those lived in all-black communities, with black storeowners, black real estate agents, and even some black police officers. Those who had moved to Harlem felt they were among their own—in a small city where they could, at long last, relax. Black poet Paul Laurence Dunbar saw Harlem as "the center of all the glory, all the wealth, and all the freedom of the world."

Though Harlem was far from the paradise that many migrants hoped for, it was a lively community bristling with new life, new ideas, and new hope for blacks everywhere. Among the millions of hopefuls who came North, many were the musicians, writers, and artists that would form the core of the Harlem Renaissance, including such notables as writer Zora Neale Hurston (from Florida), jazz musician Louis Armstrong (from Louisiana; see the chapter " 'Musical Fireworks': Jazz Lights Up the Heavens of Harlem"), and sculptor Augusta Savage (from Florida). The Northern migration became so widespread that it also swept up many blacks arriving from the West Indies, including Harlem Renaissance writer Claude McKay and Bob Douglas, founder of the world champion Renaissance Big Five (the Rens) basketball team (see the chapter " 'Fairness Creeps out of the Soul': Basketball Comes to Harlem"). In Harlem, these artists, authors, and entrepreneurs were not only welcomed, but they flourished, achieving the kind of success that would not otherwise have been possible. In Harlem, they had more than a home—they had a purpose.

But once again, there were two Harlems sharing the same space. One was the Harlem that the writers, intellectuals, and artists envisioned as a shining city on the hill, a black Camelot in which they were valiant knights fighting for the cause of "might for right" instead of the usual "white might makes right." The other Harlem was the microcosm of what life in America was like for the average workaday African-American. Those that saw the black Camelot were imagining the black America that they hoped would someday be. Writer Max Ewing rhapsodized, "Harlem is the one place that is gay and delightful however dull and depressing the downtown regions may be. Nothing affects the vitality and the freshness of Harlem." But others would have snorted at such romanticized words, especially those who struggled for their daily bread unaware of any damn Renaissance, seeing only the microcosm, black America as it now was. Yet, what made Harlem so unique and so influential was that it embraced both visions and, as a result, actually was able, at least in part, to make all of black America a little more like black Camelot.

Harlem was much too complex to be characterized by any one group of people or their visions of what Harlem should or could be. Physically, Harlem was about two square miles that resembled the shape of Utah. St. Nicholas Avenue between 114th Street and 156th Street formed the west border, 114th Street the south border, and the Harlem River the border to the north and east. Contained within these borders were the five major neighborhoods of Harlem, each with a distinctive personality: Seventh Avenue, Lenox Avenue, Strivers' Row, 135th Street, and 125th Street.

SEVENTH AVENUE: THE GREAT BLACK WAY

Seventh Avenue, the widest and most attractive of Harlem's avenues, was also known as the Great Black Way because it represented all that was attractive and cultured about Harlem. One could stand on the bricks of 125th Street and gaze all the way up to 145th Street. The lush trees and flowers planted on the median presented a virtual Garden of Eden. This paradise included not only the most prestigious churches in Harlem but also its greatest theaters, such as the Alhambra, the Lafayette, and the Roosevelt. It also boasted Harlem's ritziest hotel, the Teresa. Seventh Avenue also had its intellectual side, housing the offices of several leftist magazines as well as prominent bookstores: the Blyden and the National bookstores, both specializing in African and African-American books. Ironically, paradise's music was provided by the famed nightclub Connie's Inn at Seventh Avenue and 131st Street, which featured music by Fats Waller, but which also catered only to white patrons.

So beautiful was Seventh Avenue that it was Harlem's most popular parade route. Civic leader Marcus Garvey led the followers of his Universal Negro Improvement Association down this street, as did Father Divine, who was not only a popular civil rights activist, but also one of Harlem's wealthiest landlords. A funeral procession down Seventh Avenue proved the deceased had been a person of some prominence.

Sundays on Seventh Avenue brought out the best in people. Residents from all classes dressed in their finest clothes to simply stroll down the street. As Harlem Renaissance writer James Weldon Johnson wrote, "This was not simply going out for a walk; it is like going out for an adventure." Activist Malcolm X, a onetime resident of Harlem, echoed that sentiment: "Up and down along and between Lenox and Seventh and Eighth Avenues, Harlem was like some technicolor bazaar." Harlem Renaissance writer Wallace Thurman's 1928 account of Seventh Avenue in "Negro Life in New York's Harlem" still provides the most vivid description:

Negro Harlem is best represented by Seventh Avenue. . . . It is a grand thoroughfare into which every element of Harlem population ventures either for reasons of pleasure or of business. . . . Seventh Avenue is majestic yet warm, and it reflects both the sordid chaos and the rhythmic splendor of Harlem. From five o'clock in the evening until way past midnight, Seventh Avenue is one electric-lit line of brilliance and activity, especially during the spring, summer and early fall months. Dwelling houses are close, overcrowded and dark. Seventh

Avenue is the place to seek relief. People everywhere. Lines of people in front of the box offices of the Lafayette Theater at 132nd Street, the Renaissance motion picture theaters at 138th Street and the Roosevelt Theater at 145th Street. Knots of people in front of the Metropolitan Baptist Church at 129th Street and Salem M.E. Church, which dominates the corner at 129th Street. People going into the cabarets. People going into speakeasies and saloons. . . . It is a civilized lane with primitive traits, Harlem's most representative street.

> Seventh Avenue was indeed Harlem's Garden of Eden, filled with people trying to show what was best about their community. And every Sunday it paraded the spiritual hopes of Harlem for all to see—and emulate.

LENOX AVENUE: JUNGLE ALLEY

Seventh Avenue may have represented Harlem's spirit and soul, but it was Lenox Avenue that was Harlem's loins, exuding sensuality from every street corner and alleyway. When the sun went down, every deadly sin came out and danced openly in the streets. Brightly lit nightclubs and speakeasies tempted all within sight to enter and taste the forbidden fruits. This was the place *Collier's* magazine was referring to when in the twenties it described Harlem as "a national synonym for naughtiness" and a "jungle of jazz."

Yet, apart from the glitzy nightclubs, the rest of Lenox Avenue was mired in a sweaty struggle for daily survival. All those wonderful new apartment buildings that had been erected during the building boom were now being rented at rates much higher than comparable apartments anywhere else in Manhattan. These extortionary rates were being charged by both white and black landlords. To make things worse, the apartments were being rented to people who, on average, made less money than whites who were paying less in rent. To afford to live in these apartments, the tenants subdivided their apartments, subletting rooms or even floor space to other families. The result was massive overcrowding that left entire blocks with inadequate sanitation, high rates of unemployment, and even higher rates of crime. Once again, Harlem Renaissance writer Wallace Thurman provides a vibrant account:

Lenox Avenue knows the rumble of the subway and the rattle of the crosstown street car. It is always crowded, crowded with pedestrians seeking the subway or the street car, crowded with idlers from the many pool halls and dives along its line of march, crowded with men and women from the slum district which it borders on the west and Fifth Avenue borders on the east. Lenox Avenue is Harlem's Bowery. It is dirty and noisy, its buildings ill-used, and made shaky by the subway underneath. At 140th Street it makes its one bid for respectability. On one corner there is Tabb's Restaurant and Grill, one of Harlem's most delightful and respectable eating houses; across the street is the Savoy building, housing a first-class dance hall, a motion picture theater and many small business establishments behind its stucco front. But above 141st Street Lenox Avenue gets mean and squalid, deprived of even its crowds of people, and finally peters out into a dirt pile, before leading to a carbarn at 147th St.

But that wasn't the part of Lenox Avenue that visitors came to see. White tourists were drawn to Harlem to experience not the Garden of Eden of Seventh Avenue, but Lenox Avenue's Jungle Alley, with all the dark moral chaos the word *jungle* implies. This is where eager whites and blacks alike came in large numbers to have their most sensuous desires fulfilled, from the simple thrills of gambling and illegal speakeasies (during the Prohibition era, 1919–33), to the darker needs of hard drugs and harder prostitutes. Thurman explained the attraction: "To call yourself a New Yorker you must have been to Harlem at least once. Every up-to-date person knows Harlem, and knowing Harlem generally means that one has visited a night club or two. These night clubs are now enjoying much publicity along with the New Negro and Negro art. They are the shrines to which white sophisticates, Greenwich Village artists, Broadway revellers and provincial commuters make eager pilgrimage."

The fancy nightclubs of Lenox Avenue were the painted face of Harlem that most white outsiders saw. To many, Lenox Avenue was a nonstop party celebrating all things African-American, from the music to the food to the dance. This aspect of the black lifestyle inspired important artists of the time, including Archibald Motley and Palmer Hayden. Many blacks believed that the whites that came to Lenox Avenue to experience this joyous and artistic side of black culture could not help but see just how rich and diverse of a people they truly were. Surely that would go a long way toward promoting better race relations. Unfortunately, beneath the romanticized frivolity of Jungle Alley lurked a harsher, more terrifying truth. There were indeed two Harlems: one that did celebrate African-American culture and heritage, and one that exploited and abused it.

Jungle Alley, also known as The Street, Paradise Valley, and The Stroll, had the highest density of nightclubs and cabarets in New York City. And certainly nightclubs filled with dancing girls, famous jazz musicians, mobsters, illegal booze, and international celebrities are much more romantic than some intense young writer quietly sitting in his room scribbling about the unjust plight of the Negro. But these famous, and infamous, clubs did as much damage as good to the cause of the African-American. While they promoted and celebrated the original music of black Americans, they also promoted a false, rose-colored image that kept white America from recognizing the real problems faced by African-Americans in Harlem and across the country.

This was the notorious area that had become popularized in literature because anything was for sale here, and to keep the customers flocking in, Lenox Avenue maintained a *Picture of Dorian Gray* persona. If visitors focused on the many ritzy nightclubs that featured dynamic jazz and dancing revues, this section of Harlem seemed giddy with innocent celebration of life. But if they looked in on the buildings where the locals lived, they'd catch a glimpse of the nastier soul of the place—the run-down apartment houses and dilapidated buildings hidden in the dark shadows cast by the bright lights of the resplendent nightclubs.

But no one was interested in looking in those shadows.

These two Harlems were characterized by two of Jungle Alley's most famous, but radically different, clubs: the Cotton Club and, a couple blocks to the west, the Renaissance Casino and Ballroom. The two clubs came to define the two Harlems—Harlem Light and Harlem Dark—as clearly as the blue and gray uniforms of the Civil War. The Cotton Club symbolized how white America perceived African-Americans: as happy, dancing children, obsessed with sensuality and therefore incapable of sophisticated thoughts or actions. The Renaissance Casino and Ballroom symbolized the ideals of self-reliance and community values that the Harlem Renaissance was preaching.

The Cotton Club was part of a bizarre tradition in Harlem that included other fancy clubs such as Connie's Inn and Small's Paradise. These clubs, though operating in the heart of black Harlem, catered exclusively to white customers. Yet, in their shows and decor they still promoted an idealized but wholly inaccurate black lifestyle similar to those in minstrel shows. Menacing bouncers were stationed at the doors to make sure no black faces were admitted to the establishments, located on the same blocks where these black men and women lived. Eleven such segregated clubs were listed in *Variety*, but the most famous and popular of the group was the Cotton Club, the largest, fanciest, highest-priced, which featured the most extravagant shows.

Originally, the club was owned by a black icon who, in the eyes of other African-Americans, stood for defiance of white racism. Former heavyweight champion Jack Johnson—an amateur cellist and fiddler and frequenter of Harlem's raucous nightlife—bought the struggling Douglas Casino in 1920, changing the name to the Club Deluxe. But Johnson was unable to make the club any more successful than the predecessor. By 1923, Johnson sold it to mobster Owney Madden, who was in prison at the time for manslaughter. Madden, who also owned the popular Stork Club and Silver

Slipper, which were frequented by the rich and famous from around the world, wanted the Cotton Club to be equally renowned, so he poured a significant amount of money into renovation. For its decor, he chose to re-create, in the middle of Harlem, the plantation South and its attitude, from which so many Harlemites had fled. From their elegantly appointed tables, white patrons could view the three nightly stage shows. The shows were written exclusively for the club and they were so extravagant that they rivaled even Broadway shows. In fact, some of the shows did move on to Broadway. The revues featured some of the most famous black performers of the day, including Lena Horne, Billie Holiday, Ethel Waters, Bill "Bojangles" Robinson, Edith Wilson, and Earl "Snakehips" Tucker. Duke Ellington and his orchestra were the house band from 1927 to 1931, and again in 1933. Between 1931 and 1933, Cab Calloway took over as bandleader. Most important, the club served as the principal East Coast outlet for "Madden's No. 1" beer.

Other Harlem clubs trying to compete with the Cotton Club were sometimes met with violence. The Plantation Club tried to imitate the Cotton Club's style and venue by hiring Cab Calloway and his orchestra away from the Cotton Club. Calloway's "Minnie the Moocher" routine was famous and a big attraction. Cotton Club owner Madden was not pleased, so he sent a few of his men over to the Plantation Club to break up the place. They destroyed tables and chairs, shattered glasses, and dragged the bar out to the curb. Calloway returned to the Cotton Club.

Despite the Cotton Club's gangster origins—in fact, because of it—this became, in Lady Mountbatten's words, "The Aristocrat of Harlem" for the white elite of New York. The wealthy patrons, bedecked in their finest jewelry, hoped to be thrilled with a glimpse of Al Capone or Owen Madden. Mob bouncers met patrons at the door, enforcing the strict color code of whites only. Inside, the waiters, dancers, musicians, and stage performers were black, but were not permitted to socialize with the customers. The young girls of the chorus line had to be under twenty-one, over five feet six inches tall, and of light complexion. This discriminatory policy gained even more respectability because of the white celebrities who frequented the Cotton Club, including Mayor Jimmy Walker and singer Jimmy Durante. In his autobiography, *The Big Sea*, Langston Hughes comments on the growing resentment within the black community: "Nor did ordinary Negroes like the growing influx of whites toward Harlem after sundown, flooding the little cabarets and bars where formerly only colored people laughed and sang, and where now the strangers were given the best ringside tables to sit and stare at the Negro customers—like amusing animals in a zoo."

Rather than be outraged, the white public embraced the Cotton Club and its Uncle Remus vision of African-Americans. In 1927, CBS began broadcasting live shows from the Cotton Club, sometimes five or six a week. This created an unexpected opportunity: while the cartoonish portrayal of black culture made the Cotton Club popular enough to have a radio show, the show also provided a platform for the innovative jazz music of Duke Ellington, which led many white listeners to embrace authentic black culture and led to the dispelling of the silly stereotypes from the Cotton Club.

The Cotton Club and other segregated nightclubs didn't just slap local residents in the face, but promoted and gave respectability to a vision of African-Americans that the Harlem Renaissance was desperately combating. They not only confirmed humiliating stereotypes, but led significant numbers of blacks to embrace those same self-deprecating ideals. The conventional wisdom was that white culture and white perceptions of beauty, including lighter skin and straight hair, were somehow superior. These were the physical requirements for many of the performers at the segregated clubs. Consequently, many Harlemites chose to emulate, rather than reject, the twisted perceptions embodied by the Cotton Club.

This obsession with copying white ideals of beauty was most evident in the practices of lightening skin color and hair straightening, or conking. Even the most politically conscious magazines advertised creams that promised to lighten dark skin (products that are still widely advertised today). Ironically, one of the Harlem Renaissance's most important figures was socialite and heiress A'Leila Walker, who inherited her money from her mother, Madame C. J. Walker, the child of ex-slave sharecroppers, who built a hair-straightening empire that had made her over $2 million by her death in 1919. A'Leila Walker spent much of her hair-conking inheritance promoting African-American artists and writers of the Harlem Renaissance. In Alice Walker's novel *The Color Purple* (part of which is set during the Great Migration and the Harlem Renaissance), the character Shug comments on blacks' self-perception as symbolized by conking hair: "Somewhere in the bible it say Jesus' hair was like lamb's wool, I say. Well, say Shug, if he came to any of these churches we talking bout he'd have to have it conked before anybody paid him any attention. The last thing niggers want to think about they God is that his hair kinky."

The intellects of the Harlem Renaissance realized that before whites would see blacks as equals, first blacks had to see themselves that way—and not try to pretend to be white or adopt white ideals of beauty. And the Cotton Club, which promoted the inferiority of black identity, was a major obstacle that had to be overcome.

The other Harlem—the one that was inhabited by the black residents—was represented by nightclubs like the Lenox Club, the Plantation Inn, the Savoy Ballroom, and the Renaissance Casino and Ballroom. These establishments served the black community and were the places that Harlemites frequented for entertainment or to hold social, political, or family events. Many major local events were held at the Savoy, which boasted not only a large mixed-race clientele, but was also famous as the home of the trendy dance the Lindy Hop.

The club that in many ways most represented the ideals of the Harlem Renaissance was over on 150 West 138th Street—a two-story redbrick building called the Renaissance Casino and Ballroom. This was the place that the Cotton Club building had first been erected to compete against. And just as the name implies, this establishment embodied the heart and soul of what the Harlem Renaissance was all about. While the corrupt, mob-operated Cotton Club flaunted its patronizing attitude toward African-Americans, the black-owned-and-operated Renaissance Casino celebrated African-American achievements. This is where many of Harlem's more dignified events took place, including the annual awards dinners held by the NAACP's periodical, the *Crisis*, the magazine that had done the most to define and develop the ideals of the New Negro. Meetings of black unions and clubs were common, including the Brotherhood of Sleeping Car Porters and Business and Professional Men's Forum. Patrons danced to the jazz licks of the house band fronted by Vernon Andrade, as well as other renowned musicians and entertainers such as the Fletcher Henderson Orchestra, Louis Armstrong, Elmer Snowden's band, Rex Stewart, Dickie Wells, Cecil Scott, Roy Eldridge, and Bill "Bojangles" Robinson. While the Cotton Club rejected the black community, the Renaissance clientele reflected the black community. But most important, it celebrated the black community, from its workers to its artists to its writers.

And the Renaissance Casino and Ballroom had one other thing that the Cotton Club didn't have: an all-black championship basketball team, the Rens (see the chapter " 'Fairness Creeps out of the Soul': Basketball Comes to Harlem"). Between band sets, the dance floor would be cleared and the Rens would play basketball to the enthusiastic cheers of the patrons. When the game was over, the hoops would be stored away and the dancing would continue, sometimes with team members joining the customers on the dance floor. More important, the team barnstormed throughout the Midwest, South, and Northeast. Through the team's athleticism and courage in the face of constant racism, they helped spread the gospel of the Harlem Renaissance without even knowing it.

STRIVERS' ROW AND SUGAR HILL:
THE STREET OF THE ELITE

Officially named the St. Nicholas Historic District, the stretch between Seventh and Eighth avenues on 138th and 139th streets was commonly known as Strivers' Row. The nickname was bestowed on the area to describe its residents—African-American doctors, dentists, and bandleaders who were "striving" for a better lifestyle. These individuals were successful despite the economic and social hardships faced by African-Americans at the time. Strivers' Row specifically refers to the three rows of town houses constructed between 1891 and 1893 and developed by the first African-American architect, David H. King, who also built Madison Square Garden and the base of the Statue of Liberty. Other houses in this district were designed by some of America's most prominent architects, including the celebrated Stanford White, who planned the neo–Italian Renaissance houses on the north side of West 139th Street. Each building has a rear courtyard and gated alleyway where the owner's horses could go directly to the stables.

Despite the classy design and pedigree of the architects, the development company was at first unable to sell the houses. Black influx into Harlem and white flight left them empty for years. Finally, out of desperation, the houses were sold to blacks, but only ambitious professionals—"strivers"—were able to afford them. Musicians Eubie Blake, Fletcher Henderson, comedian Stepin Fetchit, preacher/congressman Adam Clayton Powell Jr., and W. C. Handy, the "father of the blues," all lived on Strivers' Row. Wallace Thurman barely conceals his contempt for the place in his 1928 description: "Between Seventh and Eighth Avenues, is 139th Street, known among Harlemites as 'strivers' row.' It is the most aristocratic street in Harlem. Stanford White designed the houses for a wealthy white clientele. Moneyed Negroes now own and inhabit them. When one lives on 'strivers' row' one has supposedly arrived. Harry Rills resides there, as do a number of the leading

Babbitts and professional folk of Harlem." Today, the buildings are all designated landmarks.

Like Strivers' Row, Sugar Hill became the place to live for those who had arrived at the good life. Perched on a bluff above Harlem Plains, Sugar Hill is not a hill and never had anything to do with sugar. The "sugar" nickname is thought to imply that the residents here were living the "sweet life." Jazz musician Duke Ellington, who was on the road and missing his home in Sugar Hill—"where life is sweet"—made the place famous when he cowrote, with fellow Sugar Hill resident Billy Strayhorn, "Take the 'A' Train (Up to Sugar Hill in Harlem)," which became Ellington's theme song. This upscale neighborhood was part of Hamilton Heights, extending from Edgecombe Avenue to Amsterdam Avenue, and from 145th Street to 155th Street. Harlem historian Levering Lewis (*When Harlem Was in Vogue*) described Sugar Hill as "a citadel of stately apartment buildings and liveried doormen on a rock, [that] soared above the Polo Grounds and the rest of Harlem like a city of the Incas." From those exalted heights gazed the elite of the black community, including Harlem Renaissance intellect W. E. B. Du Bois, NAACP leaders Walter White and Roy Wilkins, and civil rights leader the Reverend Adam Clayton Powell Sr.; writers Langston Hughes, Ralph Ellison, and Zora Neale Hurston; singer/actor Paul Robeson; artists Aaron Douglas and Hale Woodruff; jazz musicians Cab Calloway, Luckey Roberts, and Jimmie Lunceford; and other notables such as socialite A'Leila Walker and special counsel to the NAACP Thurgood Marshall, the first African-American U.S. Supreme Court justice. *Ebony* magazine described the residents of Sugar Hill as Harlem's most prominent men and women in law, sports, civil liberties, music, medicine, painting, business, and literature.

135TH STREET:
THE BOULEVARD OF BRAINS

If Seventh Avenue was the beautiful face of Harlem, and Lenox Avenue was its loins, then 135th Street was its brains. This is where the New Negro of the Harlem Renaissance would learn how to come into being. Here on 135th Street many of the literary elite lived, wrote, and performed. The Harlem YMCA provided not only a place to live for Langston Hughes and many other writers (before they became successful enough to move to Sugar Hill), but it also made rooms available for literary groups to share their latest creations. Harlemites would gather at the YMCA to listen to the latest works of Langston Hughes or Countee Cullen.

One of the most formative places in encouraging these artist/warriors was the 135th Street Library, which was the Harlem branch of the New York Public Library. In 1926, Arthur Schomburg, a leading figure in the Harlem Renaissance, donated his vast collection of ten thousand books, manuscripts, and artworks to the library. This magnanimous gesture resulted in the renaming of the library as the Schomburg Center for Research in Black Culture. Here, many of Harlem's literary elite studied the past—and forged their future. Nearly every writer to come out of the Harlem Renaissance did research at this library. (And it was here, thirty-eight years after its founding, a seventeen-year-old Kareem Abdul-Jabbar would wander into the building and discover the wonders of the Harlem Renaissance. See the chapter " 'Mad Medley': How Harlem Influenced My Life.")

The Schomburg Center was more than a passive repository of the past, it was an active participant in making history. Throughout the 1920s and 1930s, the library promoted various cultural activities, including commissioning African-American art for its walls. One of its most renowned commissions was Aaron Douglas's murals called *Aspects of Negro Life*. While 135th Street nurtured the Harlem Renaissance's most famous communicators, it also housed its most popular means of communication among the community.

Here, among the barbershops and beauty salons immortalized by Renaissance photographers James Van Der Zee and Morgan and Marvin Smith, word of literary events, political rallies, and social gatherings were passed along.

125TH STREET:
BASKING IN THE LIGHT OF THE APOLLO

Just a few blocks away from the literary neighborhood was Harlem's commercial hub: 125th Street. Here, among the many shops and department stores, is where much of Harlem shopped. And when they were done shopping, there was entertainment of all kinds: from the classical operas at the Harlem Opera House, to the jazz and blues at the Apollo Theater.

The 1,750-seat Apollo, "America's Finest Colored Theatre," was Harlem's most prestigious theater, featuring performers such as Louis Armstrong, Ella Fitzgerald, and Billie Holiday. A 1937 article from the *New York World-Telegram* described the Apollo:

The theatre stands behind a gaudy neon sign between a haberdashery and a leather goods store. . . . You can buy your ticket at a sidewalk booth (from fifteen cents mornings to a fifty cent top Wednesday and Saturday nights) and enter through a narrow lobby lined with bathroom tiles, glistening mirrors and photographs of such Harlem idols as Ethel Waters and Louis Armstrong. . . . On the rear wall hang three large oil paintings, each featuring several square feet of female flesh. . . . The wallpaper has a recurring motif of a nude young woman.

This is where Harlemites of all walks of life would go to see the latest African-American entertainers. And every performer knew that his or her career depended on how well he or she was received at the Apollo. Beyond providing a venue for many of the Harlem Renaissance's most famous performers who would go on to be embraced by white audiences, the Apollo gave Harlemites a sense of pride in their own culture. The theater produced over thirty shows a week and featured an amateur night that launched many careers, including that of Pearl Bailey in 1934.

SURVIVING IN HARLEM: HEAVEN ON A BUDGET

While the best and brightest of the Harlem Renaissance struggled to create a new image of African-Americans, most of the residents of Harlem didn't know anything about it and couldn't have cared less if they did. As Langston Hughes observed, "The ordinary Negroes hadn't heard of the Negro Renaissance. And if they had, it hadn't raised their wages any." Given some time, they might have appreciated the intentions of the Harlem Renaissance: to use the talents of the black artists, musicians, and writers to force white America to see blacks as intellectual, athletic, and moral equals to the whites. If only they weren't preoccupied with earning their daily bread.

Everyone wanted a piece of paradise. But the constant influx of black immigrants from the South and West Indies caused such overcrowding that residents were forced to face a whole new set of challenges. The density rate for whites in New York City was 222 per acre, while for blacks it was an astounding 336 per acre. Aside from the enormous economic toll, the housing congestion had additional fallout. More people crammed into smaller space resulted in quicker deterioration of the properties, making them less attractive and more dangerous. In addition, the high density of people meant higher rates of communicable diseases and higher mortality rates. Between 1923 and 1927, the death rate from pneumonia for whites in New York City was 124 per 100,000; for blacks in Harlem it was nearly double that, 244 per 100,000. The death rate from tuberculosis for white New Yorkers was 76 per 100,000; for black Harlemites it was 183 per 100,000. Hundreds of Harlem residents died each year for no other reason than color. For some, it was hard to tell the difference between the oppressive old South they had run away from and their new home in the North. The unnecessary death of a loved one was just as heartbreaking, whether at the hands of an angry Southern white mob—or the turned backs of a neglectful Northern white citizenry.

It would be poetic to report that such adversity resulted in the pulling together of Harlem's African-Americans into a one-for-all-and-all-for-one community. But that, too, would be Disney stereotyping. Human interactions are much grittier and more complicated. In fact, adversity sometimes turned Harlemites against each other. Ironically, much of this internal conflict was based on the color of skin and where you were from. Racism and regionalism of blacks against blacks threatened to destroy the community from within. Jervis Anderson describes the tension in his book *This Was Harlem, 1900–1950:* "Northern-born blacks looked down on the speech and manners of those who had recently arrived from the rural South; an upper class, consisting mainly of light-skinned professionals, fought to be recognized as Harlem's most representative social grouping; West Indians and black Americans often glared xenophobically at one another across borders of accent and cultural style."

The discrimination of American blacks against West Indians was especially significant since they provided so much of the talent and momentum for the Harlem Renaissance. Seventeen percent of blacks in New York City were foreign-born, yet one-third of the city's black professionals, physicians, dentists, and lawyers were foreign-born. Most of them West Indians. The West Indians who came to Harlem were in general more educated and highly trained than other immigrants. Many had left their homelands less because of racism than because of a static economy. Though they were certainly aware of the blatant racism in the United States, they came from a society in which they were the majority, so the racism was less unrelenting. In their society, people were white, black, or mulatto, so the many mulattoes who came were not prepared to suddenly be referred to and treated as black. In their countries, successful blacks held a higher social status than poor whites. The

West Indians had not been raised, as had many American blacks, with an attitude of submission and nonresistance. The result was the rise of many West Indians to prominence in the black community during the Harlem Renaissance, including activist Marcus Garvey, Rens founder and Renaissance Casino and Ballroom manager Bob Douglas, and prominent author Claude McKay.

For most of the black residents of Harlem, daily life could be summed up in one frustrating word: rent. Harlemites were paying significantly more money for housing than whites in similar neighborhoods in Manhattan. By 1938, the average apartment rent in Harlem was $30 per month, while a comparable apartment elsewhere in Manhattan went for only $18. Not only were blacks earning less money, they had to pay higher rents. Harlem renters were paying 40 percent of their income on rent alone. And if the rent wasn't paid by Sunday night, on Monday morning the landlord would have all their furniture on the street and be renting out the rooms to the next eager person. Desperate to keep their homes, residents began throwing paid-admission parties to raise the rent money.

Rent parties became a common fixture in Harlem—and a major source of community entertainment. Usually thrown on Saturday and Thursday nights, when domestics had the night off, these events were often much more elaborate than just inviting a few close friends over. Flyers were printed and distributed through pool halls, Laundromats, and even handed out to people on the street. Rooms were cleared of furniture, except for chairs that had been borrowed from the local undertaker. Strangers and friends alike paid anywhere from ten to fifty cents and were, for that amount, treated to a full night of live music and even livelier companions. And most important: the rent got paid. Wallace Thurman describes the liveliness—as well as the necessity—of the typical rent party:

There may be only piano music, there may be a piano and a drum, or a three or four-piece ensemble. Red lights, dim and suggestive, are in order. The parlor and the dining room are cleared for the dance, and one bedroom is utilized for hats and coats. In the kitchen will be found boiled pigs' feet, ham hock and cabbage, hopping John (a combination of peas and rice), and other proletarian dishes. . . . The dancers will use their bodies and the bodies of their partners without regard to the conventions. There will be little restraint. . . . And in addition to the liquor sold by the house, flasks of gin, and corn and rye will be passed around and emptied. Here "low" Harlem is in its glory, primitive and unashamed.

I have counted as many as twelve such parties in one block, five in one apartment house containing forty flats. . . . It serves a real and vital purpose, and is as essential to "low Harlem" as the cultured receptions and soirees held on "strivers' row" are to "high Harlem."

House rent parties have their evils; it is an economic evil and a social evil that makes them necessary, but they also have their virtues. . . . House rent parties do provide a source of revenue to those in difficult financial straits, and they also give lonesome Harlemites, caged in by intangible bars, some place to have their fun and forget problems of color, civilization, and economics.

While the rent party was an invaluable economic survival tool for many residents, it was also a community social event that drew the people of Harlem together. In addition, rent parties provided basic training for many of the finest jazz musicians to emerge from the Harlem Renaissance, including Willie "the Lion" Smith, Fats Waller, Duke Ellington, Luckey Roberts, Mezz Mezzrow, Eubie Blake, and James P. Johnson. Several popular songs were composed about rent parties, the most famous being "The Joint Is Jumpin'" by Fats Waller and Duke Ellington's "Saturday Night Function."

DOES IT EXPLODE?: THE LEGACY OF HARLEM

There could not have been a renaissance without Harlem. So many of the divergent rivers of history—World War I, the boll weevil, the rise of jazz, Jim Crow laws—flowed into one city at the same time, allowing all those elements to mix together and wash through Harlem like a biblical flood, only this time it was a cleansing and nurturing tide. And fed on that water, Harlem grew out of the shadows of white Manhattan—and white America—to become a cultural center that would change the rest of the country.

As it had in the past for African-Americans, change came slowly, and not without reversals. But it did come, and faster than before. Blacks across the country had found a unified voice—a voice that emanated from the neighborhoods of Harlem and spread from coast to coast as if broadcast from a powerful radio station. And, having found that voice, they were willing to raise that voice. Loudly. And often. Harlem had come to represent the distant dream of what life in America might one day be for blacks. And the congregation of minds that created the Harlem Renaissance made it clear that they would not let that dream go gentle into that good night. Langston Hughes expresses that commitment of black voices in his cautionary poem "A Dream Deferred":

What happens to a dream deferred?

Does it dry up
Like a raisin in the sun?

Or fester like a sore—
And then run?

Does it stink like rotten meat?
Or crust and sugar over—
like a syrupy sweet?

Maybe it just sags
like a heavy load.

Or does it explode?

"MAD MEDLEY"

How Harlem
Influenced My Life

BY KAREEM ABDUL-JABBAR

The Harlem I was born into in 1947 was no longer the Mecca of the New Negro, the Capital of Black America, or Pickaninny Paradise. It was just plain old Harlem, a bunch of rectangular neighborhoods, some well-off, some fallen on hard times, where most people tried their best to make a decent living and raise a decent family. Fancy limousines carrying white celebrities no longer prowled the streets looking for the next hot jazz club to experience the "jungle passions" of African-American dancers and musicians. White America had long since stopped finding Harlem exotic and was looking around for some other in vogue ethnic group to embody the sensual desires they themselves could only express through a "primitive" proxy.

The one thing my Harlem had in common with the heyday of the Harlem Renaissance was that most of the faces in Harlem were still black. The families walking on the streets were black, the teller at the bank was black, the faces on the billboards were black, even the cop on the corner was black. Having black skin didn't mean you were automatically a good human being, but at least here in Harlem you were more likely to be judged, in Dr. King's words, by the content of your character rather than the color of your skin. Writer Wallace Thurman, the Harlem Renaissance's most incisive chronicler, said that "the sight of Harlem gives any Negro a feeling of great security." That was true then, it was true when I was there, and it's still true now. Though it may no longer be the bubbling cauldron of black artistic magic that it was during the Renaissance, it is still something of a homeland for black Americans.

The Harlem of my youth isn't the Harlem of Louis Armstrong or Langston Hughes's youth; nor does the Harlem of today resemble the Harlem I used to frequent. Today there's a Starbucks, a Disney Store, an Old Navy, a Gap—and the offices of former president Bill Clinton. But it doesn't matter how trendy or mall-like it becomes on the outside, it will always be populated by people of color who know that shopping at the Gap or the Disney Store won't make them any less black in the eyes of white America. They still have to face that challenge every day. But in Harlem, surrounded by your own, it doesn't have to be faced quite so relentlessly.

During the Harlem Renaissance, tens of thousands of black people came to Harlem from the South or West Indies, all looking for a better life. Many thought it would be some kind of paradise on earth, free of the kind of soul-crushing poverty and humiliating racism they'd lived with all their lives. Among those migrants were some of the greatest teachers, intellectuals, writers, artists, and performers in American history. These men and women had a vision for the future of black Americans, and they had the dedication to try to make that vision a reality. They didn't always agree on the method, but they did agree that great change was necessary, and that they wanted to be an active part of causing that change. Though the Harlem Renaissance is long passed, that activist spirit still pulsates within Harlem. Stand at the crossroads of Malcolm X Boulevard and Dr. Martin Luther King Jr. Boulevard, named after two men with different methods but a shared vision, and you are standing at the crossroads of both the history and the future of

African-Americans. Wallace Thurman once said, "Harlem is a dream city pregnant with wide-awake realities. It is a masterpiece of contradictory elements and surprising types. There is no end to its versatile presentation of people, personalities, and institutions. It is a mad medley." That "mad medley" can still be heard and seen on the streets of Harlem. Harlem remains a place where people of color can define themselves beyond color—as individual men and women—and as members of the African-American community.

I should know, it happened to me.

I was born in Harlem in the summer of 1947; I was *re*born in Harlem in the summer of 1964.

SLOUCHING TOWARD HARLEM

If my high school coach hadn't called me a nigger, I might not have rediscovered Harlem and the Harlem Renaissance until I was much older, when it wouldn't probably have had the same dramatic effect on me.

Though I was born in Harlem, my parents moved us out when I was three. As was common at the time in overcrowded Harlem, we'd been sharing an eight-room apartment with six other tenants. My family had two front rooms, with me having my own bedroom. Then in 1950, when the Dyckman Street projects in the Inwood section of Manhattan were completed, my parents moved us there immediately. In contrast to our neighborhood in Harlem, the projects were only about 15 percent black. Our new neighbors were much more international: Russians, Puerto Ricans, Gypsies, Cubans, Scandinavians.

When I was in my junior year at Power Memorial Academy, a Catholic high school, Jack Donahue was my coach, my "agent," my friend. He had trained and guided us through a tremendous winning streak of over forty games. I was receiving a lot of letters of interest from college basketball teams, but all the letters went directly to Coach Donahue, the contents of which he never shared with me, saying only that I could attend any college I wanted. I liked the man—he pushed us, but he cared about us. More important, I trusted him.

We were playing St. Helena's, a team we should have been beating soundly. But we were up by only six points and the coach was enraged. After berating the entire team, he pointed an accusing finger at me and said, "And you! You go out there and you don't hustle. You don't move. You don't do any of the things you're supposed to do. You're acting just like a nigger!"

The air seemed to be instantly sucked out of the room and I was left sitting there, just trying to breathe. It was like waking up in the middle of the night and finding your favorite uncle pressing a pillow against your face, trying to smother you. Finally, I found my breath, we won the game, and afterward Donahue called me into his office to explain. "See, it worked!" he announced with a victorious smile. "My strategy worked. I knew that if I used that word, it'd shock you into a good second half. And it did."

Yeah, we won. We went on to win the city championship. We were voted the top Catholic high school team in the country. We were winners.

But at what cost?

Sure, Donahue didn't think he was being racist, just a motivator. For my own good. He wanted me to play up to my potential. In his heart he cared about me, but his brain should have recognized how I would react. I was big, but I was still a kid. The insult wasn't in his intention; it was in not recognizing the personal damage he was willing to risk for the sake of winning. It was in his feeling he had license to use that word with me—for any reason.

Life went on—I still had a year to play for him—but things were never the same between us. Especially that summer of '64.

Donahue ran a summer camp, mostly for kids from Power, which I'd attended for the last two summers. This year the camp had gone through some major changes: Donahue had refurbished the courts, advertised it as a basketball camp, and for the first time had paying campers. And I was a main draw. But I was going through some major changes of my own and preferred to stay in New York for the summer, not with the man who had betrayed me. However, pressure from my mother, who wanted me safely off the streets during a time of growing civil rights unrest, and a lingering sense of duty to the man, made me agree to attend his camp. Not for the full eight weeks, but three weeks at the end of summer. That left me most of the summer in the city.

Having spent the last couple years in a mostly white school, living in a mostly white neighborhood, I'd become a little removed from my own culture—so removed that I didn't even realize I was removed. I'd been well versed in the music of the African-American culture from my father, who was a jazz musician and graduate of Juilliard. He'd exposed me to some of the greatest jazz music from the Harlem Renaissance, but I no longer knew much about the *people* of Harlem. Although I'd been to Harlem several times since moving away, it was usually only for a basketball game. I'd arrive, play ball, maybe grab a bite, and immediately leave. I was more like a tourist.

Then I did something that changed my life.

That summer I signed up as part of the Harlem Youth Action Project (HARYOU-ACT), a city-sponsored antipoverty program designed both to keep kids off the streets and to teach them something about their heritage. The man in charge of our little group of overachievers was Dr. John Henrik Clarke, the head of the Heritage Teaching Program. Dr. Clarke was a well-known historian who had published notable articles such as "Africa in the Conquest of Spain" and "Harlem as Mecca and New Jerusalem," as well as books about Marcus Garvey and American Heritage's two-volume *History of Africa.*

I'd always had a fascination with history and felt fortunate that I was spending my summer with a man like Dr. Clarke rather than Coach Donahue. Dr. Clarke had gone through some similar experiences as I had in terms of questioning what I'd been taught—or rather hadn't been taught—about African-American history. When he was a young Sunday-school teacher, he'd been disturbed that he couldn't find any images of his own people in the Bible. "I began to suspect that something had gone wrong in history," he once said. "I see Moses going down to Ethiopia, where he marries Zipporah, Moses' wife, and she turns white. I see people going to the land of Kush, which is the present-day Sudan, and they got white. I see people going to Punt, which is present-day Somalia, and they got white. What are all these white people doing in Africa? There were no Africans in Africa, in the Sunday school lesson." Then one day he saw a recitalist at the high school carrying a copy of *The New Negro*, the anthology of essays, fiction, art, and poetry, compiled by Alain Locke (see the chapter "Master Intellects and Creative Giants"), that helped define the goals of the Harlem Renaissance. Young John Clarke read an essay in the book, "The Negro Digs Up His Past," and like so many black Americans who read that book, he was changed forever. "That was a key moment in my life," he said. "I made up my mind that we did have a history. For the first time, I read something on the ancient history of African people. I can't tell you how important that was to me."

Dr. Clarke, who had been so inspired by the writers of the Harlem Renaissance, shared his passion for African-American history with all of us, but somehow his messages seemed directly tailored for me. "History is not everything," Dr. Clarke once wrote, "but it is the starting point. History is a clock that people use to tell their time of day. It is a compass they use to find themselves on the map of human geography. It tells them where they are, but more importantly, what they must be." Coach Donahue had taught me how to play basketball, how to win games, but Dr. Clarke taught me how to find my place within my own community, within my own history. In a way, it was appropriate that my cultural reawakening came through the use of the n-word. I had been a little too comfortable being the young basketball star, a little out of reach of the kind of racism that others faced daily. Ironically, it was Coach Donahue who, by keeping me immersed in basketball, kept me insulated; and it was Coach Donahue who reminded me that such insulation was a fantasy that could be shattered at his discretion. That was all over now. Dr. Clarke encouraged us to explore our own past as well as what was going on in the streets now. Coach Donahue wanted us to become great basketball players, to achieve personal success; Dr. Clarke wanted us to become great African-Americans, to enlighten. Dr. Clarke hoped that training Harlem's youth in areas such as art, music, social work, photography, or journalism, those trainees would be able to make Harlem a better place when they became adults. "In regards to our precious young people," he explained, "they are really the seeds of tomorrow's crop, and our hope for immortality rests with them. They owe it to themselves, and to us, to pick out the finest things among us as examples, follow these examples and improve upon them. They are the makers of tomorrow. We changed the world once. We'll change it again."

Our job was to produce a weekly journal about Harlem life. We worked out of a tiny office in the basement of the 135th Street YMCA Annex. While the rest of Harlem enjoyed the warm sunshine of summer, we pecked away on the ancient black typewriters in the dank, windowless room. Dr. Clarke's assignments forced us to do research, some on the streets, but a lot at the Arthur Schomburg Center for Research in Black Culture. Originally, this had merely been a branch of the city library. But thanks to Puerto Rican–born black scholar and bibliophile Arturo Alfonso Schomburg, who donated his enormous collection of books on black history, the Schomburg Center was one of the world's richest sources for learning about black history. For me, walking into that building for the first time was like discovering the Holy Grail. Surrounded by all this information about the past of my people, I felt . . . unleashed. I returned again and again, with monklike devotion. I pored over every sacred scrap of information I could find about the legends of the Harlem Renaissance: black nationalist Marcus Garvey, black revolutionary W. E. B. Du Bois, the poetry of Langston Hughes and Countee Cullen, the fiction of Zora Neale Hurston and Wallace Thurman. All these talented and earnest young men and women posing all the same questions that had been bothering me all my life, but I'd never found anyone I could ask. Now I didn't have to. I could just read their insightful words and feel myself filling up, not just with knowledge, but also with pride. How could I be a senior in high school and have not even heard of the Harlem Renaissance?

Now I learned everything I could about it. After a long session in the Schomburg, I would walk out onto the streets of Harlem and notice some of the similarities between the Harlem of the Renaissance era and Harlem now. Unrest, frustration, distrust, were as thick as the humid summer air. Black militants such as Malcolm X hollered about injustice from the same soapboxes that Marcus Garvey used to speak from. Malcolm X's Nation of Islam, which advocated an aggressive approach to achieving racial equality, was at odds with the nonviolence advocated by Dr. Martin Luther King Jr. At one speech in Harlem, some Black Muslims actually stoned Dr. King. The following year Malcolm was assassinated in Manhattan by three members of the Nation of Islam. Racial tensions had gone far beyond just blacks versus whites. And gone was the respectful tolerance that the disagreeing black leaders of the Harlem Renaissance had shown toward each other.

The Civil Rights Act, which prohibited discrimination in voting, public accommodations, and employment, had just been passed, and white backlash was instantaneous—and violent. In June, three young men—James Chaney, Andrew Goodman, and Michael Schwerner—who had gone to Mississippi to help register black voters as part of what was known as Freedom Summer suddenly disappeared. Hundreds of volunteers searched for them, finally turning up their murdered bodies. Twenty men, including several police officers, were indicted. Racial tensions across the country were heating up along with the summer weather.

That same June, as a favor to Dr. Clarke, Dr. Martin Luther King Jr. addressed the participants of the HARYOU program. Dr. King was still a few months away from being awarded the Nobel Peace Prize, but he had already been announced as *Time* magazine's Man of the Year. I had always been a little skeptical of his unbending belief in nonviolence. He'd once written:

Conditions are such for Negroes in America that all Negroes ought to be fighting aggressively. . . . The nonviolent demonstrator . . . sees the misery of his people so clearly that he volunteers to suffer in their behalf and put an end to their plight. . . . Violence, even in self-defense, creates more problems than it solves. Only a refusal to hate or kill can put an end to the chain of violence in the world and lead us toward a community where men can live together without fear. Our goal is to create a beloved community and this will require a qualitative change in our souls as well as a quantitative change in our lives.

I didn't exactly believe in violence, but I had trouble believing we were ever going to get what was due us without putting up a fight. Still, like most African-Americans, I couldn't help but admire Dr. King's courage, dedication, and boundless optimism. When he spoke, all things did indeed seem possible, even "a community where men can live together without fear."

I was honored to have the opportunity to attend Dr. King's speech. Even better, I was going to cover the event as a journalist for our publication. My press credentials allowed me to take part in the press conference Dr. King held after his address. There I was, a seventeen-year-old kid huddled together with all these seasoned members of the mainstream media, scribbling away in my pad. Holding my tape recorder in my shaking hand, I finally got up the courage to ask Dr. King a question of my own: "What do you think the significance of Dr. Clarke's program is to the people of Harlem?" Dr. King replied that there was no doubt the program would be successful. In fact, it already was a success, because from that day forward, I understood what I needed to do with my life. I knew it had to be something that affected the African-American community in a positive way.

Then the inevitable happened. Just as Langston Hughes had warned in his prophetic poem "Dream Deferred," Harlem exploded.

It was July 19. A hot, muggy Sunday. Everything was sticky: my clothes, the subway seats, people's stares, even the air. After spending a lazy day at the beach, I was returning home when I decided to stop off at 125th Street to browse for jazz records before meeting up with some friends. I'd heard about a CORE (Congress of Racial Equality) rally that was supposed to take place around the same time, so I thought I'd check it out, see if there was anything newsworthy I might write about. The rally was to protest the shooting death of fifteen-year-old African-American James Powell by a white off-duty police officer, Lieutenant Thomas Gilligan. The shooting had occurred two days before and there'd been peaceful protests throughout the city ever since.

Stepping out of the subway entrance was like walking into a war zone.

Gunshots echoed. Glass shattered. A thousand desperate feet pounded past me.

I ducked behind a lamppost, wondering where the shots were coming from. People were smashing storefront windows, running wild through the streets either in fear or in rage. The riot had started outside the 123rd Street police station a couple blocks from where I was crouching. Rocks, bricks, and bottles were hurled, garbage cans were set on fire, and retail stores were looted, including those selling guns. A police officer with a megaphone had tried to calm the situation by shouting, "Go home! Go home!" One of the crowd shouted back, "We *are* home, baby!"

Now here I was, running and panting along with everyone else, scared that my height would make me an easy target for a nervous cop. Yet, I also felt part of the collective rage that emanated from the people running beside me. We were running hard and fast, fueled by anger and frustration, dragging behind us the heavy chains of history. Those thick chains scraping the pavement had caused the sparks that ignited this night. Maybe if we ran hard and fast and far enough, they'd disintegrate and we could break through the time barrier and emerge all fresh and rested in the

Harlem imagined by those visionaries of the Harlem Renaissance: a Mecca, a Paradise—a Home.

But those were the fevered dreams born of fear and anger. As much as I admired Dr. King, tonight I just wanted to pick up a brick and throw it. For the cop who shot James Powell. For Coach Donahue. For the teachers at Power who didn't think it important to teach us about anyone with a black face. Of course, I didn't. I had learned enough about history from my own studies at Schomburg Center to realize that looting and bricks didn't effect real change. Some government suits would make a sympathetic speech, create a panel that would investigate the causes, dump some money on a couple neighborhoods, plant a few trees here and there, and hope the dragon would go back to sleep for another ten years. When it would be some other politician's problem.

The next morning I showed up at the office of the journal and we decided to put out a special issue about the riots. We interviewed local residents, writing down their eyewitness accounts, chronicling for history what the white media was ignoring. While they were busy tabulating the property damage and police injuries, we were tabulating the cost to the community, to the individuals' spirits, to the hope of easing racial tensions. And that cost was high. That night the people took to the streets again, with the rioting spreading all the way to the Bedford-Stuyvesant section of Brooklyn. The city authorities declared a state of emergency in Harlem and banned all demonstrations. A "state of emergency"? Were they kidding? Harlem had been in a state of emergency for thirty years; that's why people were rioting!

The riots lasted five days, with one person being killed, 100 injured, and 520 arrested. Later, the FBI would classify the riots as an attack on "all constituted authority." Our little band of teenage journalists could have told them that much. Hell, Zora Neale Hurston said as much when she wrote, "Grab the broom of anger and drive off the beast of fear."

A week after the riots ended I was back up at Coach Donahue's Friendship Farm. After everything that had just happened, I could barely stand to look at the name of the place without wanting to break something. When my three-week sentence was up, I returned to Harlem, walking the same streets where I had so recently been running for my life. The rioting was over, much of the white press were condemning Harlemites as a bunch of thugs looking for an excuse to loot a new TV. Yeah, there was some of that. But that was like saying the Boston Tea Party was a bunch of looters after free tea. Did we really fight the American Revolution so we could get cheaper tea?

There's a famous poem called "Harlem." Nobody knows who the author is, which is appropriate because it has the plaintive feel of a silent prayer, as if anybody who lives in Harlem might be thinking it. Or everybody.

Chant another song of Harlem;
Not about the wrong of Harlem
But the worthy throng of Harlem,
Proud that they belong to Harlem;
They, the over-blamed of Harlem
Need not be ashamed of Harlem;
All is not ill-famed in Harlem,
The devil, too, is tamed in Harlem.

As I walked along the streets of Harlem, I realized that this summer had been a rite of passage for me, a leap from being a child of the projects to being a citizen of Harlem. I knew what my history was, who my people were—and where my future pointed.

THE HARLEM WITHIN

I left Harlem to attend UCLA when I was eighteen. But in the more than forty years since then, Harlem has never left me. When I think back on that summer from the heights of the giants' shoulders I have since stood on, I can see much more clearly what effect it had on me. I'm reminded of the last line in Stephen Crane's story "Open Boat." After the four survivors of a shipwreck brave a turbulent sea to make shore in their leaking lifeboat, the strongest and best person among them having drowned, they stand on the shore, looking out at the sinister water, trying to make sense of the horrible experience: "When it came night, the white waves paced to and fro in the moonlight, and the wind brought the sound of the great sea's voice to the men on shore, and they felt that they could then be interpreters."

In the end, that's the point of it all, isn't it? To not just endure hardship and turmoil, but to make sense of it all so we don't have to endure it again. So, a few lessons emerged from turmoil of that summer, lessons I've applied throughout my life. First, it isn't enough to just *read* history. That's something else I'd learned from Zora Neale Hurston: "Learning without wisdom is a load of books on a donkey's back." To read about the past for the sake of curiosity is merely gossiping disguised as study, not much different from reading a glossy magazine to find out what cologne Brad Pitt prefers. What's really important is what we do with the information we discover; how we use it to motivate ourselves into some form of action to better our own lives and the lives of those in our community. Action doesn't always have to be attending rallies or marching, it can also be much more personal, such as helping a neighbor, volunteering in a classroom, or teaching our children about our collective past and our collective values.

Second, I learned the value of educating myself. Even the well-meaning teachers at my schools taught only the same things they'd been taught, using conservative textbooks that repeated the same propaganda that had been repeated before. As Malcolm X said, "I've had enough of somebody else's propaganda. I'm for truth, no matter who tells it. I'm for justice, no matter who it is for or against. I'm a human being first and foremost, and as such I'm for whoever and whatever benefits humanity *as a whole.*" Why trust in authority figures that have time and again demonstrated their unwillingness to tell the truth? Where were the black faces in the

Bible, in my schoolbooks, in the author's photo on the novels we were assigned to read? Why was Marcus Garvey, one of the most beloved black leaders in the world, portrayed in the white press as a buffoon? Why was Malcolm X, who calmly articulated the frustrations of many of his people, referred to as a "hatemonger," "troublemaker," and "the angriest black man in America"? I would never forget that first day at the Schomburg Center as I pored over book after book about the enormous accomplishments of African-Americans in every field—the arts, science, education, politics—all at a time when everything around them conspired to discourage their achievements. After all they'd had to overcome to fulfill their dreams, wasn't it even worse to ignore them? That library was a portal through which I could see the real world, not just the one I'd been shown in carefully edited books. Every day I spent there I felt lighter, as if some unknown burden was being eased off me. When I stepped out of that building, I was energized and inspired. Seeing all that had been accomplished before me, I felt I could do no less. But what about all those black kids who only know what they've been taught by those who only know what they've been taught? What hope did they have of recognizing their talents within? I learned it isn't enough to be content with whatever paltry "facts" the school system teaches our children, we must teach them ourselves to have a curiosity about the world, a skepticism about anything they're told is true, and the skill to find out the truth for themselves.

The third thing I learned from that summer of violence was the power of words. The ability to clearly, logically, and passionately articulate ideas goes much further in effecting long-lasting change than the buy-us-off chump change politicians hand out whenever someone tosses a brick through a Circuit City window. Dr. King's "I Have a Dream" speech opened more hearts and doors than any burning car. Malcolm X's "Brotherhood" speech following his pilgrimage to Mecca brought more respect to Islam and support for civil rights than the sight of armed young Muslims in black suits. Words are not meant to placate anger or diminish it in any way. The anger was real, justified, and well earned. But the point was to use that anger to change the circumstances that caused the anger. And history showed us that wasn't going to happen by burning down our own neighborhoods, it was going to happen by registering to vote and using those votes as a currency to purchase change.

Some historians believe the economic blow of the Great Depression of the early 1930s killed the Harlem Renaissance. Some historians say the Harlem Renaissance ended not because of the Great Depression, but because Prohibition was repealed. Once liquor was available anywhere, white people stopped coming to Harlem and black fell out of vogue. Harlem Renaissance stride pianist Willie "the Lion" Smith observed, "It was legal liquor that did to Harlem what scarcer tips and shuttered warehouses had failed to do." It would be sad indeed to think that one of the greatest artistic and intellectual movements in American history was fueled only by booze. But it's no worse than believing the hard economic times meant African-Americans couldn't afford a Harlem Renaissance, just when they most needed the principles it taught.

Anyway, I don't agree. The Harlem Renaissance didn't end, only its popularity among white people ended. True, that fade from black had serious repercussions. Fewer white publishers willing to take a chance on black writers. Fewer records by black musicians sold, fewer Broadway plays by black playwrights, fewer black artists commissioned to paint murals or sculpt public statues. But in the crucible of those bad times, without the faddish support of white benefactors, the black community proved what it was made of. They endured, just as did white America, but with a lot fewer resources and opportunities. And in that atmosphere in which less is less, many African-Americans distinguished themselves. The public relations part of the Renaissance may have died, but the effects it had created were stronger than ever. Just because the gardener who planted a seed retires, that doesn't stop the plant from growing. Even though Jean Toomer, Claude McKay, and Wallace

Thurman stopped commanding attention, James Baldwin (*Go Tell It on the Mountain*, 1953), Richard Wright (*Native Son*, 1940), and Ralph Ellison (*Invisible Man*, 1952) sprouted up to take their place. Bessie Smith and Ma Rainey might have faded from view, but Billie Holiday, Dinah Washington, and Ella Fitzgerald commanded attention.

The Harlem Renaissance had pried open a lot of reluctant doors, and those who came after learned how to shoulder those doors open even wider. The guiding principles of the Renaissance survived and flourished, despite the Depression, despite the repeal of Prohibition, despite the imprisonment of Marcus Garvey, despite the assassinations of Malcolm X and Dr. Martin Luther King Jr., despite the drugs that infested the streets for three decades, despite being ignored by politicians, both black and white. Those principles still survive today and are more important than ever: (1) study your own people's history to see what greatness has been achieved and to realize what greatness you are capable of; (2) educate yourselves, not just by mimicking what your teachers or leaders say, regardless of their color, but by honing your mind to think critically; (3) dedicate yourself to your community so that when one member moves ahead, we all move ahead together; (4) and maybe most important of all, sing, dance, and laugh. The Harlem Renaissance was born out of severe repression and hardship, yet it produced some of the liveliest, most joyous music ever heard.

Life challenges us: to do the right thing when everyone else isn't; to show mercy and compassion when others show hate and spite; to be patient and steadfast when others try to push us in different directions. I've seen a lot of photos of Malcolm X looking dour or thoughtful or holding a gun. And I've seen a lot of photos of Dr. Martin Luther King Jr. looking determined or hopeful or earnest. But the photo of them that I like most—that inspires me as much as any speech either ever made—is the one in which they're standing next to each other and they are both laughing heartily as if one of them just farted. That's how I'd like to remember both of them, as embodiments of the spirit of the Harlem Renaissance that helped create them. Despite criticism and threats from whites and blacks, they never lost their dedication and commitment to their people. And rather than despair at all that needed to be done, they celebrated the good that had been accomplished, still able to laugh at what is joyous and ridiculous in life.

Fats Waller said about playing music, "You get that right tickin' rhythm, man, and it's *on!*" Same thing with life. All those lessons from the Harlem Renaissance are like possible notes we could play in the song that is our daily life. We each need to find the right rhythm.

And it's *on!*

"Master Intellects and Creative Giants"

The "Talented Tenth" Paint the World Black

- Gladly would I urge the Negro masses to take an active part in the revolution, just to see them, for one moment emerge from their innate sluggishness, massacre their ministers, and perhaps, in the interim, give birth to a few exceptional individuals capable of arising above the mob, Communism, Christianity, and all other such doctrines to become master intellects and creative giants.

  writer WALLACE THURMAN

- The Negro race, like all races, is going to be saved by its exceptional men. The problem of education, then, among Negroes must first of all deal with the Talented Tenth; it is the problem of developing the Best of this race that they may guide the Mass away from the contamination and death of the Worst, in their own and other races.

  writer and civil rights activist W. E. B. DU BOIS

IN THE BEGINNING WAS THE WORD

Every social movement needs fiery spokespersons to, as the poet says, inspire the masses to get off their asses. Without Thomas Jefferson's and Thomas Paine's impassioned political analyses, Americans might still be part of Great Britain. Without Abbie Hoffman's carefully crafted rants, the hippie movement might just have been a bad fashion statement. Without Gloria Steinem, Simone de Beauvoir, and Betty Friedan, women might still have their faces hopelessly pressed against the glass ceiling.

Yet, while these eloquent spokespersons are able to affect those who read their carefully crafted words, it is usually up to the artists to rally people to the cause in numbers large enough to effect real change. The movie and TV series *MASH* (set during the Korean War) probably did more to end the Vietnam War than any outraged speeches by impassioned activists. The spokespersons for the women's movement made a clear and articulate case for women's rights, but more men and women were brought to the ranks through the best-selling novels of Marilyn French (*The Women's Room*) and Erica Jong (*Fear of Flying*) and the TV series *Maude* than through de Beauvoir's political treatise, *The Second Sex*. In the final analysis, the effectiveness of any social message is only as strong as the artists who carry that message to the everyday people who spend most of their day earning a living.

The Harlem Renaissance was especially blessed in that it had a plethora of enormously talented spokespersons. Many of the best and brightest African-American writers, performers, artists, and activists came to Harlem to be part of a movement that had its mind set on changing America for the better. Like the Founding Fathers who had gathered 150 years before them to set this country on an irrevocable course, these creative and talented Harlemites were also dedicated to the proposition that all people were created equal and were, one way or another, going to get the equal opportunities that went with that.

THE CHANGING OF THE OLD GUARD: BOOKER T. WASHINGTON VS. W. E. B. DU BOIS

The architects of the Harlem Renaissance couldn't very well promote a New Negro unless they had an Old Negro they wanted to replace. For them, the Old Negro had outdated attitudes about who African-Americans were, what their goals should be, and how they should go about achieving those goals. In his essay "The New Negro," which became a quasi road map for much of the direction of the Harlem Renaissance, philosophy professor Alain Locke warned, "The Negro too, for his part, has idols of the tribe to smash."

The specific "idol" of the tribe they were intent on smashing was acclaimed African-American leader Booker T. Washington (1856–1915). For twenty years, author and educator Washington was the preeminent spokesperson for the African-American community. As such, his advice was sought by presidents and members of Congress concerning all things having to do with African-Americans. Since the death of abolitionist, feminist, and newspaper publisher Frederick Douglass in 1895, Washington was perhaps the most famous, and influential, black man in America. Yet, the Harlem Renaissance meant to build their New Negro on his ashes.

On the surface, Washington would appear to be the perfect model for the New Negro. Born into slavery in Virginia, he was freed when he was nine years old. At sixteen he attended college to become a teacher and nine years later became the first black head of the Tuskegee Institute in Alabama. His rise to prominence came as a result of his 1895 Atlanta Compromise address, given at the Cotton States and International Exposition in Atlanta, Georgia. This is where he laid out to a mostly white audience his principal political philosophy regarding the advancement of black Americans: "I pledge that in your effort to work out the great and intricate problem which God has laid at the doors of the South, you shall have at all times the patient, sympathetic help of my race."

This avowed policy of "patient, sympathetic help" and the promise to endure "severe and constant struggle" included the acceptance of Jim Crow laws of segregation. Though Washington privately fought against segregation laws by funding legal challenges, publicly he amassed much financial and political support from wealthy whites to help fund schools for black children because of his non-threatening political policies. His autobiography, *Up from Slavery* (1901), inspired many African-Americans to endure the struggle while at the same time made many whites more sympathetic to the black cause.

However sincere Washington's intentions and laudable his accomplishments, W. E. B. Du Bois saw an inherent danger in his policies and labeled him the Great Accommodator. Whereas Washington emphasized industrial and agricultural training for young blacks, Du Bois pushed for more classical, liberal arts education. Washington's approach was more vocational, based on his familiarity with rural Southern states. Du Bois thought that approach limiting, wanting instead to educate blacks into the white-collar professions. While Washington urged a passive conciliatory attitude toward whites, Du Bois advocated a more aggressive approach.

Clearly, each man's political philosophy was greatly influenced by his own geographical background. Washington grew up in the South, where nearly all blacks lived rural, agricultural lives. His plan to improve African-American lives focused on, taking into account their limited education, helping them gain vocational skills. Du Bois, however, believed the Great Migration had shifted the future of black culture to the cities and so focused his plan on making blacks both urban and urbane. Like himself.

Unlike Washington, William Edward Burghardt Du Bois (1868–1963) had not been born into slavery, nor even in the South. He was born in Massachusetts to a prominent black family, eventually graduating cum laude from Harvard University, where he later became only the second African-American to receive a Harvard Ph.D. Like Washington, Du Bois, too, was an educator, founding the first sociology department in the United States while teaching at Atlanta University. Before his participation in the Harlem Renaissance, he published several significant books, including *The Philadelphia Negro* (1899), *The Souls of Black Folk* (1903), and *John Brown* (1909). *The Souls of Black Folk*, a collection of essays about African-American life in America, became particularly influential in establishing the philosophical basis for the Harlem Renaissance. In one of the book's essays, "Of Mr. Booker T. Washington and Others," Du Bois details the damage done to black Americans because of Washington's policies and urges a bold new course: "Mr. Washington represents in Negro thought the old attitude of adjustment and submission. . . . Mr. Washington's programme practically accepts the alleged inferiority of the Negro races. . . . The black men of America have a duty to perform, a duty stern and delicate,—a forward movement to oppose a part of the work of their greatest leader."

In so adamantly opposing "their greatest leader" Washington, Du Bois became one of the men who replaced him—some historians claim the most important and influential one for the next twenty years. There could certainly be no disputing Du Bois's credentials as a leader. In 1905, he cofounded the Niagara Movement, a group of thirty-two African-Americans dedicated to advancing civil rights and ending racial discrimination. The group's name came from the place of their inaugural meeting, the Canadian side of the Niagara River. Together they condemned the submissive philosophy of Booker T. Washington and issued a Declaration of Principles: "Of the above grievances we do not hesitate to complain, and to complain loudly and insistently. To ignore, overlook, or apologize for these wrongs is to prove ourselves unworthy of freedom. Persistent manly agitation is the way to liberty, and toward this goal the Niagara Movement has started and asks the cooperation of all men of all races."

But in 1909, when a policy disagreement developed over whether to include whites in the group, Du Bois and others who thought whites should be included quit to form the National Association for the Advancement of Colored People (NAACP). Because of his weekly columns for prominent African-American newspapers in New York, Chicago, and Pittsburgh, as well as for the white *San Francisco Chronicle,* Du Bois's views were now being read by blacks—and whites—across the entire country. Du Bois also became the editor in chief of the NAACP publication, *The Crisis: A Record of the Darker Races,* the circulation of which rose from one thousand in 1910 to one hundred thousand by 1920, making it one of the dominant black periodicals in the country. From the editor's chair of the *Crisis,* where he sat for twenty-five years, Du Bois articulated and promoted the ideals that formed the core of the Harlem Renaissance manifesto as well as published other prominent Renaissance writers such as Langston Hughes and Jean Toomer.

W. E. B. Du Bois gave the Harlem Renaissance two things it needed most to achieve international recognition: undeniable intellectual depth and a compelling evangelical voice. His book *The Souls of Black Folk* was especially instrumental both in focusing national attention of the plight of African-Americans as well as in "recruiting" many of the seminal writers and artists who followed the promise in his voice to Harlem. If men like this lived in Harlem, they reasoned, surely that was the place to go. Historian David Levering Lewis wrote in the first of his two Pulitzer Prize–winning biographies of Du Bois that the book was "one of those events epochally dividing history into a before and an after. Like fireworks going off in a cemetery, its 14 essays were sound and light enlivening the inert and despairing. It was an electrifying manifesto, mobilizing a people for bitter, prolonged struggle to win a place in history." In the book's introduction, Du Bois explains the main issue of identity for African-Americans: "It is a peculiar sensation, this double-consciousness, this sense of always looking at one's self through the eyes of others, of measuring one's soul by the tape of a world that looks on in amused contempt and pity. One ever feels his two-ness,—an American, a Negro; two souls, two thoughts, two unreconciled strivings; two warring ideals in one dark body, whose dogged strength alone keeps it from being torn asunder."

Though his tone is mild and moderate, the reaction was anything but. A Tennessee newspaper feared that "this book is dangerous for the negro to read, for it will only excite discontent and fill his imagination with things that do not exist, or things that should not bear upon his mind." The *New York Commercial Advertiser* wrote, "At a time when racial prejudice has suddenly taken on an aggravated form, when almost every day witnesses a new outburst in some unexpected quarter, a volume of this sort, written by a negro with unwavering faith in the inherent possibilities of his race, cannot be otherwise than wholesome and inspiring."

More important than the reaction of the press, was the effect *The Souls of Black Folk* had on young blacks around the country. Poet Langston Hughes said, "My earliest memories of written words were those of W. E. B. Du Bois and the Bible." Novelist Claude McKay confessed, "The book shook me like an earthquake." This was the reaction Du Bois sought in all of his writings, for he saw the primary function of art was to persuade the reader, saying, "Thus all Art is propaganda and ever must be, despite the wailing of the purists." He argued of the importance of using art to promote the cause of African-Americans. Pleased with the impact blues and jazz were having across the country, Du Bois deliberately set about promoting black writers to achieve the same impact, stating, "A renaissance of American Negro literature is due; the material about us in the strange, heart-rending race tangle is rich beyond dream and only we can tell the tale and sing the song from the heart."

One of Du Bois's most famous and controversial essays, "The Talented Tenth," published in *The Negro Problem: A Series of Articles by Representative Negroes of Today* (1903), advocated his belief that an elite group of educated blacks would lead the rest of the black population to a better life. This would occur because (1) these exceptional individuals would prove to white society how much blacks could accomplish when given equal educational opportunities, and (2) this accomplished 10 percent of the black population (amounting to about 1 million African-Americans) would provide a solid infrastructure to allow future generations easier access to these opportunities. Du Bois's essay explains his theory: "All men cannot go to college but some men must; every isolated group or nation must have its yeast, must have for the talented few centers of training. . . . The Talented Tenth of the Negro race must be made leaders of thought and missionaries of culture among their people. No others can do this work and Negro colleges must train men for it. The Negro race, like all other races, is going to be saved by its exceptional men."

Some critics found this approach either impractical or too undemocratically elitist, the haughty belief of an Ivy League snob. But Du Bois was firm in his conviction that these men and women of color would be "an advanced guard" who would formulate and propagate a new ideology of racial assertiveness. For Du Bois, the Talented Tenth were the Great Black Hope.

Du Bois's efforts to unify both native Africans and descendants of the African diaspora into a global community fighting for a common cause earned him the nickname Father of Pan-Africanism. Eventually, his increasing radicalism brought him in conflict with other NAACP leaders until, in 1934, as the Harlem Renaissance was beginning to wind down, Du Bois quit the *Crisis* to return to teaching at Atlanta University. He remained active in politics, acting as a consultant to the U.S. delegation during the founding of the United Nations.

However, as his politics continued toward the left, his influence began to wane. He ran for U.S. Senate on the Labor Party ticket and lost. He was fired from his job as special research director at the NAACP. In 1961, when he was ninety-three, he joined the Communist Party. His increasing radicalism brought him under careful scrutiny from the U.S. government. Disappointed at being marginalized by both blacks and whites in America, Du Bois said, "I would have been hailed with approval if I had died at fifty. At seventy-five my death was practically requested." Then in 1962, the president of Ghana invited Du Bois to oversee the completion of the *Encyclopedia Africana*, but the United States refused to grant him and his wife new passports. As a result, the Du Boises renounced their U.S. citizenships and became citizens of Ghana. When he died the following year at age ninety-five, the United States sent no one to attend the state funeral Ghana provided in his honor. Du Bois once said, "I have been uplifted by the thought that what I have done will live long and justify my life." In 1992, nearly thirty years after his death, the United States issued a postage stamp featuring Du Bois's portrait.

CHARLES S. JOHNSON: THE ARTS AS WEAPONS OF MASS PERSUASION

Du Bois's advocacy of a messianic Talented Tenth found an ally in prominent black sociologist Charles S. Johnson (1893–1956), who was referred to as the Dean of the Renaissance. As research director for the National Urban League, a civil rights organization, and the editor of its influential periodical, *Opportunity*, Johnson used his editorial powers to promote young black writers not only by publishing them, but by arranging literary prizes that launched their careers into more prominence. Famed poet Langston Hughes, one of the writers that Johnson promoted, praised Johnson as the person who "did more to encourage and develop Negro writers during the 1920s than anyone else in America." Novelist Zora Neale Hurston (*Their Eyes Were Watching God*) said that the Renaissance was quite simply Johnson's "work, and only his hushmouth nature has caused it to be attributed to many others."

Johnson displayed an unwavering belief that the writers and artists would lead African-Americans to their rightful place in American society, one work of art at a time. Johnson was convinced that African-Americans could provoke sympathy and empathy in the rest of the world "by sheer force of the humanness and beauty of [their] own story." In *When Harlem Was in Vogue*, author David Levering Lewis describes Johnson's belief:

If the road to the ballot box and jobs was blocked, Johnson saw that the door to Carnegie Hall and New York publishers was ajar. Each book, play, poem, or canvas by an Afro-American would become a weapon against the old racial stereotypes. Johnson was certain that "If these beliefs, prejudices, and faulty deductions can be made accessible for examination, many of them will be corrected." . . . In the bleakness of the present, it was left to the Afro-American elite to win what assimilation it could through copyrights, concerts, and exhibitions.

Always the sociologist, Johnson researched the growth of the African-American professional class, concluding that this Talented Tenth grew by 69 percent between 1920 and 1930, justifying his and Du Bois's faith. Black-owned banks and life-insurance companies sprang up in every black community. Unfortunately, the stock market crash of 1929, followed by the Great Depression, crushed many of these businesses, sending highly educated African-Americans to work in stockrooms and elevators. Despite the financial setback, the propaganda part of the plan was still sound: great works of literature and art were being thrust into the world, and white America was responding with enthusiasm.

THE SHIPPING NEWS: MARCUS GARVEY AND THE BACK-TO-AFRICA MOVEMENT

Not everyone in Harlem during the Renaissance was optimistic about the future of blacks in America. To some, especially those blue-collar workers who weren't part of the Talented Tenth, the New Negro was still just another black person dressed up to go to a party to which he was neither invited nor welcome. Even if he was eventually allowed into the big house, rather than being treated as a respected guest, he would be seen as a mere curiosity, like a precocious child who could recite all the state capitals. Being an Old or New Negro wasn't the problem, being a Negro in America was the problem. And the only practical solution to that problem was for blacks to leave America. So argued Jamaican immigrant Marcus Moziah Garvey (1887–1940), whose back-to-Africa movement based in the heart of Harlem contradicted the heart of the Harlem Renaissance, bringing him into bitter conflict with W. E. B. Du Bois and the rest of the Talented Tenth.

Garvey was not an enthusiast of the Harlem Renaissance, yet it was the renaissance atmosphere in Harlem that gave him the inspiration and platform to launch his Universal Negro Improvement Association (UNIA). His educational background kept him from being part of the Talented Tenth (he claimed to have a doctor of civil law degree from Birkbeck College in England, though it seems that he only audited classes there), but his charisma and drive made him a popular leader among much of the other "untalented" nine-tenths of African-Americans. One Harlem observer described the barrel-bodied Garvey as "a little sawed-off, hammered down black man, with determination written all over his face, and an engaging smile that caught you and compelled you to listen to his story."

Though Garvey founded the UNIA while on a visit to Jamaica, it was in Harlem that he established his headquarters and core followers. But Garvey found little support from African-American leaders. Booker T. Washington, who had at first expressed support, did little to help Garvey's cause, and Du Bois and the NAACP were openly antagonistic to him and his plan. Yet, Garvey was not deterred, and his detractors soon realized how much they had underestimated his determination.

Invited to address the congregation at Bethel A.M.E. Church, Garvey's passionate speech there had the two thousand Harlemites shouting back with enthusiastic support. Word quickly spread throughout the Harlem community among the average workaday blacks who didn't write poetry, play jazz, sing or dance, or who didn't wear a suit to work. And they liked what they heard when

Garvey shouted, "One God, One Aim, One Destiny!" Following the incorporation of the UNIA in New York in 1918, Garvey began publishing his own weekly newspaper, the *Negro World*, to compete with Du Bois's *Crisis* and Johnson's *Opportunity*. Because of his call for blacks to abandon their racist countries to return to Africa, the *Negro World* was banned throughout most of the British and French territories. Still, Garvey's popularity grew and his speeches in Harlem commonly drew crowds of five thousand. "I have no desire to take all black people back to Africa; there are blacks who are no good here and will likewise be no good there. . . . Our success educationally, industrially and politically is based upon the protection of a nation founded by ourselves. And the nation can be nowhere else but in Africa."

Garvey's rejection of black participation in World War I garnered considerable support among the less conservative civil rights organizations, including socialists, Marxists, and black nationalists. But it also brought him under the watchful eye of the federal government. When the State Department granted permission to Du Bois to go to Versailles, France, where the peace treaties ending the war were being signed, but refused Garvey's handpicked delegation, Garvey launched a vitriolic attack against Du Bois before a rally of five thousand Harlemites. The battle lines had been drawn, and for these two men and their divergent philosophies for black Americans, there would be no peace, no Versailles. In an article in the *Crisis* entitled "Lunatic or Traitor," Du Bois called Garvey "the most dangerous threat to the Negro race." Garvey responded by calling Du Bois "purely and simply a white man's nigger." Ridiculing what he considered to be a conservative stance by Du Bois and the NAACP, Garvey wondered, "How can a Negro be conservative? What has he to conserve?"

Garvey proved just how serious he was in his back-to-Africa rhetoric when he started the Black Star Line Steamship Corporation in 1919 with the intention of purchasing the ships that would transport blacks back to their African homelands. He quickly raised $200,000, mostly from the laborers desperate to improve their lot. One poor Panamanian investor who had already bought $125 in Black Star shares wrote to Garvey to express his hopefulness: "Now I am sending thirty-five dollars for seven more shares. You might think I have money, but the truth, as I have stated before, is that I have no money now. But if I'm to die of hunger it will be all right because I'm determined to do all that's in my power to better the conditions of my race."

While Du Bois had raised the hopes of the black middle and upper classes that through hard work and education they would soon earn their rightful place at the dinner table, Garvey raised the hopes of the hourly wage earner that there was a place where they would not have to endure the daily contempt and hopelessness heaped upon them by each passing white face. White NAACP board of directors member Mary White Ovington captured Garvey's dynamic allure when she said, "Garvey was the first Negro in the United States to capture the imagination of the masses. . . . The sweeper of the subway, the elevator boy eternally carrying fat office men and perky girls up and down a shaft, knew that when night came he might march with the African army and bear a wonderful banner to be raised some day in a distant and beautiful land."

But it was not to be. For Garvey's followers, the distant land would remain distant.

Garvey's famous quote, "Look for me in the whirlwind or the storm," became prophetic for his own troubles. Garvey's Black Star Line did indeed buy ships, but they were mostly in poor condition. One blew a boiler and had to be towed, and another sank. Mismanagement, corrupt crews, and infiltration by J. Edgar Hoover's Federal Bureau of Investigation, and even the possibility of sabotage by rivals or government agents, brought the collapse of Black Star in 1922, after only three years of operation. Though the all-black crews and captains had made trips to the West Indies, none had gone to Africa. Worse, the Liberian government, which had at first been supportive of the UNIA's plans to build schools, roads, and businesses as a first step for the resettlement of Garvey's followers, withdrew its support in the 1920s under pressure from European business interests. Even in the United States, some of Garvey's supporters began to withdraw as he aligned himself with the KKK and other racist organizations to embrace separatism of the races. Defiantly, Garvey proclaimed that if one had to choose between the Klan and the "National Association for the Advancement of 'Certain' People, give me the Klan for their honesty of purpose toward the Negro." Du Bois and other black leaders responded with a "Garvey Must Go" campaign, which did much to undercut Garvey's credibility, if not among his loyal core, then among some of the sympathetic middle class that had previously given him financial support.

Finally, Garvey was convicted of mail fraud because his Black Star Line stock brochure featured a photo of a ship he did not own, though he was in negotiations to purchase it. Others were also charged, but only Garvey was found guilty. In 1925, he was sentenced to five years in Atlanta Federal Prison. Garvey's supporters launched a campaign to appeal to President Calvin Coolidge to commute the sentence, arguing that it was politically motivated. One of those supporters was Malcolm X's Baptist minister father, Earl Little. Years later, Malcolm X recalled his father's efforts on Garvey's behalf: "The image that made me proudest was his crusading and militant campaigning with the words of Marcus Garvey. . . . It was only me that he sometimes took with him to the Garvey UNIA meetings which he held quietly in different people's homes." After two years, President Coolidge commuted the sentence. Because Garvey was not a U.S. citizen and had been convicted of a felony, he was deported back to Jamaica. When he arrived in Kingston in 1927, a large crowd of supporters greeted him at the docks and then marched with him to his local UNIA headquarters.

The Harlem branch of the UNIA began in a bleak basement with Garvey, his wife Amy Jacques Garvey, and seventeen loyal members. A few years later, through sheer force of his vision, charisma, and willpower, he claimed 4 million members worldwide (though most authorities agree that number is greatly exaggerated). Although his affectations—gaudy uniforms, giving himself the title "Provisional President of Africa"—caused the Talented Tenth to ridicule him, there was no doubt he was a true folk hero to many of the rest of the black population. This was the man who, after all, had amassed one hundred thousand blacks to parade through Harlem under his distinctive UNIA flag. The NAACP couldn't claim such an accomplishment.

Although Garvey remained active in politics, he moved to England in 1935, where he spent the last five years of his life, dying at the age of fifty-three. The breadth and depth of his influence can be seen in the many buildings, schools, colleges, and highways that bear his name throughout Africa, Europe, the Caribbean, and the United States. The red, black, and green flag he designed for the UNIA is now used as the Black Liberation Flag. Those who attended UNIA meetings include a wide variety of world-shakers, including Elijah Muhammad, founder of the Nation of Islam; Vietnam's Ho Chi Minh, who while a seaman in his youth had briefly lived in New York; and Kwame Nkrumah, the first president of Ghana, who attended meetings while a student in New York and, in homage to Garvey, named Ghana's shipping company the Black Star Line.

In 1980, a bust of Garvey was presented at the Washington, D.C., Organization of American States' Hall of Heroes. His remains are kept in the Marcus Garvey National Shrine in Jamaica, where he is considered the "Father of Jamaican Independence" as well as Jamaica's first national hero. His face adorns the Jamaican half-dollar. Although Garvey did not endorse the Rastafarian movement, its followers in Jamaica believe Garvey to be a religious prophet, perhaps even the reincarnation of John the Baptist, which is why he is the topic of much reggae music.

Garvey did not see himself as part of the in-crowd that celebrated itself with the lofty term *Harlem Renaissance*, yet he certainly embodied the attributes that the Renaissance promoted. He was self-reliant, self-motivated, and a charismatic speaker who led what one historian called "the largest, most widespread, most powerful, and most influential movement among people of African descent in world history."

LOCKE OF AGES: ALAIN LOCKE INTRODUCES THE NEW NEGRO TO THE WORLD

The Talented Tenth were handed their bible and mission statement in one handy volume, *The New Negro*, produced by one of the Harlem Renaissance's most important figures (despite that he never actually lived in Harlem). Washington-based Alain LeRoy Locke (1886–1954) is credited as being the main interpreter of the Harlem Renaissance, and the man most responsible for shaping the arts that came out of that era. Because of his remarkable academic, literary, and cultural achievements, Locke not only symbolized the Talented Tenth, but became a mentor to many of the other Talented Tenth writers and artists of Harlem.

Born in Philadelphia, Locke was raised in a house that emphasized education. Locke's parents were both teachers and his father had a law degree from Harvard University. This might explain Locke's admonishment to his own students that "the highest intellectual duty is the duty to be cultured." And cultured he became, perhaps more so than any other figure in the Renaissance. In 1907, Locke graduated magna cum laude and Phi Beta Kappa from Harvard University with a degree in philosophy. Locke then became the first African-American Rhodes Scholar, allowing him to attend Oxford University in England, where he studied philosophy, Greek, and literature. After Oxford, he attended the University of Berlin from 1910 to 1911, earning an advanced degree in philosophy. These seven years of university study in America and Europe established an international perspective in Locke that he would later use in his own writings to put the accomplishments of black artists in a larger context of world history.

But before that could happen, Locke needed a job. Though he returned from Europe in 1912 with the sort of education and accomplishments that any university would ordinarily clamor for, his being black limited his options. Before accepting a teaching position at Howard University, Locke decided to take a personal tour of the South to experience firsthand the blatant and pervasive discrimination that he'd so far mostly experienced in passive and subtle ways. His trip confirmed in him a belief that the only way blacks could be treated as equals by whites was to demonstrate significant intellectual abilities and accomplishments. When he started teaching at Howard University, that's exactly what he set about to do, struggling to introduce African-American studies into the curriculum. The battle lasted for years, ending in victory only when the white president of the school was replaced by a black president. Locke later earned his Ph.D. in philosophy from Harvard, but remained a professor at Howard until he retired in 1953, one year before his death. It was during a three-year leave of absence from Howard that Locke became a predominant force in the Harlem Renaissance.

Despite being based at Howard University in Washington, D.C., Locke enjoyed frequent trips to Harlem, where he made a point to become acquainted with many of the prominent figures in Harlem's civil rights and cultural movements, especially W. E. B. Du Bois and Charles S. Johnson. His association with Johnson led to his becoming involved with the National Urban League's prestigious magazine, *Opportunity: A Journal of Negro Life*, which Johnson edited. Locke was even the master of ceremonies at the lavish 1924 dinner at New York City's Civic Club that was meant to introduce black writers to the many white publishers and magazine editors in attendance. The plan worked: as a result of the dinner party Countee Cullen's poems were published in *Harper's* magazine, and an agreement was made for a special edition of the respected sociology and political magazine *Survey Graphic* to be devoted to the "New Negro." Though the term *New Negro* had sporadically been used in the late 1890s, it became the adopted term of the Harlem Renaissance to describe its new renaissance man.

Some historians point to this March 1925 issue of *Survey Graphic*, which Locke titled "Harlem: Mecca of the New Negro," as the official start of the Harlem Renaissance, because this collection of essays, poetry, and fiction captured both the spectrum of issues facing African-Americans as well as the zeitgeist of the movement. This issue was so successful that Locke produced an expanded, book-length edition, titled *The New Negro*. Published in 1925, *The New Negro* became the acknowledged bible of the Harlem Renaissance for blacks, and a cultural shot fired over the bow of the ship piloted by the guardians of white American culture. The book was an immediate critical and commercial success—among both blacks and whites. Historian Nathan I. Huggins, in his definitive work *The Harlem Renaissance* (1971) describes the thirty-nine-year-old Locke's contribution: "Locke's editing of and contribution to this volume and his energetic championing of the intellectual achievement of Negroes in the 1920s made him the father of the New Negro and the so-called Harlem Renaissance."

Locke lacked both Du Bois's practical editing experience and credentials as an activist in civil rights politics. Where Du Bois had left academia to toil in the ruthless fields of race relations, Locke had remained the removed intellect, observing from a distance. Du Bois had already written three influential books by the time he was Locke's age, but Locke had remained content to study and teach. However, now that Locke was given this opportunity to join in the fight, he did do so with all the gusto and dedication he could muster. The result was a volume designed to include a representative group of black and white intellectuals, male and female, young and old—yet who did not veer too far to the left toward more radical attitudes. This exclusion was by choice: *The New Negro* was specifically aimed to appeal to whites as an introduction to the kind of intellectual depth and literary sophistication that black writers were capable of.

Locke's foreword reveals the book's purpose: "We speak of the offerings of this book embodying the first fruits of the Negro Renaissance." To many white readers, these "fruits" would be an exotic species never before tasted. The volume included many of the brightest literary, artistic, and intellectual stars of the Harlem firmament: fiction and poetry by Rudolph Fisher, Jean Toomer, Zora Neale Hurston, Countee Cullen, Claude McKay, James Weldon Johnson, and Langston Hughes; art by Aaron Douglas; essays by Alain Locke, W. E. B. Du Bois, Jessie Fauset, Charles S. Johnson, Walter White, and Arthur A. Schomburg—and many other leading writers and scholars. The contents avoided provocative attacks on white racism, but did not shy away from a deliberate but measured condemnation. But the book wasn't just an exposé of the obvious, it was also an effort to put blacks within a historical context of world and American history, to reveal their significant contribution to the past and promise for the future. And that promise for the future rested within the dark hands of the learned New Negro, which Locke describes in the book:

For generations in the minds of America, the Negro has been more of a formula than a human being—a something to be argued about, condemned or defended, to be "kept down" or "in his place," or "helped up," to be worried with or worried over, harassed or patronized, a social bogey or a social burden. . . . [The New Negro] now becomes a conscious contributor and lays aside the status of a beneficiary and ward for that of a collaborator and participant in American civilization. The great social gain in this is the releasing of our talented group from the arid fields of controversy and debate to the productive fields of creative expression. The especially cultural recognition they win should in turn prove the key to that revaluation of the Negro which must precede or accompany any considerable further betterment of race relations. . . . No one who . . . views the new scene with its still more abundant promise can be entirely without hope.

Predictably, controversy followed. Some saw Locke's selections as elitist, the familiar charge leveled against Du Bois, Johnson, and other self-proclaimed members of the exclusive Talented Tenth. Black journalist George Schuyler, author of an article entitled "The Negro-Art Hokum," referred to Locke as the "high priest of intellectual snobbocracy." Perhaps confirming this point is the book's deliberate snubbing of the considerable influence of Marcus Garvey. Worse, there was animosity among some of those included. Cullen's poetry style was markedly conservative compared to the more experimental work of Toomer and the jazz style of Hughes. In fact, the following year Hughes would attack Cullen in his essay "The Negro Artist and the Racial Mountain," with the claim that Cullen preferred to be known as a poet who happened to be Negro rather than as a Negro poet.

Locke himself received some of the most brutal criticism from his own contributors. Jean Toomer accused Locke of tricking and misusing him. When Locke, to avoid political fallout, and without consulting Claude McKay, changed the title of his deliberately pointed poem "White House" to the tamer "White Houses," McKay proclaimed that Locke had "destroyed every vestige of intellectual and fraternal understanding" between them. McKay lamented, "I would much prefer if you dropped me out of your contemptible book."

One clear sign that the community of black writers was not quite as unified as Locke wanted the world to believe was the publication the following year of *Fire!!*, a magazine produced by Wallace Thurman and including the work of Langston Hughes, Countee Cullen, Zora Neale Hurston, and Aaron Douglas. They saw Locke's work as more of a public relations publication and wanted to create one that dealt with the real-life issues of Harlem blacks generally ignored by the more genteel Talented Tenth, including jazz and homosexuality. Thurman later described the purpose of his magazine in "Negro Artists and the Negro": *"Fire*, like Mr. Hughes' poetry, was experimental. It was not interested in sociological problems or propaganda. It was purely artistic in intent and conception. Its contributors went to the proletariat rather than to the bourgeois for characters and material. They were interested in people who still retained some individual race qualities and who were not totally white American in every respect save color of skin."

The magazine pointedly did not list Locke as one of the nine patrons, signaling a clear break from Locke's vision. However, *Fire!!* failed to capture the public's interest, folding after only one issue. In contrast, Locke's *The New Negro* continues to be read, not merely as a cold and dusty historical document, but for its vibrant style and hopeful attitude. In his introduction to the 1992 edition of *The New Negro*, author Arnold Rampersad assesses the book's impact: "The New Negro exudes more than energy—it exudes a quality suspiciously like joy, the great quality that J. A. Rogers [a contributor to the anthology] sees in jazz. . . . Even today it remains a reliable index to the black American sensibility at that point where art and politics meet, as well as to the events in Harlem and elsewhere among blacks in the 1920s."

One might think producing the so-called bible of the Harlem Renaissance would be contribution enough, but Locke's influence was even more significant in his role as guardian at the gates of eccentric philanthropist Charlotte Osgood Mason. Mason, in her seventies and white, had money to give to worthy black writers and artists to help support them while they produced their works. Locke selected those he deemed worthy of such support and introduced them to Mason, who insisted upon being called "Godmother" to those she helped. Mason's gifts, however, came with the knowledge that she would have considerable say in one's career, even going so far as to edit one's works. Mason had a clear, though clearly patronizing, agenda for the kind of art she would support. She saw blacks as a spiritually superior people because their primitiveness had been uncorrupted by Western culture. Ironically, some of the quintessential works of the Harlem Renaissance were funded and guided by this elderly woman from her Park Avenue penthouse. She paid for Langston Hughes to attend Lincoln University in 1926, then urged him to write the novel *Not Without Laughter*. Years later, after an argument, Hughes broke from her. Zora Neale Hurston also received Mason's money—and editorial influence. In Hurston's autobiography, *Dust Tracks on a Road*, she describes, with some affection, Mason's editorial process: "Godmother could be as tender as mother-love when she felt that you had been right spiritually. But anything in you, however clever, that felt like insincerity to her, called forth her well-known 'This is nothing! It has no soul in it. You have broken the law!'"

Artist Aaron Douglas was also unable to refuse the Godmother's offer—to his regret. Mason forced Douglas to turn down or withdraw from lucrative commissions whenever she felt they weren't what she deemed "proper Negro art." Douglas, too, eventually broke away. Yet, Locke remained, ushering new artists to her lair, convincing her to subsidize them, trying to balance his personal and racial integrity with the knowledge that many of these artists' works might not ever come to fruition without her financial support.

WRITERS ON THE STORM: THE GREAT EIGHT

Though Du Bois, Johnson, and Locke published important works regarding black culture, they were smart enough to realize the limited appeal of their academic works. They were preaching to the choir, but the choir was small. To reach the larger audience that could help improve life for African-Americans, skilled literary writers of prose, poetry, and fiction would be required. Through their respective magazines, Du Bois (*The Crisis*), Johnson (*Opportunity*), and Locke (*Survey Graphic*) were able to maintain relatively tight control over whose voices would be heard.

Black intellectual and author Frantz Fanon (*The Wretched of the Earth*, 1961) wrote, "Each generation out of relative obscurity must discover their mission, fulfill it or betray it." Certainly most of the writers of the Harlem Renaissance came from obscurity and were handpicked because of their talents and dedication to fulfill the mission. Du Bois laid out the spiritual message in his essay "Strivings of the Negro People":

The history of the American Negro is the history of this strife,—this longing to attain self-conscious manhood, to merge his double self into a better and truer self. In this merging he wishes neither of the older selves to be lost. He would not Africanize America, for America has too much to teach the world and Africa. He would not bleach his Negro soul in a flood of white Americanism, for he knows that Negro blood has a message for the world. He simply wishes to make it possible for a man to be both a Negro and an American, without being cursed and spit upon by his fellows, without having the doors of Opportunity closed roughly in his face.

From statements such as this, Harlem Renaissance writer Sterling Brown (*Southern Road*) categorized five major literary themes of the Renaissance writers: (1) Africa as a source of race pride, (2) black American heroes, (3) racial political propaganda, (4) the black folk tradition, and (5) candid self-revelation. Following these rough guidelines, serious literary writers would give Harlem the cultural heft and gravitas necessary to make it not only a geographical location but also to imbue it with the sheen of hope and historical context.

In the short story "City of Refuge," Harlem writer Rudolph Fisher does just that. Upon first seeing Harlem, the protagonist, a naive immigrant from the rural South, exclaims, "Done died and woke up in Heaven." As he looks around at the bustling black residents of Lenox Avenue, he concludes, "In Harlem black was white. You had rights that could not be denied you; you had privileges, protected by the law. And you had money. Everybody in Harlem had money." Of course, this romanticized vision of Harlem was only partially true. Many hopefuls did first see Harlem that way; but most Harlemites did not have the money or prestige that some writers described. That became one of the controversies among the writers—and other artists—of the Renaissance: Was their art to be used merely as a propaganda tool to promote the ideals of the black intelligentsia, or did they have a responsibility to portray the grittier warts-and-all Harlem life—and of African-Americans in general?

Ironically, one of the first novels to portray the more realistic and gritty side of Harlem, *Nigger Heaven* (1926), was written by a white man, Carl Van Vechten (1880–1964), who had frequented Harlem and was friends with many black writers. The controversial title is a slang phrase for movie theater balconies where blacks were forced to sit. Set during the Harlem Renaissance, the novel portrays a rather simplistic love story between a black couple. The book divided the black literary circles, with Langston Hughes, Nella Larsen, and Wallace Thurman supporting it, and Countee Cullen, W. E. B. Du Bois, and Alain Locke arguing that it was an "affront to the hospitality of black folk." Despite its lack of literary ambition, and detractors among some black leaders, the novel became a huge best seller, succeeding at fulfilling the mandate of the Renaissance intellects: it introduced blacks as intelligent, talented, and sympathetic characters to a mostly white audience. Though it must have stung some to have a white man come in and seemingly steal their material to write a best seller, black writers were also heartened to see, and have white publishers see, that there was a paying market for their stories. They wasted no time setting about to tell those stories.

It would be a mistake to think that just because these talented writers, whom Zora Neale Hurston referred to as the Niggerati, shared the same skin color they also shared the same ideals and beliefs. Nor were they above criticizing each other for reasons both intellectual and petty. Like any large family, there was a lot of competing for attention. Nor were their targets only the injustices of the white society. They also attacked the complacent upper-class African-Americans, whom they called "dicty blacks." And they pointed out the rampant racism within their own community, as light-skinned blacks looked down on those with dark skins.

While many significant writers came out of the Harlem Renaissance, eight giants stand out as having contributed the most. Brief descriptions of each are presented below in order of date of birth because, in most cases, that dictated when they joined the literary circles of the Renaissance.

1. "LIFT EVERY VOICE AND SING": JAMES WELDON JOHNSON

James Weldon Johnson (1871–1938) was an accomplished renaissance man long before there was any kind of movement in Harlem. His staggering list of accomplishments made him the perfect mentor to many of Harlem's writers. At twenty-four he'd founded a high school for African-Americans; he edited the United States' first black-oriented daily newspaper, the *Daily American* (1895–96); he was the first black admitted to the Florida bar; as a result of writing a popular campaign song for Teddy Roosevelt, he was appointed the American consul in Venezuela and Nicaragua (1906–12); he cowrote over two hundred songs, including the unofficial "Negro national anthem," "Lift Every Voice and Sing"; he'd written the successful novel *The Autobiography of an ExColored Man* (1912), published anonymously and with great influence on upcoming young black writers. Booker T. Washington was so impressed with Johnson that he hired him to write editorials for the *New York Age*. But W. E. B. Du Bois, seeing in Johnson a kindred Talented Tenth, persuaded him to come to the NAACP, where Johnson was its chief executive officer until he left in 1931 to teach at Fisk University.

Johnson's breadth of life experiences had brought him in contact with the elite of both the white and black communities. Recognizing that Jews and blacks shared a common struggle against discrimination, he enlisted the help of several wealthy Jewish philanthropists to help finance the fight against racism. His contacts with white publishers made it easier for young black writers to be published. In his 1922 preface to *The Book of American Negro Poetry*, Johnson defined the goals of the Harlem Renaissance as well as presented a manifesto for writers to follow:

A people may become great through many means, but there is only one measure by which its greatness is recognized and acknowledged. The final measure of the greatness of all peoples is the amount and standard of the literature and art they have produced. The world does not know that a people is great until that people produces great literature and art. No people that has produced great literature and art has ever been looked upon by the world as distinctly inferior.

Though Johnson's impact can clearly be seen in the pages of many of the writers he influenced, his real impact upon African-Americans is clearer in this reminiscence by literary critic Amin Sharif:

I am old enough to remember when every black child was required to memorize and recite the poems of Langston Hughes or James Weldon Johnson. The recitation of these works usually took place at church or in school. And these occasions came as close to a rite of passage as anything possessed by the Black Community in those days. Each child practiced for weeks to stand before parents and friends to recite the words of these two great poets. And woe unto the child who forgot his lines or who gave a recitation that did not move those assembled. For the younger children, Langston Hughes was more than appropriate. But for those in the upper grades, James Weldon Johnson's works were the only ones that would suffice.

2. WITHOUT CONFUSION: JESSIE REDMON FAUSET

Jessie Redmon Fauset (1882–1961) was unique in being both an editor to many of Harlem's best writers as well as a successful novelist in her own right. Not only was she the most published novelist of the Harlem Renaissance, but she published the first novel of the Renaissance, *There Is Confusion* (1924). As with many of the Talented Tenth, she excelled at academics, becoming the first black woman at Cornell University to be elected to Phi Beta Kappa and later attending the Sorbonne in Paris. Feeling that her abilities and ambitions were slowly being siphoned away as a high school French teacher, she wrote letters to her hero, W. E. B. Du Bois, explaining, "I have had to let people know that we too possess some of the best, or else allow my own personality to be submerged."

Impressed by her intellect and passion, Du Bois offered the thirty-seven-year-old Fauset the position of literary editor at the *Crisis*, where she served from 1919 to 1926. During this time she nurtured and guided such literary talents as Claude McKay, Jean Toomer, Countee Cullen, and Langston Hughes, while beginning the writing of what would be seventy-seven published works, including the novels *Plum Bun* (1928), *The Chinaberry Tree: A Novel of American Life* (1931), and *Comedy: American Style* (1933). Du Bois also assigned her to edit the magazine *Brownies' Book*, an NAACP publication aimed at instilling racial pride in children. Du Bois felt that black children were inundated with images of white people being successful and rarely with black people as role models. Said Du Bois, "The result is that all of the Negro child's idealism, all his sense of the good, the great and the beautiful is associated entirely with white people." Fauset set about to change all that by providing African-American children with stories, poems, plays, songs, and images of heroic and admirable blacks.

Fauset's own adult fiction focused on the more genteel strata of black society and often brought the criticism that she was comparable to Jane Austen or Edith Wharton rather than having a more distinctive black voice. Alain Locke was one of her harshest critics, which she reciprocated by describing his essays in *The New Negro* as being "stuffed with pedantry which fails to conceal their poverty of thought." This animosity may also have sprung from Locke's having used the Civic Club party celebrating the publication of *There Is Confusion* to promote *The New Negro*.

After leaving the *Crisis* in 1926, Fauset devoted herself to writing and teaching, both professions that she felt would elevate African-Americans.

3. REAL-WORLD HARLEM: CLAUDE MCKAY

Claude McKay (1889–1948) represented a group of the Talented Tenth—including Langston Hughes and Wallace Thurman—that bristled under that self-important title. Like some critics, they found both the term and the ideology too elitist and exclusive. Though they agreed with the fundamental goal of elevating the image of African-Americans, they didn't want to gloss the image. Black was beautiful, even if every black was not. Plus, they wanted to include the average African-American as an active participant in the struggle. This put these writers at odds with the old guard of Du Bois, Locke, and Charles S. Johnson, but it made them popular among the younger readers.

McKay struggled greatly with the balance between his art and his political polemics. Born and raised in Jamaica, he published his first volume of poetry there at the age of twenty-three (*Songs of Jamaica*, 1912). His second volume, *Constab Ballads*, published the same year, featured poems about his experiences as a Jamaican police officer. He traveled to the United States to study at Booker T. Washington's Tuskegee Institute in Alabama, but was shocked at the level of racism he encountered in the South. McKay left the South to study at Kansas State University, but the lure of Harlem, inspired in part by reading Du Bois's *The Souls of Black Folk*, pulled him away before he could finish his degree. About his abrupt departure from school, he wrote, "If I would not graduate as a bachelor of arts, I would graduate as a poet."

In Harlem, McKay worked as a waiter on the railways while continuing to write and occasionally publish his poetry. "Harlem was my first positive reaction to American life," he wrote. ". . . It was like entering a paradise of my own people." McKay's exposure to American racism had radicalized his politics to the degree that he rejected both Marcus Garvey and the elitism of his hero Du Bois and the NAACP. Instead, he embraced communism, helping found the revolutionary group the African Blood Brotherhood. He began to write for the radical socialist magazine the *Liberator*, which published his poem "If We Must Die" (see the chapter " 'Some Technicolor Bazaar': How Harlem Became the Center of the Universe"), his response to the rash of race riots across the country in the summer of 1919. His poem articulated the rage that most blacks felt, instantly thrusting McKay into the forefront as both a writer and spokesperson for disillusioned African-Americans. "That one grand outburst," he wrote in his autobiography, "is their sole standard of appraising my poetry."

McKay then traveled to London, England, where he studied Marx more closely. He became a paid journalist for the socialist newspaper the *Workers' Dreadnought*, which some historians claim made him England's first black journalist. After a year, he returned to Harlem, ready to take his place among the literary greats that fostered awareness of the Harlem Renaissance. He quickly published his first American book of poetry, *Harlem Shadows* (1922). His interaction with the master intellects of the Renaissance left him ill at ease. "And now that I was legging along with the intellectual gang," he recounted, "Harlem for me did not hold quite the same thrill and glamour as before." Still conflicted between his literary success and his commitment to revolutionary politics, he decided to travel to the Soviet Union to attend the Third Communist International. He did not return to the United States for twelve years. He explained his need to travel in his autobiography: "Color consciousness was the fundamental of my restlessness. . . . My white fellow-expatriates could sympathize but . . . they could not altogether understand. . . . Unable to see deep into the profundity of blackness, some even thought . . . I might have preferred to be white like them. . . . They couldn't understand the instinctive . . . pride of a black person resolute in being himself and yet living a simple civilized life like themselves."

In 1928, McKay's most acclaimed work appeared, the novel *Home to Harlem*, which won the prestigious Harmon Gold Award for Literature. The best-selling novel presented a realistic and unvarnished view of Harlem street life, which influenced black writers and intellectuals throughout the United States, the Caribbean, West Africa, and Europe. White critics hailed it as "the real stuff, the lowdown on Harlem, the dope from the inside." However, the novel's honest portrayal of sexuality and the darker side of Harlem's nightlife drew harsh criticism from McKay's former hero

Du Bois, who stated, *"Home to Harlem . . .* for the most part nause-ates me, and after the dirtier parts of its filth I feel distinctly like taking a bath." For Du Bois, any art that didn't serve the propa-ganda needs of promoting the New Negro wasn't art at all. Yet, the young black writers who worshipped art for art's sake praised the novel. Langston Hughes embraced it as "the finest thing 'we've' done yet." The public agreed: within two weeks of publication, McKay's gritty book became the first best-selling novel by an African-American writer. McKay also published two other novels, *Banjo* (1929) and *Banana Bottom* (1933); a collection of short sto-ries, *Gingertown* (1932); and two autobiographies, *A Long Way from Home* (1937) and *Harlem: Negro Metropolis* (1940).

Claude McKay's commitment to instilling pride and self-reliance can be experienced in the opening lines of his poem "White House" (the poem that caused his angry response to Alain Locke, who changed the title for inclusion in *The New Negro*):

Your door is shut against my tightened face,
And I am sharp as steel with discontent;
But I possess the courage and the grace
To bear my anger proudly and unbent.

4. THEIR EYES WERE WATCHING: ZORA NEALE HURSTON

The black woman writing during the Harlem Renaissance had two reluctant audiences to win over: the white reader and the male reader, white and black. For her message wasn't just about the prejudice against color, it was also about the prejudice against gen-der. Janie Crawford, the protagonist of Zora Neale Hurston's (1891–1960) most famous novel, *Their Eyes Were Watching God* (1937), explains, with resignation, the pecking order of her world:

"Honey, de white man is de ruler of everything as fur as Ah been able tub find out. Maybe it's some place off in de ocean where de black man is in power, but we don't know nothin' but we see. So de white man throw down de load and tell de nigger man tuh pick it up. He pick it up because he have to, but he don't tote it. He hand it to his womenfolks. De nigger woman is de mule uh de world so far as Ah can see."

This message is not necessarily the one people wanted to hear, especially those associated with the political activism of the Harlem Renaissance. Feminism, even as mild as this, would have to wait another thirty years before it became a widely accepted theme in fiction. But Zora Neale Hurston chose to go her own way—as a woman, as an artist, and as an African-American—which brought her both praise and condemnation from those who expected her to follow their lead regarding what to write about and how to write about it. Despite these obstacles, Hurston became the most prolific and well-known black woman writer in America.

Hurston was born in Eatonville, Florida, where her father was both the town's mayor and Baptist minister. Her mother offered her advice that young Zora took to heart: "Jump at the sun. We might not land on the sun, but at least we would get off the ground." Her mother's death when Hurston was nine left the eight children with an unstable home life. She went to live with various relatives, eventually attending Howard University, where her short stories caught the attention of Professor Alain Locke. Impressed with her knowledge of black folk heritage, Locke recommended her to Charles S. Johnson, editor of *Opportunity* magazine. In the fall of 1924, Johnson invited Hurston to come to Harlem.

Only a few months later, Hurston made her literary debut at the *Opportunity* awards dinner in the spring of 1925. This event was Charles S. Johnson's masterpiece of public relations, designed to launch "a new period in creative expression among Negroes." Awards were to be given for the best poems, short stories, essays, and plays by black writers. Among the judges were the distinguished white literary icons Fannie Hurst, Robert Benchley, and Alexander Woollcott. That evening, Hurston won more awards than any other writer. It also set the course of her life for the next several years. Best-selling author Fannie Hurst (*Imitation of Life*, 1933) hired Hurston as her personal secretary and chauffeur, and

Annie Nathan Meyer, the founder of Barnard College, gave Hurston a scholarship to attend Barnard, where she became that school's first black graduate.

Hurston enthusiastically embraced the lifestyle of the rising literary star, attending rent parties and literary gatherings with equal joy. "I am just running wild in every direction," she confessed, "trying to see everything at once." Many were impressed with the maturity of someone so young, not realizing that Hurston had deliberately shaved ten years off her age, a fact not discovered until after her death. Maybe awareness of her real age helped convince Hurston to take advantage of the opportunities she was finally receiving because, for the first time in her academic career, she also began to take her studies seriously. At Barnard, she studied anthropology under world-renowned anthropologist Franz Boas. Boas encouraged her to collect the black folktales that she had grown up with. The result was life-altering for Hurston, who before Boas had felt confined by her knowledge of black folklore. Hurston's folklore studies brought her the patronage of wealthy white philanthropist Charlotte Osgood Mason. To encourage Hurston's anthropological collection of folklore in the South, Mason drew up a contract in which she promised to provide Hurston with $200 a month, a movie camera, and a car in exchange for "all of said information, data, transcripts of music, etc., which she shall have obtained."

Hurston's belief that "folk were creating an art that didn't need the sanction of art to affirm its beauty" helped shape her subsequent fiction writing. Rather than write about educated, middle-class characters as did Jessie Fauset and some of the other Harlem writers, she chose not only to write about the poor, working-class Southern blacks she'd grown up with, she also wrote in their slang. Ironically, Hurston's writing was criticized more by black readers than white readers, because they didn't think she was harsh enough in her condemnation of the treatment of blacks in the South. Black critics also accused her of portraying poor blacks in a way that would hold all blacks up to ridicule. Once again, the debate over art and propaganda had come crashing into the literary world, though this time, the attacks seemed more personal.

In 1937, in a fever of inspiration, Hurston wrote in only seven weeks what would become her most famous novel. *Their Eyes Were Watching God*, clearly autobiographical, is more about the plight of being a woman than being black, which is part of the reason her work was criticized by black male critics. Two years later, following the publication of another book on folklore, she published *Moses, Man of the Mountain* (1939), a blending of fiction, folklore, religion, and comedy. Despite critical praise, the book did not sell well. At the request of her publisher, Hurston reluctantly began work on her autobiography, *Dust Tracks on a Road* (1942), which sold well and made her in demand again. However, the next few novels she wrote were rejected by her publisher as not being of high enough quality.

The next few years proved to be overwhelming for Hurston. Her next published novel, *Seraph on the Swanee* (1948), was about white people. Hurston had written to Carl Van Vechten, "I have hopes of breaking that old silly rule about Negroes not writing about white people." Her daring artistic choice brought predictable backlash from black writers who interpreted this as yet another sign that she had abandoned her race. Though the book sold well, Hurston felt even more marginalized by the black community. The final blow came on September 13, 1948, when Hurston was arrested in New York, charged with committing an immoral act with the ten-year-old son of her landlady. Hurston proved she was out of the country when the supposed attack took place, but the subsequent stories in the press devastated her. She couldn't help but wonder whether the readiness to believe the false story was punishment for not writing what some wanted her to write.

Although Hurston continued to publish articles, she never published another novel. Indeed, her situation continued to deteriorate. Broke, she moved back to Florida, where out of desperation she took a job as a maid. When her employers discovered who she was, they called the newspapers and another humiliating headline spit in her face. She immediately claimed that she was merely doing research for a book about domestics, but it was clear that she was struggling to survive. For the rest of her life she worked at temporary jobs such as reporter and librarian, publishing the occasional magazine article. Hurston further alienated African-American civil rights leaders when she wrote a letter to the *Orlando Sentinel* condemning the 1954 landmark U.S. Supreme Court *Brown v. Board of Education* decision, which declared school segregation unconstitutional. For Hurston the decision was a slap in the face to "the self-respect of my people": "How much satisfaction can I get from a court order for somebody to associate with me who does not wish me near them? . . . It is a contradiction in terms to scream race pride and equality while at the same time spurning Negro teachers and self-association."

After a stroke in October of 1959, Hurston was forced to enter the Saint Lucie County Welfare Home, where she died three months later. She was buried in an unmarked grave in a segregated cemetery. A collection was taken up to pay for her funeral. One of the most promising and successful writers of the Harlem Renaissance had died in poverty and obscurity, some critics claim, as a result of her determination to write beyond the confines of what the male African-American intelligentsia demanded. But because of this determination, Hurston was rediscovered in the 1970s, thanks in large part to writer Alice Walker (*The Color Purple*), whose 1975 article for *Ms.* magazine, "In Search of Zora Neale Hurston," caused Hurston's work to be rediscovered and republished. (Walker had a headstone placed on Hurston's grave with the inscription "A Genius of the South.") A 2005 TV movie of *Their Eyes Were Watching God*, starring Halle Berry and produced by Oprah Winfrey, has further increased Hurston's popularity as both a writer and a woman of independent thinking. Janie, the protagonist of *Their Eyes Were Watching God*, may have summed up Hurston's own attitude of living without regret: "If yuh kin see de light at daybreak, you don't keer if you die at dusk. It's so many people never seen de light at all. Ah wuz fumblin' round and God opened de door."

5. THE CANE THAT WAS ABLE: JEAN TOOMER

Nathan Eugene Toomer (1894–1967) struggled with identity issues his whole life. Light-skinned enough to sometimes pass for white, he nevertheless was eager to embrace his black heritage. Yet, at times, he also wanted to distance himself from that heritage. He wanted to be a literary writer, but he didn't always like the elitist circle of other writers it brought him in contact with. He saw himself as of the common people, though he still sometimes placed himself above them.

Born in Washington, D.C., Toomer had the distinction of being the grandson of the first African-American governor in the United States, Pinckney Pinchback of Louisiana. When his father abandoned the family, his mother moved them into her father's autocratic household in Washington, where he attended an all-black school. His mother remarried in 1906, moving the family to an all-white neighborhood in New Rochelle, New York, where Toomer attended an all-white school. Following the death of his mother in 1909, he returned to Washington and attended the all-black Paul Dunbar High School, where Jessie Fauset had taught. His early educational experiences played havoc with his sense of racial identity and cultural heritage, so that by the time he graduated high school in 1914, he'd made the dramatic and naive decision to reject any racial category and live only as an American.

The next seven years were spent wandering the country in search of a personal identity and purpose. For three of those years he became a vagabond student, studying agriculture, physical education, psychology, and literature at various schools. However, despite his great hunger for learning, he never completed a degree. When not attending school, he spent time as a bodybuilder, a welder, a Ford salesman, a physical education instructor, and a hobo. By 1919, the toll of such an undirected and chaotic life resulted in a bout of nervous exhaustion. He was desperate for something to give his life meaningful direction.

In 1920, while attending a party in the Greenwich Village home of Irish-born poet Lola Ridge (*The Ghetto and Other Poems*, 1918), Toomer met a group of writers that he considered to be the "aristocracy of culture, of spirit and character, of ideas, of true nobility." Finally comfortable among a group of people, Toomer quickly became friends with many notable writers, including Edwin Arlington Robinson, Witter Bynner, Hart Crane, Sherwood Anderson, and Malcolm Cowley. Inspired, Toomer returned to Washington, where he would care for his ailing grandfather and begin his own literary career. He wrote relentlessly, churning out plays, poems, essays, and reviews. His poem "The First American" expressed his previous declaration of moving beyond racial classifications: "I wrote a poem called 'The First American,' the idea of which was that here in America we are in the process of forming a new race, that I was one of the first conscious members of this race. . . . I had seen the divisions, the separatisms and antagonisms . . . [yet] a new type of man was arising in this country—not European, not African, not Asiatic—but American. And in this American I saw the divisions mended, the differences reconciled."

In 1921, Toomer underwent an experience that changed his racial attitudes. He moved to Sparta, Georgia, for a job as the temporary principal of the Sparta Agricultural and Industrial Institute. For the first time, he lived among rural Southern blacks and experienced their lives: "There for the first time I really saw the Negro, not as pseudo-urbanized and vulgarized, a semi-Americanized product, but the Negro peasant, strong with the tang of fields and soil." For the two months he spent in Sparta, he studied his surroundings with the same intensity he'd studied everything else. When he emerged, he felt he had finally resolved his own questions of racial identity: "When I live with the blacks, I'm a Negro. When I live with the whites, I'm white, or better, a foreigner. I used to puzzle my own brain with the question. But now I'm done with it."

Not quite done. Toomer used his own spiritual and racial re-birth to write one of the most influential novels of the period, *Cane* (1923). Like himself, the novel defied strict categorization and was hailed as both a seminal work of the Harlem Renaissance because of its focus on race consciousness, and a shining exam-ple of the Lost Generation because of its experimental technique (merging short stories, poetry, plays, and prose) and disillusion-ment with postwar values. Following *Cane*'s publication, Toomer was embraced by the movers and shakers of the Harlem Renais-sance and hailed as the most promising African-American writer of his time. His friend and fellow novelist Waldo Frank rhap-sodized, "[*Cane*] is a harbinger of the South's literary maturity. . . . And, as the initial work of a man of 27, it is a harbinger of a literary force of whose incalculable future I believe no reader of this book will be in doubt." Black critic and writer William Stanley Braithwaite was even more exhuberant: "Jean Toomer . . . artist of the race . . . can write about the Negro with-out the surrender or the compromise of the artist's vision. . . . He would write just as well . . . about the peasants of Russia or . . . Ireland, had experience given him the knowledge of their existence. *Cane* is a book of gold . . . and Jean Toomer is a bright morning star of a new day of the race in literature."

However, Toomer was not comfortable being a part of the movement. To identify himself as part of the Harlem Renaissance meant labeling himself a Negro, which he felt was too confining as both a man and as an artist. He complained to his publisher about referring to him as a Negro writer, stating that "you never use such a word, such a thought again." He confessed to James Weldon Johnson that the "Negro Art movement . . . is for those who have and will benefit by it . . . [but] is not for me." Like Claude McKay, Toomer was more concerned with the bigger picture of class than with color. Color was a distraction, he thought, when the real hope of blacks was to join with other workers to bring about real social change. For Toomer, many of the black elite of the Harlem Re-naissance were fighting to join an already corrupt society that only had room at the banquet for a Talented Tenth. All others, white and black, would always be dining on table scraps.

Despite being hailed as a promising writer, and despite a prolific output of poems, plays, autobiographies, novels, and articles, Toomer never again published with a commercial house. Publishers found his writing after *Cane* to be boring and indulgent, and they pointed out that *Cane* had sold less than five hundred copies. Toomer continued his spiritual quest as well, finally joining the Society of Friends and devoting the rest of his life to activities within the Quaker community.

6. THE SWEET HARVEST OF WALLACE THURMAN

While the old guard of Alain Locke and W. E. B. Du Bois were carefully crafting a cadre of accomplished literary talents to parade proudly down the wide boulevard of white culture, a few of the younger African-American writers who were either denied entry or who were uncomfortable being among the anointed were looking for other means to express their views. In 1925, Wallace Thurman (1902–34), a talented writer and influential editor, arrived in Harlem at the age of twenty-three boldly ready to gather those misfits into their own literary circle to make their views widely known.

Like Jean Toomer and Claude McKay, Thurman rejected the notion that the Harlem Renaissance should be nothing more than a publicity machine to promote politics regardless of the quality of the writing. Like Toomer, he was especially sensitive about racial identity, but in Thurman's case, he resented the prejudice within the black community, which obviously valued lighter skin versus the darker skin that Thurman had. One of his most dramatic encounters with this kind of prejudice occurred when his friend Langston Hughes introduced him to writer and artist Richard Bruce Nugent at a cafeteria. Light-skinned Nugent was shocked by the darkness of Thurman's skin to the point that he later admitted he couldn't eat. (This scene is portrayed in the dramatic film *Brother to Brother*, 2004.) "How dare he be so black," Nugent recalled thinking. Though they became good friends, collaborators, and roommates, that encounter left its mark on Thurman.

To Thurman, this kind of skin color bias among African-Americans proved a much deeper brainwashing than could be scrubbed away by a few novels about educated blacks that were hailed by educated whites. Thurman argued that chasing after the approval of white critics was especially detrimental because they used lower standards to judge black writing. This is why, he complained, the Harlem Renaissance wasn't a true literary movement. If anything, it was keeping the real talented black writers from being discovered. So, when Du Bois attacked writer Rudolph Fisher for not providing "glimpses of a better class of Negroes" in his realistic novel *The Walls of Jericho,* Thurman wrote exactly what was wrong with Du Bois's narrow criteria and the damage that was doing to the black aesthetic:

Were [Du Bois] a denizen of "Striver's Row," scuttling hard up the social ladder, with nothing more important to think about than making money and keeping a high yellow wife bleached out and marcelled, one would laugh at such nonsense and dismiss it from one's mind. But Dr. Du Bois is not this. He is one of the outstanding Negroes of this or any other generation. He has served his race well; so well, in fact, that the artist in him has been stifled in order that the propagandist may thrive. No one will object to this being called noble and necessary sacrifice, but the days for such sacrifices are gone. The time has come now when the Negro artist can be his true self and pander to the stupidities of no one, either white or black.

Thurman's feelings of being an outsider from the mainstream renaissance movement was further complicated by his open homosexuality. Some of the Renaissance's most respected literary figures were also homosexual or bisexual, including Claude McKay, Countee Cullen, Alain Locke, Richard Bruce Nugent, and, some say, Langston Hughes, who wrote extensively about gay Harlem. Explains a homosexual character in Blair Niles's 1931 novel, *Strange Brother,* "In Harlem I found courage and joy and tolerance.

I can be myself there . . . They know all about me and I don't have to lie." In fact, Harlem featured several clubs where gays and lesbians could mingle freely and safely, including Rockland Palace, the Garden of Joy Club, and the Clam House. Performers at these clubs—including Gladys Bentley, Alberta Hunter, Jackie "Moms" Mabley, Mabel Hampton, Ma Rainey, Ethel Waters, and Bessie Smith—sang sensual songs with double-entendre lyrics about gay and lesbian love. Like the hippie movement of the 1960s, the Harlem Renaissance was a time of sexual, as well as artistic and political, experimentation. However, experimentation doesn't mean acceptance. Mainstream African-Americans were no more tolerant (some historians say even less so) than whites regarding homosexuality. And the old guard decided that their goal of promoting blacks as equals to whites might be compromised, or at least distracted, by support of homosexuality in their writings. Thurman hoped to change that, too.

Born in Salt Lake City, Thurman was raised in Los Angeles, where he tried to emulate the Harlem Renaissance by launching his own publication for the New Negro, the *Outlet*. The magazine ceased after six months, and in 1925 Thurman decided to move to Harlem, where he became managing editor of the radical magazine the *Messenger*, publishing works by pals Langston Hughes and Zora Neale Hurston. He left to take a job as the first black editorial assistant on a white publication, the *World Tomorrow*. That summer, Langston Hughes and Bruce Nugent approached Thurman to edit and help finance their new magazine, *Fire!!*, which was to feature the young writers and artists of the Harlem Renaissance, with its goal "to satisfy pagan thirst unadorned." By presenting literature for its own sake, with no social or political agenda, they would publicly distance themselves somewhat from the more rigid artistic ideals of Du Bois and Locke. The magazine, which offered works by Hughes, Thurman, Nugent, Hurston, and Countee Cullen and was illustrated by Aaron Douglas, made a bold literary statement, though it folded after the first issue. But the gauntlet had been thrown down in no uncertain terms, which Thurman reiterated in an editorial in his next magazine, *Harlem: A Forum of Negro Life* (which also folded after a single issue), when he declared that he and the writers in the magazine spoke for the *new* New Negro. Now Thurman and his tight circle of writers and artists would have to prove that their voices spoke more truthfully for their fellow African-Americans.

The rooming house where Thurman lived on West 136th Street was owned by Iolanthe Sydney, who allowed young artists and writers to stay rent-free because she believed being poor was a necessary ingredient to the artistic impulse. Because of the frequent gatherings here of the new generation of black artists and literary lions—Hurston and Hughes lived here briefly—Hurston nicknamed the place Niggerati Manor (which Thurman portrays in his 1932 novel *Infants of the Spring*). The bohemian lifestyle within those walls became infamous. One frequent guest claimed that, despite Prohibition, "the bathtubs in the house were always packed with sourmash, while the gin flowed from all the water taps and the flush boxes were filled with needle beer [so named from the practice of injecting alcohol with a needle through the cork of nonalcoholic beer]."

Thurman's first play, *Harlem: A Melodrama of Negro Life in Harlem* (1929), had a successful run, though it received the kind of reviews that were to be expected whenever a black writer wrote an unflattering portrait of Harlem. Theater critic R. Dana Skinner was disturbed by "the particular way in which this melodrama exploits the worst features of the Negro and depends for its effects solely on the explosions of lust and sensuality." Other critics found it "exciting" and "constantly entertaining." This demarcation of responses followed Thurman throughout his literary life. His novels, plays, even the screenplays he wrote when he went back to California for a brief time, never achieved the unqualified acclaim others achieved. His middling literary acceptance, combined with his outsider feelings due to his sexual preference and skin color, left him racked with self-doubt, which was further complicated by poor health due to tuberculosis and alcoholism. When his doctor advised him that his health had deteriorated to such a degree that he needed to immediately quit drinking, Thurman instead returned to New York for a solid month of drinking and partying. His final six months of life were spent in the Welfare Island City Hospital, which he had written an exposé about in his novel *The Interne* (1932). Like his friend Zora Neale Hurston, he died in poverty. And like Hurston, neither poverty nor death (at the age of thirty-two) prevented him from influencing not only his own generation, but also generation after generation of writers that followed.

In his 1929 novel, *The Blacker the Berry*, which comes from the folk saying "The blacker the berry, the sweeter the juice," Thurman explains, through this monologue by a character symbolically named Truman, his conviction that prejudice among African-Americans reveals their deep need to achieve acceptance by the white community and white standards, a flaw that ultimately doomed the Harlem Renaissance to fail:

"Color prejudice and religion are akin in one respect. Some folks have it and some don't, and the kernel that is responsible for it is present in all of us, which is to say, that potentially we are all color-prejudiced as long as we remain in this environment."

7. THE MARVEL THAT IS COUNTEE CULLEN

One of the great ironies of the Harlem Renaissance was that, although it was a movement that tried to both unify African-Americans and present a unified image of black Americans, several of its most outstanding spokespersons were individuals who often felt alienated from both the black and white cultures. Countee Cullen (1903–46), considered one of the best poets to emerge from the Harlem Renaissance, was raised and educated in a mostly white community. This left him somewhat alienated from the usual experiences of African-Americans, which is why he often refrained in his writing from exploring the typical racial themes, though the poems considered his best dealt directly and eloquently with race. He preferred to be known as a poet rather than a black poet, wanting his audience to focus on the timeless themes of his work rather than limiting them to a particular date and place in history:

If I am going to be a poet at all, I am going to be POET and not NEGRO POET. This is what has hindered the development of artists among us. Their one note has been the concern with their race. That is all very well, none of us can get away from it. I cannot at times. . . . But what I mean is this: I shall not write of negro subjects for the purpose of propaganda. That is not what a poet is concerned with. Of course, when the emotion rising out of the fact that I am a negro is strong, I express it. But that is another matter.

Born in New York City, Cullen was adopted by the Reverend and Mrs. Frederick Ashbury Cullen, who raised him with strong Methodist values. In 1922, he attended New York University, where, for three consecutive years, he won national poetry contests open to all American students. He graduated Phi Beta Kappa in 1925 with degrees in English and French, immediately entering Harvard University to begin work on his master's degree. By now, he had already published poetry in the black community's two most important magazines, the *Crisis* and *Opportunity*. By 1924, his poetry had also appeared in important white publications such as *Harper's*, *Century*, *American Mercury*, and *Bookman*. The same year he graduated college, his first book of poetry, *Color*, was published to the kind of rave reviews writers don't dare dream of. Alain Locke declared, "Ladies and gentleman! A genius! Posterity will laugh at us if we do not proclaim him now." The critic at the *Yale Review* was even more enamored: "There is no point in measuring him merely by . . . other Negro poets of the past and present: he must stand or fail beside Shakespeare and Keats and Masefield, Whitman and Poe and Robinson."

With such accolades from both black and white critics, with his strong Christian values, and with his neat, formal attire (and his Phi Beta Kappa key always clearly visible), Cullen was quickly embraced by the leaders of the Harlem Renaissance. They had found their poster boy for the Talented Tenth. If he had a morose streak in his poetry, and if he rejected being called a "Negro poet," those were small concessions to be able to display his black face above the label "New Negro" for all the white world to see and admire.

To make his storybook ascendancy to Harlem intellectual royalty complete, in 1928 Cullen married Yolande Du Bois, the daughter of W. E. B. Du Bois, in one of the most spectacular weddings Harlem had ever seen. Over a dozen police officers kept order on the streets as a crowd of three thousand guests attended. Cullen saw it as "the symbolic march of young and black America . . . it was a new race, a new thought, a new thing rejoicing in a ceremony as old as the world." Unfortunately, the marriage existed only as a symbol: two months after the wedding, Cullen, who was in love with Harold Jackman, his best man and friend since high school, left with Jackman for Europe—without Yolande. The divorce was finalized two years later.

By 1930, after producing some of the most memorable poetry of the time, the brightest flame of the Harlem Renaissance was already flickering out. His reliance on traditional poetic forms such as sonnets, which had made him popular in the beginning, was now criticized as being too mired in white culture. His writing was nothing like the jazz-inspired work of friend and rival Langston Hughes. Even after he was no longer Harlem's Golden Child, he was popular as a speaker, his poems were studied in universities, and much of his verse was set to music by popular composers. Yet, none of this was enough to pay the bills.

Eventually, he was forced to take a job teaching French and English in Frederick Douglass High School, where he proved to be an inspiration to at least one of his students, future literary great James Baldwin. Though Cullen continued to write poetry and published a novel, *One Way to Heaven* (1932), he also produced children's literature that was "coauthored" by his cat, Christopher (*The Lost Zoo*, 1940 and *My Lives and How I Lost Them*, 1942).

In 1940, Cullen married Ida Mae Robertson. During the last years of his life, Cullen worked arduously on a play, *St. Louis Woman*, a musical adaptation of fellow Harlem Renaissance writer

Arna Bontemps's novel *God Sends Sunday*, with music by Harold Arlen ("Over the Rainbow") and lyrics by Johnny Mercer (*Seven Brides for Seven Brothers*), both white. Opening on Broadway in 1946, the show was reviled by Walter White of the NAACP and other civil rights activists for its unflattering portrayal of African-Americans, a charge that Cullen was not used to receiving since he himself was being presented, like a work of art, as the most flattering portrayal of African-Americans.

Cullen had always been suspicious of the mixture of race themes with art. He worried that the artist could be cast aside when his art didn't match the political needs of his supporters. But history has a more democratic way of judging an artist: by the power of his work. And never was Countee Cullen more powerful then in his signature poem, "Yet Do I Marvel," which still inspires poets eighty years after it was read aloud at the Harlem YMCA:

I doubt not God is good, well-meaning, kind,
And did He stoop to quibble could tell why
The little buried mole continues blind,
Why flesh that mirrors Him must someday die,
Make plain the reason tortured Tantalus
Is baited by the fickle fruit, declare
If merely brute caprice dooms Sisyphus
To struggle up a never-ending stair,
Inscrutable His ways are, and immune
To catechism by a mind too strewn
With petty cares to slightly understand
What awful brain compels His awful hand.
Yet do I marvel at this curious thing:
To make a poet black, and bid him sing!

8. THE WORLD SPEAKS OF LANGSTON HUGHES

Upon first meeting Langston Hughes (1902–67) in 1925, writer/artist Richard Bruce Nugent described his stunned reaction: "He was a made-to-order Hero for me. He had done everything—

all the things young men dream of but never quite get done—worked on ships, gone to exotic places." This reaction is similar to how Hughes affected almost everyone he met, which, along with his prodigious talent and prolific output, helped make him the most enduringly famous and popular writer to come out of the Harlem Renaissance. It was part of Hughes's genius that he balanced being a great artist with the ability to move with such ease and respect among the various factions of the Harlem Renaissance, both black and white.

Hughes was born in Joplin, Missouri, but spent much of his youth traveling, partially a result of his parents' lifestyle and partially because of his own wanderlust. His attorney father, convinced that there was no opportunity for blacks in America, moved to Mexico City when Hughes was a child. At first, Hughes's mother refused to follow; but when Hughes was six years old, she and her son joined her husband in Mexico City. But after an earthquake shook the city, she returned to the United States, dropping young Langston off with her mother while she continued traveling. His grandmother raised him with a strong sense of political awareness: her first husband had died at Harpers Ferry, a member of John Brown's fighters; her second husband had been a staunch abolitionist. Several years later, after his mother had remarried and had another son, Hughes joined her in Lincoln, Illinois. The family then moved to Cleveland, Ohio, where his mother divorced her second husband and moved to Chicago with her son Kit. Hughes remained in Cleveland, alone and on his own at fourteen. This abandonment and subsequent loneliness, he later recalled, drove him to find comfort with "books, and the wonderful world in books." It also drove him to write, because "when I felt bad, writing kept me from feeling worse."

In his junior year of high school Hughes's gift for poetry emerged. He was named editor of the school yearbook and Class Poet in his senior year. More remarkable, one of his poems, "The Negro Speaks of Rivers," which he had scribbled on an envelope while crossing the Mississippi on a train to visit his father, was published in the *Crisis*. Jessie Fauset later recalled, "I took the beautiful dignified creation to Dr. Du Bois and said, 'What colored person is there, do you suppose, in the United States who writes like that and yet is unknown to us?'" Hughes would never be unknown again. (The poem, one of his most famous, was recited at his funeral.)

After the publication of his poem, Hughes was eager to travel to Harlem. Upon graduation in 1921, he did just that. When he came out of the subway and saw Harlem for the first time, it was as if he'd entered an enchanted land: "Hundreds of colored people! I wanted to shake hands with them, speak to them. I hadn't seen any colored people for so long." He began studies at Columbia University, but soon dropped out to work menial jobs while writing his poetry. Finally, anxious to be on the move again, twenty-one-year-old Hughes took work aboard a cargo ship bound for Africa. From the ship's deck, Hughes tossed into the sea the books he'd studied at Columbia, keeping only Walt Whitman's *Leaves of Grass*.

Hughes approached Africa with a great sense of awe, not unlike his first sighting of Harlem. But the reality was disillusioning: poverty, children being sold, and, worse, when he spoke to native Africans about his and their similarities, they merely pointed to his light skin and wavy hair and said, "You white man! You white man!" He also received a different perspective on Harlem politics: everywhere he stopped, he heard locals speak of Marcus Garvey, "and the Africans did not laugh at Marcus Garvey, as so many people laughed in New York." Hughes did not travel to Africa with Du Bois's or Garvey's grand pan-African agenda, yet when he returned in 1924, he had already seen more of Africa than either of them from their offices in Harlem.

After only four months, Hughes took work on a ship bound for Holland. He then made his way to Paris, where he lived by working odd jobs. He returned to Harlem and went straight to his friend Countee Cullen's house. Together they attended an NAACP benefit where Hughes was warmly welcomed by W. E. B. Du Bois and the rest of the Renaissance literati. However, within a few weeks, the close friendship between Cullen and Hughes was shattered; though both wrote about the pain the break caused each of them, neither revealed the specific cause.

In quick succession, Hughes published two collections of poetry, *The Weary Blues* (1926) and *Fine Clothes to the Jew* (1927), both merging jazz and blues with more traditional forms of poetry. Like McKay, Toomer, and Thurman, he was attacked by some black critics who thought his portrayal of life among lower-class blacks was a betrayal to the New Negro image. In 1926, Hughes responded in the *Nation* with his now famous artistic manifesto, "The Negro Artist and the Racial Mountain." In this excerpt, he answers the question of why his poems use so much jazz, a question, Hughes believed, that showed an inherent self-hatred in blacks who asked it:

But jazz to me is one of the inherent expressions of Negro life in America: the eternal tom-tom beating in the Negro soul—the tom-tom of revolt against weariness in a white world, a world of subway trains, and work, work, work; the tom-tom of joy and laughter, and pain swallowed in a smile. Yet the Philadelphia clubwoman is ashamed to say that her race created it and she does not like me to write about it. The old subconscious "white is best" runs through her mind. Years of study under white teachers, a lifetime of white books, pictures, and papers, and white manners, morals, and Puritan standards made her dislike the spirituals. And now she turns up her nose at jazz and all its manifestations—likewise almost everything else distinctly racial. She doesn't care for the Winold Reiss portraits of Negroes because they are "too Negro." She does not want a true picture of herself from anybody. She wants the artist to flatter her, to make the white world believe that all Negroes are as smug and as near white in soul as she wants to be. But, to my mind, it is the duty of the younger Negro artist, if he accepts any duties at all from outsiders, to change through the force of his art that old whispering "I want to be white," hidden in the aspirations of his people, to "Why should I want to be white? I am a Negro—and beautiful!"

Like Zora Neale Hurston, Hughes was not able to survive on the admiration of reviewers and in 1927 accepted financial support from wealthy white philanthropist Charlotte Mason. She supported his return to college at Lincoln University in Pennsylvania, which he graduated from in 1929, and encouraged him to write a novel, *Not Without Laughter* (1930). By the time the novel was published, Hughes had pulled away from Mason, and his relationships with Hurston and Locke had also crumbled. He began another period of travel, first spending seven months barnstorming through the Deep South, where he read his poems (at one point, through the bars to the Scottsboro Boys) and sold inexpensive collections of his poetry to audiences. His firsthand experiences with Jim Crow laws radicalized his political beliefs. When he finished his tour, he joined a twenty-two person delegation to Russia to make a film about American racial relations. The film was never made, but Hughes spent fourteen months traveling across Russia, becoming, according to one observer, "the traveling star of colored America."

Hughes's writing also became more political, as he produced polemic essays and poems, yet earned a living writing Broadway plays (*Mulatto*, 1935) as well as children's verse and fiction for commercial magazines. During the Harlem Renaissance, he had actively fought the artistic restraints of using writers for propaganda, but now he encouraged it. "It is the social duty of Negro writers," he wrote, "to reveal to the people the deep reservoirs of heroism within the race." A younger, less jaded Hughes would have remarked that just by being talented, articulate, and insightful, the African-American writer was already being heroic.

Unlike many of his Harlem Renaissance colleagues, Hughes continued to be prolific and widely read long after the Renaissance had "officially" ended. He wrote many plays, poems, essays, and stories as well as two autobiographies, *The Big Sea* (1940) and *I Wonder as I Wander* (1956). Although his political views became much more moderate following World War II, he was still called before the House Un-American Activities Committee in 1953. Hughes refused to give the committee any names, but he did renounce some of his earlier radical positions. By the end, he was dismissed as a "friendly witness." Eighty-three-year-old W. E. B. Du Bois, on the other hand, remained defiant and unrepentant before the committee.

Hughes's final years were spent living in a brownstone in Harlem, where he continued his prolific output. One of his most memorable literary achievements is a collection of stories featuring the Harlem character Jesse B. Semple, referred to as Simple, whose direct and honest views, mostly about race issues, given to the reserved narrator at a neighborhood bar, resulted in five popular collections, beginning with *Simple Speaks His Mind* (1950). He also produced his most political book of poetry, *The Panther and the Lash* (1967). In 1967, suffering from severe abdominal pains, he checked himself into a hospital under the name James L. Hughes, not telling anyone that he was there. He died two weeks later.

Langston Hughes's funeral service was a celebration of the fruits of the Harlem Renaissance he had come to embody: jazz and blues music were played, poems were recited, and Duke Ellington's "Do Nothing Until You Hear from Me" ended the service. Later, as his body was being cremated, his dearest friends recited his first published poem, "The Negro Speaks of Rivers." And, while that poem is rich with youthful intensity and longing for heritage, a poem more representative of Hughes's wit, charm, and razor-cut observation, "Dinner Guest: Me," places him enjoying the admiration of his white hosts, yet ever aware of being the outsider:

I know I am
The Negro Problem
Being wined and dined,
Answering the usual questions
That come to white mind
Which seeks demurely
To probe in polite way
The why and wherewithal
Of darkness U.S.A.—

Wondering how things got this way
In current democratic night,
Murmuring gently
Over fraise du bois,
"I'm so ashamed of being white."
The lobster is delicious.
The wine divine,
And center of attention
At the damask table, mine.
To be a Problem on
Park Avenue at eight
Is not so bad.
Solutions to the Problem,
Of course, wait.

WORDS OF THE WISE:
THE LEGACY OF THE HARLEM WRITERS

Langston Hughes's closest friends holding hands and reciting a
defining poem in African-American history as his body is fed to
the flames of the crematorium. What a wonderful metaphor that
could be: a symbolic choir of the Talented Tenth singing the
gospel of the spirit of the Harlem Renaissance as its final surviving
minister is laid to rest, his shining words echoing from their hopeful lips into history. Then we could catalog all the names of the famous African-Americans and white Americans that have been
inspired by those words. How poetic! How uplifting!

How insulting.

These giants of the Harlem Renaissance weren't heroes because they were flawless. They were heroes because, despite petty
jealousies, philosophical differences, and romantic disappointments among themselves, they still found ways to express enduring
principles, values, and beliefs that they thought would benefit their
community, whether that be the African-American community, or

the American community, or the world community. They had a vision beyond themselves for a better world. Sometimes the vision burned bright their whole lives and they continued to carry that torch right up until the end; sometimes it burned too bright and they confused their own ambitions with those of their vision and it incinerated them. They were uncommon people dedicated to a common cause—and that cause made them great. But, if the Harlem Renaissance teaches us anything, it is to see each of them as a human being, not just an icon of color. And to marvel that sometimes human beings can translate into words the chaos of passions, frustrations, and hopes we hold for the future—and make those words echo forever, not just in dusty tomes of history, but in the richest need in our hearts.

The Great Black Migration. The Harlem Renaissance became possible, if not necessary, because of the influx of millions of African-Americans from the South to the North. Many of the key men and women of the Renaissance were such immigrants. The three main reasons for the mass immigration were the failure of the cotton crop, which caused economic devastation in the South; the harsh and discriminatory Jim Crow laws, and the onset of World War I, which caused a shortage of workers in Northern factories. (Clockwise from top left: Southern family migrating to the North; black soldiers in trenches during World War I; segregation sign; editorial cartoon from *The Crisis* (1920) showing a black man leaving the South and lynching behind.)

The Savoy

The Renaissance Casino & Ballroom

Jungle Alley. The popularity of Harlem among monied whites was due in large part to Jungle Alley, the patch of 133rd Street between Lenox Avenue and Seventh Avenue that hosted the most nightclubs in New York City. While the Savoy and Renaissance Casino and Ballroom served the black community, the Cotton Club, Small's Paradise, and Connie's Inn were whites-only clubs. Though founding fathers of the Harlem Renaissance W. E. B. DuBois, Charles S. Johnson, and Alain Locke tried to downplay the seedier side of Harlem life in Jungle Alley as an embarrassing by-product of progress, younger writers such as Claude McKay, Wallace Thurman, and Langston Hughes wrote extensively about it as a celebration of a suppressed people finally emerging from the invisibility of racism. Jungle Alley was where jazz took root and spread across the country, thanks to national radio broadcasts from places such as the Cotton Club.

The Cotton Club

Connie's Inn

Small's Paradise

The lynching of four unidentified African-Americans, circa 1900. Lynching was a common method of terrorizing the black community into submission, as well as stemming the Great Black Migration from the South. Between 1889 and 1918, 2,522 blacks were lynched, 79% in Southern communities. Causes for being lynched included everything from homicide to theft to "insult to a white person." Until 1918, not one person in the South was punished for participating in a lynching. This situation spurred more blacks to migrate north. "Every time a lynching takes place in a community down South," said Chicago's Urban League President T. Arnold Hall, "you can depend on it that colored people will arrive in Chicago within two weeks."

10

Harlem Riots of 1964. The riots lasted five days, with 1 person being killed, 100 injured, and 520 arrested. Seventeen-year-old Kareem unwittingly stepped into the middle of the chaos and began to run for his life. This event helped shape Kareem's political awareness.

11

The Curse of Blackface. The Harlem Renaissance fought hard to erase the racist image that white Americans had of African-Americans. To a large part, the stereotypes that were so firmly lodged in the white consciousness were the result of the minstrel shows in which whites pretended to be blacks in order to ridicule their behavior. These derogatory attitudes were legitimized when beloved celebrities donned blackface to continue the practice. (Clockwise: A 1900 minstrel show poster; advertisement for the popular *Amos 'n' Andy Show*; Bing Crosby in blackface in *Dixie* [1943]; Judy Garland in blackface.)

12

13

14

15

Kareem, ten, towers above his team-mates at St. Jude's Day Camp, 1958. Although his first love was baseball, Kareem's height made it inevitable that he would give basketball a chance. At first awkward and clumsy, he began practicing by himself in order to develop the skills he would need.

16

17

Kareem, Power Memorial, 1964. Despite his realization that the school offered very little teaching about African-American history or culture, Kareem was an accomplished student, earning high grades.

Kareem, Power Memorial, ca. 1964. With only one black teacher at the Catholic school, Kareem often felt out of place.

18

Left: The only face-to-face meeting between Malcolm X and Dr. Martin Luther King Jr., 1964. Despite conflicting approaches to solving the civil rights problem, both men represented ideologies rose to prominence during the Harlem Renaissance. Their individual beliefs sprang directly from the political writings of Garvey, Du Bois, and Locke. Both men deeply influenced Kareem's religious and political development. Right: High-school journalism student Kareem covering a press conference with Dr. Martin Luther King Jr.

Movers and Shakers. These three men did the most to promote the Harlem Renaissance ideals of black self-reliance, achievement, and political solidarity. Their influence was felt not just throughout the United States but also across most of the world. Because of them, African-American writers, artists, intellectuals, athletes, and politicians were accorded greater acclaim and respect. Right: W. E. B. Du Bois (1868–1963), c.1910. Editor of the influential periodical *Crisis*, Du Bois discovered and promoted most of the prominent writers, artists, and intellectuals of the Harlem Renaissance. He avidly promoted the "New Negro" Movement with such conviction that most blacks and whites saw him as the movement's spokesperson.

Charles S. Johnson. Along with Du Bois and Locke, Johnson (1893–1956) formed the "holy trinity" of Harlem Renaissance founding activists. Though more conservative than Du Bois, Johnson tried to work behind the scenes to effect change. Born in Virginia, he moved north as part of the Great Black Migration, eventually distinguishing himself as the first black president of historically black Fisk University. As editor of the National Urban League's periodical, *Opportunity*, he guided many young writers of the Harlem Renaissance.

Alain Locke (1886–1954), 1926. Locke was a philosopher, educator, writer, and one of the prime proponents of the Harlem Renaissance. The first black Rhodes scholar, he also edited the "bible" of the Renaissance, *The New Negro* (1925), an anthology of essays, stories, poetry, and art that defined the goals of the movement.

James Weldon Johnson. A prominent author, poet, civil rights activist, and leader of the Harlem Renaissance, Weldon (1871–1938) brought his vast experience to the movement. He was the first black accepted to the Florida bar, served as U.S. consul to Venezuela and Nicaragua, and was one of the first black professors at New York University. His novel, *The Autobiography of an Ex-Colored Man* (1912) and book of verse, *God's Trombones* (1927) are classics of the era. He also wrote the lyrics (his brother wrote the music) for "Lift Ev'ry Voice and Sing," commonly known as the "Black National anthem."

24

Claude McKay. Jamaican-born McKay (1889–1948) was one of the first Harlem Renaissance writers to produce a bestselling novel, *Home to Harlem* (1928). His early work, a collection of poems called *Harlem Shadows* (1922), was one of the first Harlem Renaissance works published. Frustrated with the slow progress of civil rights movement in America, McKay became a communist and traveled the world promoting black nationalism and civil rights.

25

Jean Toomer, 1916. Toomer's (1894–1967) light skin allowed him to attend both all-white and all-black schools. His restlessness led him to attend many colleges, but graduate from none, as well as work a variety of jobs, from car salesman to bodybuilder. During a teaching job in the South, he experienced his first exposure to the Jim Crow South. The experience resulted in the novel *Cane* (1923), considered a major contribution to the literature of both the Harlem Renaissance and the Lost Generation.

26

Wallace Thurman, 1928. Thurman (1902–34) was one of the Harlem Renaissance's most energetic writers. His most famous work, the novel *The Blacker the Berry: A Novel of Negro Life* (1929), explores the discrimination based on skin color within the black community, something he experienced due to his dark skin. His depiction of the underbelly of Harlem life earned him both praise and criticism from the black community.

27

Countee Cullen, 1925. Cullen (1903–46) proved to be one of the most popular poets of the Harlem Renaissance. He started writing poetry at fourteen, and was soon publishing in magazines such as *Harper's*, *Century Magazine*, *Poetry*, *Opportunity*, and *Crisis*. He received his master's degree from Harvard University.

28

29

Langston Hughes (1902–67) as a busboy at Wardman Park Hotel, Washington, D.C., 1925. It was here that the famous poet Vachel Lindsay was dining before giving a public poetry reading. While working as a busboy, Hughes is said to have dropped his poems beside Lindsay's plate. The poet was so impressed that during his reading that night, he also read some of Hughes's poems. Interviews with the "busboy poet" followed. Soon after, Hughes quit his job and moved to New York City.

Legacy of the Harlem Renaissance. Right: Langston Hughes signing autographs for children during Negro History Week. Until his death in 1967, Hughes remained the most popular and recognizable writer to come out of the Harlem Renaissance.

30

31

Teenage Kareem riding the subway. As a youth, Kareem was an avid reader, exceptional student, and burgeoning journalist. He spent many hours at the library studying the Harlem Renaissance.

Kareem and friend Michael Bendik
playing around, ca. 1964–65.

Zora Neale Hurston, 1935. Hurston (1891–1960) was involved in every aspect of the Renaissance, from the wild parties at Wallace Thurman's apartment, to the collecting of important historical folk tales from Southern blacks, to producing some of the most acclaimed literary works of the era. One of the most vital and influential writers of the Harlem Renaissance, her novels, including (*Their Eyes Were Watching God*), and anthropological works are still widely read.

33

34

Jessie Fauset, Langston Hughes, Zora Neale Hurston at grave of Booker T. Washington, 1927. Three of America's most dominant literary influences pay homage to Booker T. Washington, the leading spokesperson for African-Americans before the Harlem Renaissance. Ironically, the Renaissance's political goals were in direct opposition to Washington's own philosophy.

35

The Talented Tenth, 1924. Langston Hughes, Charles S. Johnson (editor of the influential National Urban League periodical *Opportunity: A Journal of Negro Life*), sociologist E. Franklin Frazier (author of *The Negro Family in the United States*), Rudolph Fisher (physician and author of the first black detective novel, *The Conjure-Man Dies*), Hubert T. Delaney (attorney and judge) at a party honoring Hughes.

Marcus Garvey (1887–1940). Tireless crusader for black nationalism, Jamaican-born Garvey founded the Universal Negro Improvement Association and African Communities League (UNIA-ACL). Though his back-to-Africa shipping line ended disastrously, his impact on civil rights activism was enormous. Garvey was often at odds with other Harlem Renaissance leaders, such as Du Bois, because his gaudy uniform and fiery speeches appealed to the working classes, while Du Bois and Locke promoted the more educated image of the Talented Tenth.

36

"The Gifts That My Ancestors Gave"

How Harlem Writers Influenced My Life

BY KAREEM ABDUL-JABBAR

■ When I read great literature, great drama, speeches, or sermons, I feel that the human mind has not achieved anything greater than the ability to share feelings and thoughts through language.

JAMES EARL JONES

I used to play basketball.

Since retiring as a professional basketball player eighteen years ago, I've done many things: sports announcing, scouting, acting, coaching. But the occupation I feel most defines all the aspects of who I am at this time in my life is writer.

What surprises people about me so much isn't that I'm a writer. Lots of celebrities write books, mostly about how they became celebrities or how you, too, can cook, do yoga, or stay young like a celebrity. What surprises people is that I write books about history. Granted, three of my books were autobiographical, but that, too, is a form of history. My history. And in each I tried to do more than just detail my relationship with basketball. *Giant Steps* (1983) explores the complicated coming-of-age process of how I became a man—a man who also happened to be a professional basketball player. *Kareem* (1990), a diary of my farewell season in 1989, focuses on how being an African-American in this society brought me from two obscure rooms in Harlem to that well-publicized last season. *A Season on the Reservation: My Sojourn with the White Mountain Apaches* (2000) was not so much about me as about the White Mountain Apache high school basketball team I helped coach for a season. While I recounted my trials, triumphs, and shortcomings as a coach, mostly I wanted the book to be about the high school team in the context of their rich Native American history and my involvement with them in the context of my equally rich African-American history. Not so much a collision of two cultures, but a wary dance of sorts as our pasts sniffed each other's present—and found a way to respectfully learn from the other. Though the details in each of those books were indeed my personal history, the real story was about my small place in a much larger canvas of African-American history.

My other two books are pure Kareem-less history. *Black Profiles in Courage: A Legacy of African-American Achievement* (1996) presented a group of outstanding African-American role models for children of color who are forced to read history books in school that mostly ignore black achievements. How can black children grow up with a strong sense of self-respect and hope if they rarely see people like them honored and exalted? Sure, they can go to the sports arena and see black athletes chasing different-shaped balls, turn on MTV and see a variety of black performers singing and dancing, or go to the movies and see a few black leading actors. But our history is so much richer than that of performers. It's filled with inspiring examples of heroism, creativity, ingenuity, and genius. I wrote that book because I wanted kids to see the broader spectrum of opportunities. To see the many paths open to them by profiling admirable historical figures to act as their trail guides.

Brothers in Arms: The Epic Story of the 761st Tank Battalion, WWII's Forgotten Heroes (2004) recounts the heroic exploits of the 676 enlisted men and 36 officers of an all-black tank battalion. Despite a horrendous casualty rate of 50 percent and unrelenting racism from white commanding officers and fellow enlisted men, these men never balked, never gave up. Recent war movies have shown the faces of courage when they look like Mel Gibson (*We Were Soldiers*) or Bruce Willis (*Tears of the Sun*). The highly decorated warriors in *Brothers in Arms* showed the world what the face of bravery looked like when it was black.

My interest in history is less academic and much more practical. I'm not interested in gathering amusing tidbits of historical trivia so people can sit around a fancy restaurant table sniffing the bouquet of their wine while repeating the information to entertain each other. The people I write about fought and struggled and suffered, and I want all that to count for something. I want their history to inform and excite and inspire the reader. As it did me. Harlem Renaissance leader Marcus Garvey said, "A people without the knowledge of their past history, origin and culture is like a tree without roots." This has been my guiding principle in choosing what to write and how to approach the material. For some, history is a drab and dusty subject; for me it is a powerful stimulant, arousing our passions about past injustices and infusing us with strength to fight present ones. The only way I know how to share my passion about history and its power to affect our lives is to write these books.

Which brings us to *On the Shoulders of Giants*. Once again, I'm relating some autobiographical material, but only with a specific focus: how a particular time in history opened my eyes about who I was—as an American, as an African-American—and inspired me to become more than I might otherwise have become. Yes, I was seven feet tall, and had I not discovered the Harlem Renaissance, I would probably still have become a successful professional basketball player and had a role in *Airplane!* But having a successful career is not nearly enough to make one happy or fulfilled. If the pinnacle of my influence as a human being was perfecting the skyhook, I would not feel very satisfied. Learning about the Harlem Renaissance allowed me to enjoy my success because I could understand it better and use it to do more. There's an old saying, "A rising tide lifts all boats." The Harlem Renaissance taught me that my success could also be others' success.

Despite my having written several best-selling books, people don't come up to me on the street and say, "Hey, Kareem, got any suggestions about what I should read next?" They don't corner me at the airport and ask, "What's up with James Baldwin saying, 'Artists are here to disturb the peace'? What'd he mean by that?" Interviewers don't want to know my take on the pan-African movement. They want to discuss the Lakers, the current crop of NBA rookies, a shot I took in a game twenty years ago. The NCAA instead of the NAACP. And I don't resent it one bit. I consider myself lucky that anyone wants my opinion about anything. But the Harlem Renaissance taught me not to be afraid to use whatever celebrity status I have to benefit my community. If people gather around to hear about basketball and I happen to slip in a story about some great figure in African-American history, then I'm doing what Maya Angelou describes in her poem "Still I Rise":

Bringing the gifts that my ancestors gave,
I am the dream and the hope of the slave.
I rise
I rise
I rise.

I used to play basketball. Now I am a writer. I didn't become either one by myself.

I didn't rise alone.

IDENTITY THEFT: BEAUTY OR THE BEAST

As long as the colored man look to white folks to put the crown on what he say . . . as long as he looks to white folks for approval . . . then he ain't never gonna find out who he is and what he's about.

AUGUST WILSON JR., *Ma Rainey's Black Bottom*

The main struggle that the writers of the Harlem Renaissance faced was trying to convince white Americans to change their long-held perceptions of black Americans. This was similar to the problem microbiologist Louis Pasteur had trying to convince the world that some diseases were caused by germs instead of just spontaneously popping up. People didn't want to believe Pasteur because they were used to seeing the world a certain way—no matter how wrong it was, no matter how dangerous to themselves and their loved ones their stupidity was. History is filled with those heroes who accepted the daunting task of trying to change people's petrified minds: mold could be penicillin, women could be equals, something heavier than air could fly. The public's first reaction to change is always a resounding "Get lost!"

Which is exactly the challenge the Harlem Renaissance writers faced in the 1920s and 1930s. Southern whites had had too many smug generations of seeing blacks as disposable property to suddenly slap their foreheads and say, "Gosh, what was I thinking? Of course we're all brothers and sisters under the skin." And poor whites, barely scratching an existence out of the unforgiving soil, desperately needed to cling to their skewed perception of blacks— they needed *someone* they could feel superior to in order to keep away despair. Whites from other parts of the country usually had little exposure to blacks, so their perceptions were formed by casual observation of the shoeshine man or hotel maid combined with how blacks were portrayed in the arts. Minstrel shows had featured whites in blackface—and even blacks in blackface—shuffling and jiving around the stage, perpetuating the familiar stereotypes of the lazy, stupid, childlike African-American (see the chapter " 'Musical Fireworks': Jazz Lights Up the Heavens of Harlem" for the history of minstrel shows). Cartoons, novels, radio shows, advertisements, newspapers, movies, and even children's games perpetuated these portrayals. Judy Garland, Mickey Rooney, and Bing Crosby, among others, wore blackface in several of their films, including Crosby in the 1942 Christmas favorite, *Holiday Inn* (giving new meaning to the phrase *white Christmas*).

They might have heard a rumor of an educated black who was a doctor or lawyer, but they saw that as a freak of nature, akin to a circus oddity, probably having more to do with some white blood in the veins from a frisky slave owner.

All these attitudes about blacks were based on a firm belief that whites were biologically superior to blacks. Throughout the eighteenth, nineteenth, and twentieth centuries, plenty of "scientific" studies were published to support this conclusion. German anthropologist Johann Friedrich Blumenbach (1752–1840) was the first to come up with the idea of dividing people into five "races": Caucasian (whites), Mongolian (yellow), Malayan (brown), Negro/Ethiopian (black), and American (red). In addition to skin color, he categorized people according to various physical traits: fair skin and high brows of Caucasians were proof of higher intelligence and more generous spirit; Mongolians, with their narrow eyes and sallow skin color were crafty and literal-minded; sloping craniums and dark skin of Negroes revealed how close they were to primates (although, it's interesting to note that if you shave the hair off a chimpanzee or gorilla, their skin is whiter than that of a Caucasian).

Most scientists today discount the practice of race categories as a phony distinction used by one group of people to justify dominating another group, just as Adolf Hitler used Blumenbach to justify his persecution of those he considered "racially inferior." While discarding the crackpot idea of race might seem a step in the right direction for dispelling racial stereotypes, first society has to *want* to know the truth. Yet, in some ways society hasn't changed that much since those "Yassir, Mr. Bones" minstrel days. The publication in 1994 of Richard J. Herrnstein and Charles Murray's *The Bell Curve* was one of the more recent pseudo scientific "proofs" of black inferiority. What's significant here isn't that *The Bell Curve* proposed such scientifically outdated ideas at the close of the twentieth century—people will never stop trying to justify their prejudices. What's significant is that the book was *a major best seller in America.* A lot of people *wanted* to believe it.

So, while it may be of some comfort that scientists say there is no such thing as "race," it's not scientists that have to be convinced. It's the average white person walking down the street, clutching his wallet when a black teenager approaches; sitting on a jury a little more certain the defendant is guilty because he's black; waiting in a hospital hoping the black doctor approaching isn't going to be his. To overcome these automatic reflexes of perception, as quick and thoughtless as blinking when a fly approaches the eye, requires a Herculean effort from both sides: one side to mount convincing propaganda, the other side to open themselves up to being convinced.

That is what the writers of the Harlem Renaissance faced every time they sat down at their desks. Behind them stood the 10 million African-Americans anxiously awaiting their opportunities at the American Dream; before them stood the 90 million whites wondering what was in it for them if they changed their attitudes. As if writing wasn't hard enough, each novel, each essay, each poem, each *word*, carried the hopes of an entire community. Under such circumstances, it was an act of heroism to write anything. But write they did, producing some of the greatest works in American literature.

BLACK BY ANY OTHER NAME

I am America. I am the part you won't recognize. But get used to me. Black, confident, cocky; my name, not yours; my religion, not yours; my goals, my own; get used to me.

MUHAMMAD ALI

I used to be Lew Alcindor.

Now I'm Kareem Abdul-Jabbar. The change isn't just in name. It signifies the change in me from how I perceived myself as a boy who was unwittingly influenced by white perceptions of who I should be—and how I perceived myself as a man who had abandoned those perceptions. I can trace the genealogy of my change in name—and change in heart—directly to the Harlem Renaissance.

Writers know how important words are in manipulating an audience. Choose one word and the audience weeps, choose another and they are angered, choose another and they are thoughtful. One of the words that the Harlem Renaissance concerned itself with was what to call black people. Blacks had a long history of being called by words meant to hurt, humiliate, and subjugate. So whatever they chose had to project an image of respectability, capability, and intelligence, not just to whites, but also to blacks who could feel pride in such a word. W. E. B. Du Bois argued in favor of *Negro*, as long as the word was capitalized. As a result, the Harlem Renaissance promoted what they called the New Negro: an educated, disciplined, talented black person whose example whites would admire and blacks would emulate.

Richard Moore *strongly* disagreed. Moore was a respected Harlem Renaissance soapbox orator and civil rights activist, whose beliefs and example led the way for many African-Americans during the civil rights push of the 1960s. He was involved with the Harlem Education Forum, which organized debates and lectures, and the Associated Colored Employees of America, a job opportunity organization. In 1919, he joined the African Blood Brotherhood, a national secret organization that promoted self-defense, race pride, and self-determination for African-Americans. He founded the Afro-American Institute and owned the Frederick Douglass Book Center in Harlem for thirty years. Moore also led the fight to use the term *Afro-American*. In his popular book, *The Name "Negro": Its Origin and Evil Use* (1960), Moore rejects the word *Negro* because of its sinister origin. He argues that *negro* can be traced back through Spanish and Latin to the Greek word *necro*, which means "death." This connection stems from when the Greeks went to Egypt to study their advanced civilization (including writing, medicine, science, and religion) and mistakenly thought the many temples honoring dead ancestors meant the Egyptians were preoccupied with death. Hence, *necro*. "So there you have it," Moore writes, "the negro— a race of dead people with a dead history and no hope for resurrection as long as they remained ignorant of their past. This was a triple death—the death of the mind, body, and spirit of the African people."

What's in a name? Everything.

Were W. E. B. Du Bois, Alain Locke, Charles S. Johnson, and some of the other geniuses of the Harlem Renaissance wrong? Was their use of the word *Negro* compounding the problem of image? Not at all. History is a series of causes and effects. There is no sudden overnight change from Injustice to Justice. Du Bois and the others knew the audience they were addressing and approached them with words that wouldn't automatically close their minds. And it worked. White people listened, rallied, supported them. Black people from across the country were inspired to achieve more, to walk among whites a little prouder. Du Bois and others made it possible for Moore and others to find another name that more effectively addressed their target audience, for whom the word *Negro* had lost some of its former power. The time was then right for the next step, for a new name. As Moore said, "The name that you respond to determines the amount of your self-worth. Similarly, the way a group of people collectively responds to a name can have devastating effects on their lives, particularly if they did not choose the name." So the black community itself debates: *black* or *Black*? *Afro-American* or *African-American*? *People of color* or *colored*? The name selected is less important than the fact that it's the community itself choosing their own name. Moore emphasized how important it was that black people name themselves because "dogs and slaves are named by their masters; free men name themselves!"

So, I named myself Kareem Abdul-Jabbar. Here's why.

When I was still Lew Alcindor, I was influenced by Harlem Renaissance leader Marcus Garvey. Garvey wasn't one of the in-crowd of the Renaissance; in fact, while Du Bois and Locke were touting the Talented Tenth, Garvey was gathering followers from the working-class blacks who didn't care about the thinkers and writers and artists who would *eventually* bring about change; they cared about being treated like human beings *right now*. The intellectuals of the Renaissance thought Garvey to be something of a clown, with his gaudy marching-band uniforms and elaborate parades and back-to-Africa shipping line. But average black people throughout the United States, the Caribbean, and even Africa felt a surge of pride and hopefulness because of him that they had not felt before.

Like Garvey, my family was also from the Caribbean. They arrived in New York City from Trinidad in 1917. My dad told me how my grandparents would often discuss Garvey's ideas at the dinner table. One night while I was in high school, I went to hear Malcolm X speak at the corner of 125th Street and Seventh Avenue. Unfortunately, Malcolm canceled that evening, but the speakers who did show up were from the African Nationalist Pioneer Movement (ANPM). The ANPM, organized by Carlos A. Cooks, were followers of the late Marcus Garvey, who had died in 1940. Their theme for the evening was "Buy Black," which I found interesting and so decided to stay.

The orator, Charles Peaker, argued that by patronizing black merchants we would be building a solvent foundation for our children while helping to create employment and independence for all black people. In fact, the preamble to the ANPM Constitution states: "We submit that the Black people of Harlem and all other Homo-geneous African communities, have the same natural and moral right to be clannish in their patronage as all other people have drama-tised that they are. We advocate as a matter of sound racial economics, the BUY BLACK CAMPAIGN. Patronize the merchants of your own race."

Peaker outlined in detail the methods that were used to economically exploit black people. He spoke about the way blacks were the last hired and first fired, and how credit and loans were not available unless the terms were exorbitant. To combat this exploitation, whenever possible black people should patronize black businesses and black landlords and spend their money in the black community. Although the idea was sound in theory, it was hard to practice due to the lack of black business. At the end of the speech, Mr. Peaker heaped praise on Marcus Garvey for being an early advocate of black economic independence. From that night on, I wanted to know more about Marcus Garvey, but I was unable to get any of his published works until *Philosophy and Opinions* was published in the early or midseventies, when I was in my twenties and playing for the Milwaukee Bucks. Reading his powerful words on the page, I could only imagine the impact he must have had in person.

I have a vision of the future, and I see before me a picture of a redeemed Africa, with her dotted cities, with her beautiful civilization, with her millions of happy children, going to and fro. Why should I lose hope, why should I give up and take a back place in this age of progress? Remember that you are men, that God created you Lords of this creation. Lift up yourselves, men, take yourselves out of the mire and hitch your hopes to the stars; yes, rise as high as the very stars themselves.

I have no doubt that Garvey's back-to-Africa movement was sincere. His entire life was a testament to his commitment to the African-American community. However, Garvey's program was doomed from the beginning by poor planning and a lack of competent execution. One hindrance was that there was no model for him to emulate in reaching his goals, the problem most pioneers face. It's always the people who come afterward who benefit by their forbearers' failures. But Garvey's visions would have gone a long way to gaining black political and economic power if they could have been executed in a competent fashion. The economic aspect of his plan is something black movements have never fully understood, but which black Americans could still benefit from today. As much as I admired his beliefs and writings, the one area that does not work for me is the attempt to get blacks to leave the United States. Back-to-Africa plans have not worked ever since the time when Liberia was established in 1847. Mostly this is for two reasons: (1) no African country would necessarily want the political or economic destabilization caused by the sudden influx of millions of people with voting privileges and housing and job needs; and (2) there's a fundamental injustice in people uprooting their lives, even voluntarily, and moving to another country because they can't secure their human rights in the country where they were born; it's a form of surrender that seems cowardly.

Despite this flaw, Garvey's influence was monumental during the Harlem Renaissance. One person who was affected by Garvey's teachings was Malcolm X, whose father, Baptist preacher Earl Little, was a member of Garvey's Universal Negro Improvement Association. In *The Autobiography of Malcolm X*, Malcolm recalled the price his family paid for supporting Garvey:

When my mother was pregnant with me, she told me later, a party of hooded Ku Klux Klan riders galloped up to our home in Omaha, Nebraska, one night. Surrounding the house, brandishing their shotguns and rifles, they shouted for my father to come out. My mother went to the front door and opened it. Standing where they could see her pregnant condition, she told them that she was alone with her three small children, and that my father was away, preaching in Milwaukee. The Klansmen shouted threats and warnings at her that we had better get out of town because "the good Christian white people" were not going to stand for my father's "spreading trouble" among the "good" Negroes of Omaha with the "back to Africa" preachings of Marcus Garvey.

Earl Little moved his family to Michigan, where he continued preaching the gospel of Garvey. This time, reaction was swift and violent: members of the black-robed Black Legion, a part of the KKK, burned the Littles' home to the ground. As a young man, Malcolm studied Garvey, whose writings helped form the basis for the teachings of the Nation of Islam and even Stokely Carmichael, leader of Student Nonviolent Coordinating Committee (SNCC). Even the Black Arts Movement of the 1960s got its start following the teachings of Garvey. A group of young high school musicians formed the Jazz-Art Society, which they renamed the African Jazz-Art Society in honor of Marcus Garvey. One of their goals was to adapt the teachings of the ANPM lectures into a jazz form that would be more accessible to the average person wary of rhetoric. They launched their first concert on December 24, 1956, appropriately at Small's Paradise, one of the leading clubs during the Harlem Renaissance. Just as the writers, musicians, artists, and performers of the Harlem Renaissance had used their artistic skills, whether knowingly or unknowingly, to promote the message of racial equality and the promise of the New Negro, so were these originators of the Black Arts Movement carrying on that same tradition.

Nobody rises alone. We do it on the shoulders—and sometimes the weary backs and broken bodies—of others. Booker T. Washington influenced Marcus Garvey, Garvey influenced Malcolm X, and in turn Malcolm's *The Autobiography of Malcolm X* (1965) had a profound influence on me. Malcolm embraced Richard Moore's attitude about the importance of naming ourselves. He advocated that the "so called Negro" be referred to as "Black." Perhaps a rose by any other name does not smell as sweet—at least to the rose. And when he submitted himself to Islam and renamed himself Malcolm X from Malcolm Little, I also became a Muslim and took a new name for myself: Kareem ("generous") Abdul ("servant of Allah") Jabbar ("powerful").

Contrary to what some critics thought, the teachings of the Harlem Renaissance had not become diluted with time, they had become even more potent.

ON THE SAME PAGE: HARLEM WRITERS WHO MOST INFLUENCED ME

Got one mind for the white folks see, another mind I know is me.

blues song that opens *Real Cool Killers* by CHESTER HIMES

The thinkers behind the Harlem Renaissance were on a mission. They realized that white America had a biased view of all African-Americans as biologically inferior. They believed that the only way to convince whites that their entrenched opinion was inaccurate was to excel at everything that the conventional white wisdom said blacks couldn't do. Conventional White Wisdom said blacks weren't athletic, so blacks went about competing successfully in sports. Conventional White Wisdom said blacks weren't smart, so they excelled in medicine, law, and business. Conventional White Wisdom said blacks weren't creative, so they went about creating dynamic art, literature, and theater. Conventional White Wisdom said blacks couldn't understand the complexities of music, so they originated the blues and jazz and spun white America across the dance floor. The Harlem Renaissance produced so many successful and popular African-Americans that the Conventional White Wisdom took a serious beating.

As a result of this revolution in image, several black writers became the toast of the literary world. Two of the most famous and respected of the Harlem Renaissance writers, Claude McKay and Jean Toomer, wrote with great intensity and sensitivity about the struggles of being black in the early part of the twentieth century. Yet, they resented being referred to as "Negro writers." Both wanted to be judged on their merits as writers, not as symbols of a race, forgiven any imperfections as artists because of the righteousness—or faddishness—of their cause. But people want to see you one way, a way that they are familiar and comfortable with. For years after the Emancipation Proclamation, blacks settled for that Conventional White Wisdom image; some even bought into it themselves. If whites thought they weren't smart, many blacks figured maybe they were right. But when the Harlem Renaissance produced so many examples of successful black writers, artists, intellectuals, musicians, and businesspeople, the rest of black America could for the first time feel as if they were finally being seen. They were no longer invisible, one lump of dark faces, interchangeable.

It was the writers of the Harlem Renaissance that shone the light on those dark faces hidden in the shadows—that made America see them, feel them, understand them, on both an emotional *and* intellectual level. They described the hardships and injustices, the successes and accomplishments, with such precision and passion that black America could no longer be ignored. And these skilled writers articulated the fears, frustrations, and hopes with such poetry and power that they armed black Americans with vivid words to express both their dissatisfaction and goals.

For many people, literature falls somewhere between candy and medicine: a delicious confection easily forgotten or a bitter tonic that must be endured because it's good for you. The founders of the Harlem Renaissance saw it as a means to a righteous end—propaganda to demonstrate the talents of the New Negro. Many writers bristled under those restraints and sought to tell whatever stories they thought needed telling, regardless of how white people reacted. For me, literature is much more. You remember those adventure movies in which the hero winds up in a dark cave unable to see his way to safety. He's surrounded by snakes, bears, genetically altered monsters, magical beasts—things with sharp teeth. How will he survive? He somehow creates a makeshift torch from moss and the femur of the last guy caught in the cave, rubs his zipper along the stone wall to create a spark that fires up the torch, and stumbles forward in his tiny aura of light. That's literature to me. Each story, novel, poem, and play presents a vision of the world that illuminates the dark cave of life we stumble through. We can see better where we're going, what sudden drop to avoid, where the cool water is running. Several of the writers of the Harlem Renaissance became particular favorites of mine because they helped me find the words I needed to define myself, and they illuminated the path that helped me go where I wanted to go.

I first read the poetry of Langston Hughes when I was too young to really appreciate it—or poetry in general. Only later did I come to admire the bold honesty of his writing, both in his poetry and essays, turning his critical eye on white America with such subtlety and intensity that white America was forced to react with a mixture of surprise, anger, and shame. And his willingness to accurately describe the grittiness of Harlem life, despite the disapproval of the forefathers of the Harlem Renaissance (Du Bois, Johnson, and Locke) who insisted on publicizing only the uplifting in Harlem, showed even more courage. John Wooden, my coach at UCLA, used to recite Hughes's poetry by heart, which helped foster a bond between us. Hughes was one of the few writers from that era who kept writing and publishing throughout his life, always providing a clear and resonant voice, like a bell in a dense fog, to guide black America. His lifelong devotion to the black community in the face of overwhelming odds, as well as his dedication to his art as a writer, inspired me in both areas.

Zora Neale Hurston's work provides a vivid picture of the daily life during the Renaissance. I especially appreciate her work in documenting black folk stories, preserving an important part of Black Americana. During her lifetime, she endured some nasty criticism from other blacks for writing in the slang of the Southern blacks she had grown up among. Not until later did the world came to appreciate that she wasn't poking fun at them, but rather honoring them. As a writer, Hurston took on a double burden: not only did she have to convince the white reader that blacks were their equal, she had to convince men of all colors that women were their equals. That she succeeded as much as she did is remarkable. While I could never fully understand her criticism of the Supreme Court decision to end school desegregation, she did create some honest and questioning debate, which is necessary for any progress to take place. She once said, "I have been in Sorrow's kitchen and licked out all the pots. Then I have stood on the peaky mountain wrapped in rainbows, with a harp and a sword in my hands." She faced both triumph and defeat with the kind of grace, intelligence, and wit that the rest of us can only hope to emulate.

James Baldwin was born in 1924, during the height of the Harlem Renaissance, so technically he's not really a Renaissance writer. But his themes are the distillation of all that his predecessors were writing about. Though separated by a couple decades, the Harlem he wrote about had the same problems as the Harlem of Thurman, Hurston, and Hughes. In fact, one of Baldwin's most famous stories, "Sonny's Blues," echoes the same lesson as Langston Hughes's poem "Weary Blues." In both, characters are deadened by their daily struggle on the "killing streets" to survive in an unrelentingly racist society—their hopes, their confidence, their identities as men drying up, as Hughes said in another of his poems, "like a raisin in the sun." Only when they experience the release from jazz music do they see a path that will allow them to transcend the inevitable suffering. Baldwin said, "Not everything that is faced can be changed. But nothing can be changed until it is faced." In those words, it's as if Baldwin had snatched the flag of the Harlem Renaissance from one of its fallen writers and was waving it for his generation to follow. And follow it I have.

Like James Baldwin, Chester Himes was born during the Harlem Renaissance, but wasn't strictly a part of it. Yet, his gritty crime novels succeeded in doing what so many writers of the Renaissance had set out to do: portray the wide array of Harlem characters beyond stereotypes, convey the harsh realties of Harlem life as well as the joyous aspects, and do so in books that became popular enough among both white and black readers to actually have an impact. His characters reflect different strata of Harlem life: from the respectable preachers, teachers, laborers, and housewives to the underside of Harlem with its con men, gamblers, petty thieves, drug dealers, and exotic dancers. Part of Himes's appeal for me is in his life story: raised in a middle-class home in Ohio, goes to college, gets kicked out for playing a prank, commits armed robbery, and is sent to prison for twenty-five years at the age of nineteen. Reading famed mystery writer Dashiell Hammett (*The Maltese Falcon*) in prison, Himes taught himself to write and was soon selling his stories to magazines like *Esquire*. Paroled after seven years, Himes continued writing, publishing various stories and novels (*If He Hollers Let Him Go*) that addressed racism and its destructive effects on the black community. But it wasn't until Himes moved to France that his biggest success came. A French publisher asked him to write a series of hard-boiled detective novels in the tradition of Dashiell Hammett and Raymond Chandler. What Himes produced was unlike anything ever seen before in the genre. His characters, two tough Harlem cops named Coffin Ed Johnson and Grave Digger Jones, were inspired, Himes said, more by William Faulkner's "ripe violence and absurdist view of life" than by Hammett's urbane world. This series—which included *A Rage in Harlem*, *The Crazy Kill*, *Cotton Comes to Harlem*, and *Blind Man with a Pistol*—made Himes famous and brought him literary awards in France. In America, the books were regarded as mere pulp fiction, though today he is regarded as an influential literary author, whose work had a great impact on subsequent black writers, including Ishmael Reed and Walter Mosley. Several movies have been made from this series, the most famous being *Cotton Comes to Harlem* (1970). While I appreciate Himes's re-creation of Harlem life, I also enjoy his absurdist humor and vivid action scenes, complete with shoot-outs and chases and fights. Himes obviously loves Harlem, and his stories are a tribute to the diversity of black life.

WHY THE PAGE IS MORE THAN BLACK AND WHITE

> But there are certain very practical things American Negro writers can do. And must do. There's a song that says, "the time ain't long." That song is right. Something has got to change in America—and change soon. We must help that change to come.
>
> LANGSTON HUGHES

I am a Harlem Renaissance Man, not because of my achievements, but because of my goals. And right now, my goal as a writer is to offer books that use the past to illuminate the future. To unearth and put on display all the broad, black shoulders for future generations to climb upon and see what they are capable of. For example, what is the first full-length feature film directed, written, and produced by an African-American? If you answered Ossie Davis, Eddie Murphy, or Bill Cosby, you're wrong. The first was Oscar Micheaux, the son of former slaves, who was born in 1884. While working as a homesteader in South Dakota, he wrote, published, and distributed his first novel, *The Conquest* (1913). When a film company offered to produce his novel *The Homesteader* (1919), Micheaux agreed. But when he became dissatisfied with their approach, he decided to found his own production company and wrote, directed, and produced the movie himself. He was the first. He was also the first African-American filmmaker to produce a sound film, *The Exile* (1931). His 1920 film, *Within Our Gates*, was an angry response to D. W. Griffith's *The Birth of a Nation* (1915), which is credited with reviving the Ku Klux Klan. Micheaux's film cleverly counters Griffith's racist portrayals of blacks by replicating a rape scene from *The Birth of a Nation*. Using the same lighting, blocking, and setting as Griffith, Micheaux instead replaces the drunken black rapists attacking a white woman with a white man assaulting a black woman.

Is knowing how many points I scored in my career going to change any lives? No. Is knowing about Oscar Micheaux going to change any lives?

Yes, I think it will.

Year after year, studies among educators reveal the same conclusions. African-American students do much better in classes in which they read about positive role models who are also African-American. One study evaluated twenty-four hundred children's books published from 1937 to 1990 and concluded that African-American characters appeared in only 15 percent of them. And it's not just the quantity, it's also the quality of representation that's damaging. Let's face it, it's hard to encourage a positive self-image if you're reading *Mary Poppins*, in which Mary meets two African-Americans, who have this to say: "Ah bin 'specting you a long time

"FAIRNESS CREEPS
OUT OF THE SOUL"

Basketball

Comes to Harlem

■ When it's played the way it's spozed to be played, basketball happens in the air; flying, floating, elevated above the floor, levitating the way oppressed peoples of this earth imagine themselves in their dreams.

JOHN EDGAR WIDEMAN author of *Brothers and Keepers*

THE FIRST WORLD CHAMPIONSHIP OF BASKETBALL

On March 28, 1939, eight young black men from Harlem anxiously stood on the polished wooden floor of the Chicago Coliseum facing eight white men in the final championship game of the first-ever World Professional Basketball Tournament. Surrounding them was a sold-out crowd of three thousand raucous fans—most of them white, most of them shouting out the name of their favorites: the all-white Oshkosh All-Stars.

The black team, the New York Renaissance Big Five, known in Harlem as simply the Rens, tried to ignore the boisterous crowd while waiting nervously for the game to begin. After all, they had finished the season with a remarkable record of 112 wins against only 7 losses. So far in this tournament they had beaten two other all-white teams as well as their archrivals, the Harlem Globetrotters. But the Oshkosh All-Stars had an impressive record, too. And not only were they the National Basketball League's Western Division Champions, but they were local Midwestern sons with the crowd enthusiastically behind them.

The stakes had never been higher for these young players. The winning team would receive $1,000—and be crowned the first-ever World Champions of Basketball. Even though 1939 was at the tail end of the Great Depression, $1,000 still wasn't a huge sum, only about $13,000 in current money. Today's NBA players make that much just for lacing up their endorsement shoes before a game. But these two teams couldn't have been more determined to win if they'd been playing for $10 million. At stake was something far more precious than money; because this was the first ever basketball tournament that included both white and black teams, the winners would be the acknowledged basketball champions of the world.

For the Oshkosh All-Stars, a victory would be a fitting culmination for the team that had been perpetual bridesmaids: for the past three years they had been Western Division Champions in the racially segregated National Basketball League, but had yet to win a national title. If they were ever going to be national champions, it would be today, with the crowd solidly behind them. For the Renaissance Big Five, winning would be a vindication for sixteen years of capturing many Colored Basketball World Championships, but never being allowed to play against white teams in national championship games because no professional leagues wanted to see a black team as champions.

For the sixteen players awaiting the opening whistle, this game was the climax of a sports rivalry dating back several years. But for the enthusiastic crowd screaming and stomping from the stands, this game was a race rivalry dating back hundreds of years. Each side knew exactly whom they wanted to win. And, for most, their reasons had nothing to do with basketball.

WHEN A GAME ISN'T JUST A GAME: THE GREAT BLACK HOPE

For African-Americans across the United States who had hoped that the start of the twentieth century would bring enlightenment and opportunity, so far it had been mostly decade after decade of bitter disappointment. Racism wasn't just a matter of public debate among politicians and academics in editorials and at cocktail parties, it was a harsh reality that blacks in the United States had to struggle with daily. Aside from the long list of Jim Crow laws meant to subjugate and humiliate, there was always the real possibility in some places of lynching. Between 1882 and 1930, a black man, woman, or child was hanged by white mobs at an average of once a week.

This final game, then, wasn't just about which team of young, energetic men would put the ball through the hoop more times than the other. For many of the 118 million whites in America, winning would be further proof of the superiority of the white man, physically, mentally, and morally. But for the 13 million blacks in America, winning would provide empirical evidence that, given a chance to compete on a level playing field, African-Americans were equal to whites in every way. As many black parents knew, this wasn't a lesson just for whites, it was something their own young children had to recognize, if they were to grow up with any hope of having their voices heard and their dreams realized.

Sometimes a game is only a game. But sometimes, such as this time, it was so much more.

THE COLOR OF COMPETITION: BLACK VERSUS WHITE IN SPORTS

Up to this point, America's record concerning black athletes (with the exception of boxing) had been consistent: allow blacks to compete against other blacks for colored championships; allow blacks to compete against whites to pump up the ticket sales (black-vs.-white games had higher attendance); but never, ever, *ever* let blacks compete against whites for national titles because these titles carried not only more money, but the immeasurable treasure of white pride. At first, this formula was the result of the common attitude among whites that blacks were too lazy and undisciplined to excel at sports. Later, as blacks began demonstrating exceptional achievements in most sports, the formula became a sort of Jockstrap Curtain, designed to keep black athletes on one side, barnstorming for loose change, while on the other side the high salaries and higher prize money remained in white hands. "How long is this state of affairs going to exist?" asked the black newspaper *New York Age* in 1920, referring to segregation in baseball. "Are our ball players—despite the active part they took in the war for Democracy, despite their gentlemanly behavior on the diamond and in civil life—to be forever confronted with this unsurmountable color barrier? Is there no conscience in the white solon's hearts? Will there never be any way out for the Negro?"

Baseball began excluding black players in 1867, when the National Association of Base Ball Players (NABBP) formally banned any African-Americans from participating. When the NABBP folded a couple years later, the major league American Association accepted as members the Toledo Blue Stockings, whose catcher, "Fleet" Walker, became the first professional black baseball player. However, Walker faced enormous player resistance, even from his own team. "He was the best catcher I ever worked with," admitted teammate Tony Mullane, but "I disliked a Negro and whenever I had to pitch to him I used anything I wanted without looking at his signals." As a result of this kind of attitude, the American Association bowed to public pressure and returned to segregation in 1887, followed by the International League in 1890, the year Fleet Walker retired. American baseball would remain segregated until Jackie Robinson joined the Brooklyn Dodgers in 1947. Still, it took another thirteen years until the last holdout, the Boston Red Sox, integrated.

Football followed a similar pattern. In the beginning, a few exceptionally talented African-Americans were permitted to play on the college and professional level. The American Professional Football Association was founded in 1920, changing its name to the National Football League (NFL) in 1922. The NFL permitted a few notable black players, including Frederick Douglass "Fritz" Pollard, who had been the first black college player to compete in the Rose Bowl; Robert "Rube" Marshall; and Paul Robeson, who would later become even more famous as a singer/actor/political activist. In 1933, the NFL also became exclusively white, banning all blacks until 1946, when Kenny Washington and Woody Strode (who later became a respected actor, appearing in *Spartacus* opposite Kirk Douglas) joined the Los Angeles Rams, and Marion Motley and Bill Willis joined the Cleveland Browns.

Professional basketball, though popular in the black community, was also largely segregated. The American Basketball Association, founded in 1925, banned black players. Although blacks became continually more prominent in college play, it wasn't until 1942 that the professionals followed suit when the National Basketball League accepted Bill Jones and three other African-American players on the Toledo Jim White Chevrolet team, as well as five ex–Harlem Globetrotters on the Chicago Studebakers. Two years later, in 1944, West Coast professional leagues began admitting African-American players: Kenny Washington, who would two years later make history in the NFL, made history this year by joining the Hollywood Bears; Jackie Robinson, who three years later would shatter the color line in baseball, shattered it this year by joining the Los Angeles Bulldogs. But when it came to a whites-only policy, basketball proved to be more tenacious than most other professional sports. When the Basketball Association of America formed in 1946, they banned black players. Then in 1950, Chuck Cooper became the first African-American in the draft of the newly formed National Basketball Association (NBA). Cooper was picked by the Boston Celtics.

The average American didn't seem to notice the irony in our

national celebration over the fifty-six U.S. medals in the 1936 Olympics in Berlin, Germany. Many Americans took particular pride in humiliating Adolf Hitler and his smug philosophy of Aryan superiority as Ohio State University's Jesse Owens and seventeen other African-American athletes won fourteen of those fifty-six medals. Owens himself captured four gold medals and set seven world records. He was the first American to win four gold medals in track and field in a single Olympics. Yet, Owens's return to America was anything but triumphant. Because he was black, he received no endorsement contracts, and to earn money to care for his family, he was forced to abandon college in his senior year and use his remarkable speed in bizarre exhibitions. He raced everything from people, to horses, to motorcycles. He was a familiar sight around the Negro Baseball League where, before games, he would sometimes race thoroughbred horses. Other times he would race the teams' fastest runners, each time giving them a ten-yard advantage before speeding past them to victory.

At first glance, boxing seemed to be the exception to this pattern of racism. After all, when African-American heavyweight Jack Johnson defeated Jim Jeffries in 1910 to claim the championship title, he won what was the largest boxing purse in history: $117,000. It wasn't that boxing was color-blind—in fact, just the opposite. Promoters exploited racism to build attendance. All other sports were metaphoric regarding race rivalry, but in boxing two men pummeled each other until one was left standing, and that said it all. Fists to the face spoke more directly to the fans' racial attitudes than did the more stylized sports that involved chasing a ball. Jim Jeffries made that clear when he came out of retirement to put this upstart black man in his place. Said Jeffries at the time, "I am going into this fight for the sole purpose of proving that a white man is better than a Negro." At ringside, a band played the popular song "All Coons Look Alike to Me," while promoters led the mostly white crowd in chants of "Kill the nigger!" After Johnson easily knocked out Jeffries, race riots ensued across the country as white lynch mobs attempted to breach black neighborhoods. Nevertheless, black Americans across the country felt a jolt of pride in his accomplishment. Whites had demanded proof of black equality—and they got two fistfuls of it. Jack Johnson's flamboyant lifestyle of outspokenness, partying, and marrying white women (at a time when interracial marriages were illegal in most states) further outraged whites—and many conservative blacks. Finally, in 1912 Johnson was convicted of transporting his wife across state lines before they were married and he fled the country. These troubles didn't diminish Johnson's importance in the black community. If anything, they enhanced his image, because it proved that whites would do anything to destroy a black man who challenged their notions of racial superiority.

Heavyweight champion Joe Louis, the "Brown Bomber," was determined not to suffer Johnson's fate of being triumphant in the ring only to be knocked out by public opinion. He followed strict rules of behavior to avoid being characterized as threatening, which included never being photographed with a white woman, never going clubbing by himself, and never speaking unless spoken to. Despite all his effort to present a docile public face, Louis became the focal point of the most racially charged bout in world history. On June 19, 1936, undefeated Joe Louis fought Germany's Max Schmeling, who was personally endorsed by Nazi leader Adolf Hitler to prove white supremacy to the world. When Schmeling did the impossible and knocked Louis out, Germany's press celebrated with endless propaganda that this was conclusive evidence of white superiority to all people of color. Perhaps less expected was when some American newspapers joined in to echo the Nazis. A columnist in the *New Orleans Picayune* said, "I guess this proves who really is the master race."

Two months later at the Berlin Olympics, Jesse Owens would make those master-race proponents swallow their words when he proved to be America's master racer. Undoubtedly, that contributed to the hype that accompanied the Schmeling-Louis rematch in 1938. So confident was Hitler in the outcome that he ordered all the movie theaters to close, forcing the public to stay home to listen to the fight on their radios. But, when Louis instantly began pounding Schmeling right from the opening bell, Hitler cut the power to the radios. Louis knocked out Schmeling only 124 seconds into the first round. That sports figures were icons of more than just winning for their own glory is clear in what Joe Louis meant to African-Americans everywhere. Said poet Maya Angelou, "The one invincible Negro, the one who stood up to the white man and beat him down with his fists. He in a sense carried so many of our hopes, and maybe even our dreams of vengeance."

During the first half of the twentieth century, when professional sports were becoming more popular—and lucrative—one thing was abundantly clear to all African-American athletes: if they wanted to compete at all, they would have to form their own teams and leagues and compete among each other. Even though most of the white owners, managers, and players did everything to keep sports, and the money involved, to themselves, a few enterprising black men and women made black sports not only profitable, but a pulpit from which the gospel of equality was not only preached, but demonstrated again and again. These pulpits were hardwood floors with baskets, or diamond-shaped fields with bases, or hundred-yard fields with goalposts, and it was on them that white Americans *experienced* what no sermon on civil rights would ever be able to articulate. Ed Henderson, the first black man to teach physical education in an American school, and the founder of the first black basketball league, explained how important black athletes were to the movement for racial equality when in 1927 he told a reporter, "I doubt much whether the mere acquisition of hundreds of degrees or academic honors have influenced the mass mind of America as much as the soul appeal made in a thrilling run for a touchdown by a colored athlete. . . . Fairness creeps out of the soul in the athletic world to a larger extent than anywhere else."

If "fairness" was ever going to happen, this is where it would start.

The Father of Black Basketball: Smilin' Bob Douglas

When this wall of segregation in sports seemed both impenetrable and insurmountable, one entrepreneur of both the wallet and the soul, Robert "Smilin' Bob" Douglas, began to chip away at that wall. At first glance, he seemed like an unlikely challenger to Jericho's gated community. Born in 1882 in St. Kitts, British West Indies, Douglas was only nineteen years old when he emigrated to New York City in 1901. For the next four years he worked twelve hours a day as a doorman, earning only $4 a week. But, like many of his fellow Caribbean immigrants, he wanted to be a businessman. This entrepreneurial spirit, more common among Caribbean immigrants than those who had migrated from the South, caused its own brand of racism in Harlem. Many Harlemites resented both the ambition and success of their West Indian neighbors, refusing to patronize their stores. So, for Bob Douglas to succeed, he would have to overcome the prejudice of white America as well as that of black Harlem.

The first step to success was to find something to be passionate about. For Bob that came in 1905, when a coworker took him to visit an upstairs gymnasium on Fifty-second Street and Tenth Avenue. As a child on St. Kitts, he had been a mediocre player of the island's most popular sports of soccer and cricket. But when Bob walked into that gym and saw his first basketball game, he knew he had finally found his passion. "I knew it was the greatest thing in the world," he later commented. "You couldn't keep me off the court after that."

This newfound passion inspired him to form a partnership with George Abbott and J. Foster Phillips to found the Spartan Field Club in 1908. The club provided black children with a place to compete in amateur sports such as soccer, cricket, track, and basketball. But Douglas had bigger ambitions, for both the club and basketball. He put together his own club team, the Spartan Braves, which, under his leadership as the manager as well as a player, became a leading amateur team in New York City. In 1918, at the age of thirty-six, Bob Douglas retired as an active player to become the general manager of the Spartan Field Club. For the next three years, the Spartan Braves were a dominant amateur team in New York City, easily winning the Eastern Championship in 1921.

During this time, Douglas got his first taste of professional basketball, a taste that proved somewhat bitter. Although the Spartan Braves were successful against other amateur clubs, when they faced the Loendi Big Five, Cumberland Posey's professional team from Pittsburgh, in February of 1921, they were humiliated by a twenty-point loss. A month later the Spartan Braves would face Loendi in a grudge match, and again they would lose, this time by a more modest 30–25. Thus began a sports rivalry between Bob Douglas and Cumberland Posey that would endure for several years, raising the profile of black basketball while raising the quality of black players.

Eight years younger than Bob Douglas, Cumberland Posey (1890–1946) was already a legendary figure in both baseball and basketball. A star basketball player in college, he had gone on to become a star semipro baseball player. Like Douglas, Posey had business ambitions beyond the sweaty uniforms and fleeting glory. He became owner of the powerful and profitable Homestead Grays baseball team, as well as a guiding force of the Negro National League. In 1912, he founded the Loendi Big Five professional basketball team, for which he also played. By the time Douglas's Spartan Braves played them, they had already won two Colored Basketball Championships in a row—and would go on to win the next two years as well for an unprecedented four-peat. His baseball team was equally successful, winning nine consecutive pennants from 1937 to 1945. He was a savvy businessman who oversaw a dynasty in two sports. Certainly Bob Douglas was respectful, if not downright jealous, of his more successful rival from Pittsburgh. Losing to his team on the court only rubbed salt in the wound—and seasoned his taste for victory. That taste would go unfulfilled the next year when, before a crowd of four thousand fans, Posey's Loendi Big Five again defeated the Spartan Braves.

"THE SPORT SUPREME" TURNS PRO

From the size of the crowds, it was now clear, according to the *New York Age*, that basketball reigned as "the sport supreme among the colored people of Harlem." With that popularity came business opportunity. Many amateur players, as well as managers, wanted to turn pro. The Metropolitan Basketball Association (MBA), the regulating organization of amateur basketball in New York City, fought hard against what they considered to be the increasing corrupting influence of professionalism. The MBA promoted the ideal that amateur sports built strong bodies and strong moral character, whereas professional sports was, according to the *Chicago Defender*, a road "which in the long run leads nowhere."

The line between professional and amateur basketball became blurred as players jumped from team to team. The MBA, trying to plug the crumbling dike of amateurism, began punishing teams who added professional players to their roster. Douglas's Spartan Braves were fined for using a former Loendi player, James Sessoms. In 1921, two professional black teams tried to make a go of it. The Lincoln Stars played the champion all-white Original Celtics at Madison Square Garden, only to lose by a score of 30–16. Meanwhile the newly formed New York Colored Leaguers were barely holding their own with a mediocre record of seven wins against sixteen losses. The MBA quickly announced that any MBA player who played for the Stars would be banned from MBA teams forever.

This battle between amateurs and professionals took its toll on Bob Douglas and his Spartan Braves. When the Spartans met their Loendi rivals again, Douglas was forced to bench his top players, James Sessoms and Frank Forbes, because the MBA had determined they were pros. The Spartans lost again, for the third time in a row, this time by only four points (30–26). Douglas arranged for games outside the MBA, but the Spartans were on a downward slide. The Defender Athletic Club handed the Spartans their worst loss: 31–9. When the MBA finally banned Sessoms from play, things just kept getting worse, with more losses piling up. And, if Douglas had any hopes of revenge against the Loendi team, that hope died when the MBA declared the Loendi Five to be "a menace to amateur basketball" and banned all member teams from playing against them. Becoming ever more desperate, the MBA also suspended some of its own teams. In the end, the MBA didn't have enough fingers for all the holes in this dike, and their attempts to hold back the future just nudged it along even faster.

As the crowds became bigger, the games became more than sporting events, they became social events. Many games were held at casinos and nightclubs, with full orchestras or jazz bands providing music before and after the games as the fans danced late into the night. Both teams and club owners were making increasingly more money. Given this atmosphere, amateur play inevitably gave way to the professionals. To speed that transition along, in the fall of 1922 the McMahon brothers, successful white boxing promoters based in Harlem (and grandfather and granduncle of Vince McMahon, the current chairman and majority owner of the World Wrestling Entertainment Inc. empire), formed their own professional black basketball team, the Commonwealth Big Five, named after their Commonwealth Casino. A former Spartan Brave, Frank "Strangler" Forbes, was the captain/manager. When they defeated the Monarch Lodge of Elks team, led by Cumberland Posey and banned Spartan Brave James Sessoms, black professional basketball had clearly arrived. And black amateurs everywhere took that final whistle as a call to arms to join the ranks of the pros.

Ironically, Bob Douglas remained with the MBA for the 1922–23 season. But tightening restrictions by the MBA resulted in lackluster play from his team, finally forcing Douglas to withdraw the Spartan Braves from the amateur league and turn professional. Afterward, a domino effect set in, with other teams and players turning pro. By 1923, most amateur players turning pro were hired guns, offering to play nightly depending on who offered the most money. This practice was already common among pros, with many playing on several competing teams in the same season. Between 1918 and 1922, Joe Lapchick, the white powerhouse who eventually played for the Original Celtics, was commanding $75 to $100 per game and playing for four different teams. Before this, he'd earned a total of $33 for two years' work.

THE RENAISSANCE OF BOB DOUGLAS

The two-story redbrick Renaissance Casino and Ballroom at 138th Street and Seventh Avenue opened in 1923 to the clamor of controversy between two of Harlem's most famous political leaders. Built by the black-owned Sarco Realty Company, the building was lauded by acclaimed activist and scholar W. E. B. Du Bois for being a black-owned business. Not only was the second-floor ballroom one of the finest in Harlem, the bottom floor boasted the only black-owned department store in New York City. However, in his publication *Negro World*, Marcus Garvey, the charismatic leader of the popular "back to Africa" movement, accused Sarco Realty of being a front, and that the Renaissance building was instead owned by Jewish investors. Sarco Realty angrily denied the charge and demanded a retraction.

Where others saw controversy, Bob Douglas saw opportunity. He quickly made a deal with Sarco Reality Company owner William Roach, a fellow Caribbean immigrant: in exchange for practice and playing space, Douglas would pay Roach a generous percentage of the admission take. In addition, the Spartan Braves would now be called the Renaissance Big Five, thereby providing advertising for the casino. Privately, Douglas admitted that he didn't like the new name, which he felt was too long and awkward to pronounce. But business was business and the simple name change brought them a new home where every Saturday night his "Rens" could play against the best teams while patrons danced to the orchestra before, after, and at halftime of each game—all for only fifty-five cents admission. Douglas knew just how important that fifty-five cents was to his business plan, because he wasn't throwing together just another black basketball team, he was making history: the Rens were the first ever black-owned, full-salaried, black professional basketball team. The rest of the world—especially the world of black basketball players—were watching to see whether Douglas's venture was a solid business plan that they could copy, or a romantic pipe dream to be crushed and forgotten.

Douglas's new enterprise was significantly helped by Romeo Dougherty, the sports and theater editor of the black *New York Amsterdam News*. Known as the "Sage of Union Hall Street," Dougherty was well respected as a journalist for his efforts to support black artists and athletes in the community. Also an immigrant from the West Indies, and an admirer of Douglas's business savvy, Dougherty used his column to promote the Rens. Certainly part of the team's success was due to many years of Dougherty's unflaggingly loyal articles about Douglas and his Rens. When the formation of the Rens was first announced, Dougherty endorsed Douglas.

Douglas took advantage of it on Saturday, November 3, 1923, when the Rens (also called the Renaissance Big Five, the "Big R" Five, and the Harlem Rens) played their first game as a team in their new home. The team consisted of Leon Monde, Hilton "Kid" Slocum, Frank "Strangler" Forbes, Zack Anderson, Hy Monte, Harold Mayers, Tucker Wardell, and Harold Jenkins. Even though these players were well-known in Harlem, the newspaper advertisements didn't carry their names, but rather promoted an even greater selling point, stating that the team was "under the personal management of Smilin' 'Bob' Douglas."

The game was played on the ballroom's dance floor, with two portable baskets erected at either end, and folding wooden chairs set up for spectators. "The floor was very slippery," recalled future

Rens star William "Pop" Gates, "and they outlined the sidelines and foul lines. It wasn't a big floor. It was far from being a regular basketball floor. Other than high schools or armories, they had very few places to play at." The Rens defeated the all-white Collegiate Five, 28–22. At the conclusion of the game, around eleven o'clock, the baskets were removed, the Theatre Orchestra began playing, and the fans, dressed in formal suits and gowns, danced far into the morning. Douglas's new team—and business venture—were off to a great start.

But there was no time to rest on his laurels. If he was going to keep the team profitable, Douglas would have to arrange games that would draw big crowds. Because the competition in Harlem was so fierce—and because the Renaissance Casino held fewer fans and therefore made less money—Douglas could not afford a bad night's attendance. His pal Romeo Dougherty worried, "Two [financial] failures at the Renaissance and the team will go to pieces."

THE BATTLE FOR HARLEM

Dougherty's prediction was never tested. The Rens drew large crowds of around two thousand, even when they suffered a three-game losing streak. Even though new professional black teams seemed to be announced weekly, the Rens remained popular, defeating a vast majority of their opponents, most of them white. These "race matches" pitting black teams against white teams brought in much larger crowds in Harlem than when black teams faced each other. Romeo Dougherty was quick to hype the Rens' second game, this time against the all-white Bridgeport Separates, as another opportunity for black players to prove themselves against whites: "Instead of picking easy ones for his men, Douglas is seeking the hardest combinations among white teams, and Bridgeport is truly representative of the best white teams. This action lends confidence to the local team, as the people [of Harlem] know they will do their best to stop these fast white players."

When it came to winning, especially against white teams, Douglas's Rens and the McMahons' Commonwealth Five were considered the two best teams in Harlem, making a showdown between them inevitable. Despite their successful record of wins, the Commonwealth Five were not pulling in the crowds that the Rens were, forcing the McMahons to lower the ticket price from seventy-five cents to fifty cents. If the team didn't start becoming profitable, the McMahons would disband them. One step toward that profitability was a three-game series against the popular Rens team.

The first game was scheduled for February 24, 1924. But first the Commonwealth team had to face the biggest obstacle of all professional teams, black or white: the Original Celtics. This all-white team seemed nearly unbeatable, and every time a black team lost against them, it seemed like a harsh reminder of what it was like for African-Americans to compete in a white world. The Original Celtics came to the Commonwealth Casino having just won 108 of their last 110 games. The McMahons didn't have to worry about drawing a crowd for this game: three thousand fans paid a dollar each in hopes of seeing black faces jumping in victory. Instead, the Original Celtics defeated Commonwealth, then beat them again in the second game of the series.

This made the McMahons' team even hungrier when they finally faced the Rens for what was called the grand finale championship of Harlem. In the first game, the Commonwealth Five outshot the Rens to post a 38–35 win. In the second game, the Commonwealth team squashed the Rens by ten points, 31–21. Smilin' Bob Douglas's highly touted and popular Renaissance Five suddenly seemed poised for extinction.

The Rens' salvation came from the unlikeliest of saviors: the McMahon brothers. Defeating the Rens may have been a moral victory, but the McMahons were devotees of the bottom line. Despite a successful season on paper, the Commonwealth team had failed to defeat either Cumberland Posey's Loendi team or the Original Celtics. Worse, they had failed to draw fans in large enough numbers to justify the expense. After only two seasons, the McMahons disbanded the Commonwealth Five to focus on their known moneymaker, boxing. Cumberland Posey's Loendi team in Pittsburgh wasn't faring much better. The Loendi Social and Literary Club, which had sponsored the team, complained that the players didn't have regular day jobs and only wanted to "play basketball and [have] a good time." They pointed out that all the players on the Coffey Club team worked full-time jobs, and yet the Loendi had failed to defeat them in the past season. Loss of the club's support forced the team to disband. With the two top professional black teams now gone, the Rens went from the verge of dissolution to now being poised to take over Harlem's basketball scene.

THE RENS TAKE ON THE WORLD (1924–29)

Douglas took immediate advantage of the breakup of the Commonwealth team by snagging two of their top players, Georgie Fiall and Clarence "Fats" Jenkins. The Rens were strengthened further with the addition of Pappy Ricks, the "Jersey Kangaroo." Freshly motivated, the Rens went on an exceptional winning streak, taking every game at home. Dougherty praised the team, writing, "No colored team today stands a chance with the crack players under guidance of the astute Bob Douglas." No one doubted Douglas's drive to win, but what made him such a respected manager was that he didn't want to win at any cost (as was often said about Cumberland Posey). When a game against the all-white Xavier Five proved too violent, Douglas took his team off the court after only nine minutes and forfeited the game. His style paid off. The Rens steamrolled over most teams. Wrote Dougherty of the Rens' winning streak, "It is a race between white teams to see which one can defeat the colored players on their home court, but so far, none of them have been successful."

Though the Rens lost a few games on the road, they won every game they played at the Renaissance Casino. Except one. The Original Celtics, who had defeated them earlier in the season, defeated them again at home, 49–38. Despite the Rens' impressive record, the bigger, stronger, more experienced Celtics still loomed over Harlem.

Douglas agreed to yet another game against the Original Celtics. Three thousand fans, five hundred of them black, crowded into the Orange Armory in New Jersey on a cold December evening to root for their race as much as for any team. Once again, the Original Celtics defeated the hopes of blacks everywhere when they beat the Rens, 31–29. Another game with the Original Celtics was scheduled for later in the month, but two additional losses to other teams by the Rens brought a scolding by Dougherty in the *New York Amsterdam News*, blaming the losses on the team's off-court behavior, including carousing with women, frequenting nightclubs, and missing practice.

Three thousand anxious fans pushed into the Manhattan Casino to witness this meeting between the Rens and the Celtics, in what was being called "the battle of the gods." Another thousand fans that had been denied entrance, huddled outside in the cold, waiting for the results. Their long wait—and faith—was finally rewarded as the Rens defeated the Celtics, 37–30. After all this time, Romeo Dougherty wrote the column he'd been waiting three years to write: "Championships in those lines of sports where the color line is drawn remain with the whites, because they deny the colored brother a chance to compete with them, but once they let down the bars they prove the fallacy of their claims of a superiority which only the white race enjoys. All Negroes have asked is a fair chance, and when given that chance, they have more than made good."

A month later, after twenty-six consecutive wins at home, the Rens again played the Original Celtics at the Orange Armory in New Jersey, the site of their last defeat at the hands of the Celtics. The Celtics jumped out to a quick lead, but the Rens fought back to win, 32–28. Now black Americans everywhere were counting on the Rens.

But the Rens and the Celtics were not yet finished with each other. In February they met again, this time at the Regiment Armory, which was large enough to hold the ten thousand spectators, the largest crowd ever to watch a black basketball team. This time, the Rens were unable to overcome their rivals, and the Celtics handed the Rens a devastating loss, 46–21.

During this time, the country's first real professional basketball league, the American Basketball League (ABL), was formed. While the National Basketball League (NBL) consisted of teams from rural small towns, the ABL was made up of teams from urban areas. Even though their players were mainly the sons of first-generation Irish, Jewish, and Italian immigrants, league officials banned blacks from joining. Supported by numerous editorials and columns in black newspapers, Bob Douglas attempted to join the ABL on several occasions, but each time he and the Rens were refused. (They would be denied membership for twenty-two more years, until 1948.) Though the Original Celtics' owner, Jim Furey, had been invited to join the ABL, he turned them down. Some basketball historians claim that Furey's refusal was based in part on the ABL's rejection of his friendly rivals the Rens. Perhaps so, but undoubtedly a bigger incentive was that, by staying out of the league, he could book the Celtics to play anyone he chose, which translated into much more money than he would make in the league.

The ABL's racism seemed contagious. In 1927, the National Basketball Officials Committee suddenly, and without explanation, failed to renew memberships for four black officials. Jesse McMahon, the white owner of the defunct Commonwealth Five, was suspended from his job at Madison Square Garden as boxing matchmaker. Before McMahon's tenure at the Garden, few black fighters were booked; since he'd arrived, nearly half the fighters were black. Most white newspapers, including the prestigious *New York Times*, ignored black sports altogether. The

Rens' Clarence "Fats" Jenkins was continually singled out by black and white sportswriters as one of the greatest, but overlooked, players in a game that reportedly involved 15 million people. Lamented the *Pittsburg Courier*, "Were his epidermis the color of alabaster he would have so many offers from basketball teams to play that he could write his own ticket and name his own price." Even the white newspaper the *New York News* declared Jenkins to be "a basketball team within himself." But, no matter how good he was or who sang his praises, he was black and could therefore only play on black teams. Meanwhile, the Original Celtics had been bought by the Madison Square Garden Corporation and forced to join the ABL. They would play home games at the Garden, where only white teams were permitted to play basketball. The idealists of the Harlem Renaissance still had a long way to go in convincing white America to tear down the color barrier. And a lot of African-Americans were betting their hopes that, if anyone could smash that barrier, it would be the Rens, who, according to Douglas, had already proven themselves to be the best black team: "The Renaissance does not CLAIM to be the World's Colored Champions. They ARE the champions because they have defeated in home and home series every recognized colored basketball team in the country."

The Rens justified many of those hopes as they faced every top white team available—and beat them. For Bob Douglas, beating white teams wasn't so much a political statement as it was a financial necessity: nine out of ten games that the Rens had won against other black teams had been financial failures. Playing white teams was the only sure way to make money. And the white team that was most profitable to play was still their nemesis, the Original Celtics. Early in their 1927 season they had defeated the Original Celtics, 38–25. At the end of the season, after the Celtics had won the ABL championship, the Rens faced them again in a three-game series for what many considered the unofficial world championship. The Celtics beat the Rens at the Renaissance Casino, 37–28, then beat them again a week later, 47–31. African-

Americans would just have to do what they had so much practice at doing. Wait. Wait and hope.

By the 1928–29 season, the Rens' popularity was so great that their home games were broadcast on the radio by New York City's WPCH. Their popularity had spread beyond Harlem to such a degree that Bob Douglas decided that, in addition to their weekly home game at the Renaissance casino, the Rens would now also play every Monday night at the Palais Royal in Philadelphia, making them the "home" team for blacks in two cities. Despite the extensive traveling and the brutal schedule, the Rens won 95 of their 107 games. So, when the season was over, they were again ready to face the Celtics, once again managed by Jim Furey, in another postseason unofficial championship duel.

The crowd of ten thousand, the most spectators ever at a professional basketball game in New York, watched as Celtics Nat Holman, Dutch Dehnert, Joe Lapchick, and Pete Barry led the team to a 38–31 victory over the Rens. A few days later the Celtics beat the Rens 30–25, and four days after that the Celtics defeated the Rens for the third time, 26–23.

And Harlem waited.

THE LONG AND WINDING ROAD:
THE BARNSTORMING YEARS

Harlem had other, more serious problems. The year 1929 was the beginning of the America's Great Depression, the longest and most devastating economic catastrophe that any Western industrialized nation had ever faced. So severe was the Great Depression that it would last for ten years, during which eleven thousand of the twenty-five thousand U.S. banks would fail, stocks would lose 80 percent of their value, manufacturing output would be cut in half, and 25 to 30 percent of the workforce (12–15 million people) would be thrown out of work, with little hope of finding jobs elsewhere. Harlem felt the impact immediately. Rents were nearly doubled, forcing tenants to move in together in ever-increasingly crowded apartments. Unemployment rose to nearly 50 percent.

The beginning of the Great Depression also brought the greatest challenge ever to the Rens, but not in the form of racism or a superior team. Jim Furey, manager of the Original Celtics (who were now owned by the Central Opera House), tried to lure several Rens players away from Bob Douglas in an effort to start a new team called the Original Renaissance Five. When word of this was made public, fans from all over offered both moral and financial support to keep the Rens together. Although a few players did sign contracts with Furey, Douglas was not about to go gentle into that good fight. He told the *New York Amsterdam News*, "It is indeed strange that the same people who bought the franchise of an almost defunct athletic club [the Original Celtics], but because we are Negroes failed to do us the honor of making an offer for the franchise of the Renaissance Five." While the Rens fought all comers on the basketball court, Douglas fought off the Celtics raiders in the legal court, beating them soundly. The Rens quickly put the controversy behind them and went on to win a string of consecutive victories over the top white teams.

The Original Celtics did not fare so well. Even though they were a championship team, they were not as profitable as the Rens, losing almost $20,000 in the first two weeks of the new season. Jim Furey was forced to replace his top players with rookies who were less experienced but a lot cheaper. Even then, the Celtics weren't able to generate enough income and were disbanded. This made clear to everyone that Furey's attempts to start an Original Renaissance Five team was a desperate move for solvency. Basketball's most unbeatable team finally fell, not to the color line that the Rens faced, but to the bottom line, which the Rens had consistently defeated.

But a healthy bottom line came with a healthy price. The Depression was getting worse: 38 percent of African-Americans were unemployed (compared to 17 percent of whites). With unemployment in Harlem rising, basketball attendance began to diminish.

Where before the Rens had drawn as many as ten thousand fans in a single night, now they were drawing less than two thousand over five nights. Douglas lamented in a letter that "basketball in New York is not what it used to be. I don't know whether the people are tired of the game or whether it is the economic conditions of the City. My crowd has fallen off more than 50%, even at reduced prices." Perhaps he saw the irony that his letterhead bragged, "Greatest Drawing Card in Basketball Today. Book the 'R' and Increase Your Gate Ten-fold."

The Rens played almost every night of the week just to keep the team afloat. The Renaissance Casino suddenly found itself on the verge of bankruptcy due to poor management. Bob Douglas had to do something or the Rens would go the way of so many other black basketball teams—into oblivion. And the casino also needed saving, not just because it was the Rens' home, but because it was the only nightclub in Harlem entirely owned and managed by African-Americans. Douglas made two crucial decisions: first, he convinced the owners to let him take over as manager of the Renaissance Casino; second, he sent the Rens on barnstorming tours for weeks at a time. Although the Rens were used to playing games on the road, they had never before gone on such extended trips. And never before had the tour included the Southern states. On previous tours, Douglas had usually accompanied the team, but now that he had management duties at the casino, he would have to stay home and do all his booking from there.

"We'd leave [Harlem] right after New Year's and wouldn't come back until April," said Rens player John "Boy Wonder" Isaacs (1936–41). "We were barnstorming."

ROAD RAGE: RACISM ON TOUR

On the road, the Rens faced much more racism than they had at home. During one game in Chicago against the Bruins, the Rens had eighteen fouls called against them, while the Bruins had none. This was so common that, whenever the Rens played against white teams, they knew they had to jump to at least a ten-point lead as quickly as possible due to the bias of the white referees. "You got ten points as fast as you could," said John Isaacs, "because you assumed those were the ten points you weren't going to get from officiating." After one particularly violent game, in which Rens road manager Eric Illidge protested a ref's unfair call, Illidge remembered, "That's when all hell broke loose. We had to form a circle in the middle of the floor and fight back to back. I had my pistol out and Fat Jenkins pulled out the knife he kept hidden in his sock. We were ready to fight our way out, but the riot squad came and saved our lives."

A newly formed Celtics team continued the rivalry just where they had left off. The two teams battled back and forth season after season, with neither one being fully dominant. Despite the intensity, the two teams respected each other. "The Rens learned a lot from the Celtics," admitted John Isaacs. "They played with their heads. And when we played other teams, we instituted a lot of their stuff—playing smart basketball, setting each other up." Because they played so many games in dance halls on highly waxed floors that were dangerously slippery to run on, both the Celtics and the Rens adjusted by developing a passing game, for which they both became famous. Bounce passes were to be avoided because the large thirty-two-inch circumference balls were held together with lumpy stitches that made the direction of the ball's bounce unpredictable.

Celtics-Rens matchups were so popular that on Thanksgiving Day of 1934 they played each other twice, once in the Bronx and again at the Renaissance Casino (with the Rens winning both games). Because both teams realized how necessary the other was to their financial success, they both considered taking the show on the road through the South, traveling to play against each other in other states. That idea was eventually rejected because they feared the South wouldn't accept the black-versus-white rivalry. "Once you passed D.C.," recalled John Isaacs, "you weren't known by what your name was, you became 'nigger' or 'boy.'" Nevertheless, the Rens added most of the Southern states to their schedule and took to the road with renewed gusto. With Douglas managing the casino, Eric Illidge became the Rens' financial manager while they toured, and "Fats" Jenkins became the player-coach. By the late thirties, the Rens were each earning about $150 to $250 a month (with $3 a day for food), with Fats Jenkins pulling in between $1,500 and $2,000 per season. Beating the Celtics brought a bonus of $25 to $50.

The Southern tour proved vastly successful. Traveling over three thousand miles on their bus, the Old Blue Goose, the Rens took on all challengers, including college, club, and professional teams—provided they were black—and beat every team on the tour. In order to be invited back for rematches, the Rens devised the formula of running up the score in the first half, then allowing the opposing team to get within ten points by the end of the game. Even though they didn't play white teams, their games were attended by both blacks and whites. By silently letting their athleticism do the talking, the Rens became the best spokespersons around for promoting equal rights. Romeo Dougherty praised the Rens, saying, "The good will the team established has done much to establish the outfit as one of the greatest basketball aggregations yet assembled." That goodwill sometimes translated into breaking longtime racial barriers: after winning an unprecedented eighty-eight consecutive games in 1933, the Rens were invited to spend the night in the all-white York Athletic Club.

Following the tour of the South, the Rens barnstormed through the Midwest, running off win after win. When they played the St. Louis All-Star team, they came up against the highest-paid player in the National Basketball League in the 1930s, John Wooden. Wooden would go on to become the first person enshrined in the Basketball Hall of Fame as both a player and a coach. Many still believe Wooden to be the greatest college coach in history, having won a still unparalleled ten National Collegiate Athletic Association (NCAA) National Championships, while coaching at the University of California, Los Angeles (UCLA). Years later, Wooden described his experience playing against the Rens: "I played many games against the New York Rens in the thirties and continue to feel that they were the finest exponents of team play that I have ever seen. . . . To this day, I have never seen a team play better team basketball."

The barnstorming years tested the Rens, not just as basketball players, but as black men. While they were often warmly welcomed by the black communities, they also faced the worst kind of racism. After traveling as many as two hundred miles to play in a game, they would be banned from restaurants and hotels, often eating cold sandwiches and sleeping on their tour bus. Sometimes even the bus wasn't a refuge, when gas station owners would stand at their pumps with rifles rather than sell gas to the Rens. "Bruiser" Saitch recalled how the Rens sometimes "slept in jails because they wouldn't put us up in hotels. . . . We sometimes had over a thousand damn dollars in our pockets and we couldn't get a good goddamn meal."

The Rens were usually able to channel their rage and frustration into the game. Maybe it was the daily fires of racism that forged their skills, motivated them to prove something to the world. Gerry Archibald, owner and manager of professional teams in Warren, Pennsylvania, recalled one such incident with the Rens. Whenever the Rens came to Warren, an all-white town of fifteen thousand, they always stayed in Jamestown, New York. But one time they showed up without having made reservations and Archibald called a local hotel to book them rooms—without telling the hotel the team was black. Archibald drove the team to the hotel and went inside with a couple of the players. "I'll never forget the look in the poor girl's face at the desk when he opened the door," Archibald remembered. "She turned white as a sheet and she said, 'Mr. Archibald, I just can't do it,' and she burst out crying. Just like that, the Rens turned around and said, 'Okay, Gerry, we'll find some place.' And, boy, did they ever put on a show that night! I beat 'em a couple of times, but not that night!"

The fans often weren't any more hospitable; those who sat courtside sometimes stabbed players in the buttocks with hatpins or burned them with cigarettes. Those fans out of reach threw cigarettes, cigars, and bottles or shined lights in the eyes of shooters. In mining towns, the miners would wear their helmets and focus the lights into the eyes of the visiting team. Sometimes, if a heckler was particularly obnoxious, a Ren would stand in front of the offending fan and call for the ball. When a teammate whipped the ball to him, he would jump aside and let the ball smash into the fan's face. Recalled "Pop" Gates, "After that, they got the message and kept quiet."

Racism didn't come just from fans and local proprietors, it also came from the other teams and promoters. During play against the all-white House of David, a player hurled racial insults at Fats Jenkins. Rens manager Eric Illidge complained to the House of David management, who promptly dismissed the offending player from their team. To make sure the Rens weren't cheated by promoters, Illidge carried two important tools: a tabulator and a gun. Because the Rens were often paid a percentage of the gate, Illidge used the tabulator to personally count heads at every game. The gun was used to make sure they got paid up front. He instructed the Rens, "Never come out on the court unless I have the money." As he later explained, "We would not let anyone deny us our right to make a living."

While the Rens were on the road, Bob Douglas continued in his role as community leader in Harlem. He spent $15,000 renovating the Renaissance Casino and Ballroom, where he launched many new bands that went on to become top entertainers. In an effort to bring youth off the streets and away from crime, Douglas started two amateur teams, the Rens Cubs and the Rens Juniors, which he personally coached. The teams served as training grounds for future Rens, such as John Isaacs. In recognition of his role in the community, Douglas was appointed an honorary member of the board of trustees of Sing Sing prison. For his efforts, in a 1935 contest sponsored by the *New York Amsterdam News*, Smilin' Bob Douglas was selected the second most popular person in Harlem.

Year after year, the Rens amassed astounding win-loss records. Even their few losses were avenged with interest. In the 1932–33 season they had a record of 120–8, having lost once to Yonkers, once to the Jewels, and six times to the Celtics. But in rematches, the Rens beat both Yonkers and the Jewels twice, and defeated the Celtics eight times. The *Chicago Defender* praised them as "the nearest thing to sports perfection that you'll ever see. They are the one team that does everything right. They simply make no mistakes." The Rens used those abilities not just to amass wins, but to support causes, playing various fund-raising games for such causes as the Scottsboro Boys (nine black youths falsely convicted of rape) and the American Jewish Congress Fund. Romeo Dougherty expressed Harlem's appreciation for their basketball skill as well as their skills as African-American ambassadors: "Bob Douglas has just reason to be proud of his team which sported the royal colors of blue and gold, for they were the very cream of basketball's royalty."

It was official. The Rens had become the crown princes of Harlem.

THE RENS–HARLEM GLOBETROTTERS RIVALRY: CROWN PRINCES VERSUS CLOWN PRINCES

During this time, another team arose to challenge the Rens' supremacy. In 1926 in Chicago, twenty-four-year-old Abe Saperstein, a five-feet-three-inch white man who'd played basketball in high school, formed and coached the all-black Savoy Big Five, named after the Chicago Savoy Ballroom. With the Depression cutting into the Savoy's business, the owners agreed to permit basketball games. When that failed to significantly increase business, the Savoy dropped basketball altogether. But Saperstein did not drop basketball. He created a new team, Saperstein's New York Globetrotters. Even though the team was from Chicago, he felt that putting *New York* in the name would emphasize to the fans that they were a black team. When he thought that wasn't obvious enough, he replaced *New York* with *Harlem* and the team became known as the Harlem Globetrotters.

Like the Rens, the Globetrotters took to the road, with the whole team crammed into Saperstein's Model T Ford. They traveled through Wisconsin, Minnesota, and Iowa, maintaining the same nightly schedule of games that the Rens did. And their win-loss record was nearly as impressive. They finished their 1933–34 season with an astounding 152–2 record. As their reputation grew, so did demand for the team. Their touring radius began to extend farther and farther, until they'd pushed all the way to Puget Sound, Washington. Naturally, everyone expected a Rens-Globetrotter matchup.

Bob Douglas had reservations. There was no doubt that the Globetrotters were talented players, maybe as talented as the Rens players. "This is a fallacy that people have, that the Globetrotters were not good ballplayers," explained Rens star Pop Gates. "They were excellent ballplayers." But Douglas's approach to basketball was to play the opponents straight up, show the world that black basketball players were the equal of white players. This would demonstrate to those who watched that, if they had been wrong about the black man's athletic ability, maybe they were wrong about other biases about blacks. For Douglas, maintaining dignity was as important as winning.

Abe Saperstein's approach was to present a more docile, less threatening image of the black player. So, to make themselves more acceptable to the white audience, the Globetrotters began incorporating tricks and comic routines. In *Smashing Barriers*, author Richard Lapchick describes why the Globetrotters were so successful:

The Harlem Globetrotters had become white America's image of what a black basketball team should be. As long as blacks were clowns, tricking rather than outsmarting their opponents while speaking barely recognizable English, they were allowed to succeed. This was especially true if the profiteers of their showmanship were whites like Abe Saperstein, owner of the Globetrotters. The players were merely his field hands.

A similar approach was adopted by a black baseball team, the Zulu Cannibal Giants, who dressed in grass skirts, wore tribal paint on their faces, played in bare feet, and batted using what looked like African war clubs.

Part of the message of the Harlem Renaissance was that the time for such stereotypes had passed and a "New Negro"—educated, confident, professional—would be promoted. If the New Negro had any chance of emerging from the crowd of Jim Crow and Aunt Jemima images branded in white American's minds, then those old, comfortable images had to be erased. In 1931, the publisher of the *Pittsburgh Courier* started a public campaign to have the popular radio show *Amos 'n' Andy* taken off the air. The longest-running show in radio history, *Amos 'n' Andy* featured two black men, played by white actors, who spoke in faulty grammar and were surrounded by stereotypes of weak, lazy, crooked, and stupid blacks. The *Courier* urged its readers to protest the show to the Federal Radio Commission: "In this way you will be helping to end a nightly program of ridicule and reflection upon the Negro group." (Though this campaign failed, a similar campaign against the TV version helped get the show yanked in 1953 after only two seasons.)

For Douglas, the Harlem Globetrotters' approach seemed more like a minstrel show in the odious tradition of *Amos 'n' Andy* rather than straight basketball and threatened to set back black sports—and blacks in general—erasing everything they'd accomplished in the last few years. This sentiment was echoed by journalist Ryan Whirty in March of 2005: "Looking back, the Harlem Globetrotters did more harm to the cause of racial equality than good. . . . They [became famous] by reducing themselves to clowning, by exploiting racial stereotypes. . . . And perhaps the most unfortunate result of the 'Trotters success has been the overshadowing of the team that truly deserves recognition as perhaps the most important and influential basketball squad in history: the New York Renaissance Big Five."

Douglas himself told *Sports Illustrated* in 1979, "Abe Saperstein died a millionaire because he gave the white people what they wanted. When I go, it will be without a dime in my pocket, but with a clear conscience. I would never have burlesqued basketball. I loved it too much for that."

Despite their different approaches, both teams were formidable. Though there was plenty of chest-beating about who was better, with public announcements of challenges, the two teams would not meet until the Chicago World Championship Tournament in 1939.

THAT CHAMPIONSHIP SEASON: THE ROCKY ROAD TO THE WORLD CHAMPIONSHIP

By 1937, the Rens were firmly established as one of the best basketball teams—black or white—in the country. But the Depression was still so severe that Douglas kept them on the road rather than face low attendance at home in the Renaissance Casino. Having put on 150,000 hard-earned miles, the Old Blue Goose finally broke down, and Douglas purchased a custom-made, specially equipped $10,000 bus for the team. This was a relief to John "Boy Wonder" Isaacs, who, because he was the rookie, was forced to ride the old bus on a folding chair. But even the newer bus had its hierarchy. Aside from driver, Tex Burnett, the ten passengers—Eric Illidge, eight players, and trainer Vincent "Doc" Bryant—sat in the bus according to seniority and stature. Illidge and player-coach Fats Jenkins sat at the front. The rookies sat at the back. "But Tarzan Cooper," Pop Gates remembered, "he had the choice seat because he was the tallest, the biggest, the baddest, and the strongest and so-called best ballplayer on the team. He was at the front where all the legroom was. . . . And anything that came into the bus had to go by Tarzan Cooper first before it got to the rear. If my mother or wife or sister sent a big cake out to me, before the cake gets to me it had to go by Tarzan. He had to get his slice first."

By now, the Rens' status was so great that, this time when they toured the South, they were able to play some white teams, including the Celtics. The Cotton Curtain was tearing, but still hung stubbornly in place. Because the Rens still faced being barred from hotels and chased out of restaurants by shotgun-wielding cooks, they stayed on black college campuses or with black families. But, no matter how circumspect they were, many whites refused to accept a black team, especially one this good. Sometimes when they played the Celtics or another white team, there were race riots afterward and police had to escort both teams to safety. In Springfield, Missouri, the National Association for the Advancement of Colored People (NAACP) took legal action to stop the segregation of fans at the Rens game and put an end to the practice.

The Rens' fight against racism got some welcomed support from none other than their longtime rivals the Celtics. Before each game against the Celtics, popular Celtics center Joe Lapchick would hug Tarzan Cooper in front of the crowd, letting them know how the Celtics felt about the Rens—and racism. Given the time, this demonstration of affection was more than a casual gesture, and it resulted in years of vitriolic epithets and death threats for Lapchick. Bob Douglas described his relationship with the Celtics as one of mutual respect: "We always played in a war, but often it was a race war. When we played against most white teams, we were colored. Against the Celtics, we were men. Over those last years a real brotherhood was born out of competition and travel."

The Rens continued their tour through the Midwest, traveling over eighteen thousand miles and establishing record attendances at some games. Often, to avoid racial confrontations, they were forced to stay in areas where they would be welcome, then travel two hundred to four hundred miles to play their game that night. But the strategy worked: despite the scorched-earth devastation of the Depression, the Rens were attracting record-breaking crowds five times as large as the Celtics were drawing. Not only were they a financial success, but their style of play—very little dribbling, fast passes, quick cuts to the basket—was being imitated everywhere. White and black college coaches from the South and Midwest attended Rens games for tips and strategies.

In 1938, the season that would lead them to compete in the world championship, the Rens added two new players, Clarence "Pop" Gates and Clarence "Puggy" Bell. For Bell, this was a dream come true: "The idols of the basketball world whenever they have played, the Rens, to Harlem, their hometown, are veritable demigods of the court, and it is the dream of nine out of ten promising young basketball players in the community to get a chance to play with them." Gates was signed for $125 a month, which was significantly more than the $17 a month his father was making doing odd jobs.

Now the roster was finalized, and standing ready to face the 1938–39 season were eight men whom Harlem was counting on: terror of the court and the team bus Charles "Tarzan" Cooper (6'4"); rebounding expert William "Wee Willie" Smith (6'5"); Eyre "Bruiser" Satch (6'1"), one of the country's first black tennis stars, having twice won the National Negro Tennis Championship (and considered by female fans to be the handsomest member of the Rens); youthful John "Boy Wonder" Isaacs (6'); William "Pop" Gates (6'3"); Zack Clayton (who would one day turn boxing referee); and Clarence "Puggy" Bell. Finally, there was player-manager Clarence "Fats" Jenkins, who, at five feet seven inches and 180 pounds, was not fat, but at forty-one, and already a veteran of twenty-five years of professional basketball, was the team's oldest and most experienced player. This was the team that Harlem, and many African-Americans across the country, were pinning their hopes on for this to be the year they would put an end to the waiting. Waiting for white America to recognize the black athlete as an equal. Waiting for just one chance to play on a level playing field against the best white teams.

The Rens ended the 1938–39 season with an astounding 109 wins against only 7 losses.

Then something amazing happened: the Rens were invited to come to Chicago for the first-ever World Professional Basketball Tournament.

The waiting was finally over.

THE SHOTS HEARD ROUND THE WORLD: THE WORLD CHAMPIONSHIP OF 1939

In 1939, copromoters Harry Hannin and Harry Wilson made history by creating the World Professional Basketball Tournament. There had been other "world championships" before, but what made this one so special, and a little closer to living up to its grandiose name, was that this would be the first time both black and white teams would compete for the title. Hannin and Wilson decided they would invite the top twelve teams in basketball—if not from the entire world, then from the East Coast and Midwest. And because they weren't dependent on any leagues, they could invite whomever they wished, including teams from the NBL, the ABL, barnstorming teams, black teams, even all-star teams formed at the last minute. The first-place team would be awarded $1,000 and the title of world's best basketball team.

The twelve teams included the Chicago All-Americans (Harmons), the New York Yankees, the Harlem Globetrotters, the Clarksburgh Oilers, the Philadelphia SPHAs, the Michigan House of David, the Sheboygan Redskins, the Fort Wayne Harvesters, the Cleveland White Horses, the Oshkosh All-Stars, the Kate Smith Celtics (now owned by the "First Lady of Radio," singer

Kate Smith), and the New York Renaissance Big Five. The SPHAs, a tough team that had beaten the Rens several times that season, had to withdraw due to injuries and were replaced with the Illini Grads. The only two black teams, the Rens and the Globetrotters, were considered by most experts to be the two best teams of any color in the country. Whether it was an oversight, bad reporting, or racism, a local white newspaper, the *Chicago Daily Tribune*, wrote that the Chicago All-Americans were the only team from Chicago, even though the Globetrotters were also from Chicago. Was it also an oversight, coincidence, or racism that placed the Globetrotters and the Rens in the same bracket, thereby ensuring that there would not be two black teams in the finals?

On Sunday afternoon, March 26, 1939, at the Madison Street Armory, the Rens met their first opponents, the New York Yankees. The Yankees lost, 30–21. Following the first day of play, the *Sheboygan Press* declared, "The Renaissance displayed the most class, and to most observers, they appear to be the team to beat, although anything can happen in a tournament of this kind." That same day, the Globetrotters had to play a doubleheader, first hammering the Fort Wayne Harvesters, 41–33, then, a few hours later, beating the Chicago All-Americans (Harmons), 31–25.

Finally, after all the years of publicly taunting each other, the Rens and Globetrotters met on Monday, March 27, at the Chicago Coliseum. The crowd of seven thousand was the largest yet for the tournament. Two weeks earlier, the Globetrotters had defeated the Celtics in Chicago, something the Rens had never been able to do. That must have been on Bob Douglas's mind as he paced the sidelines, chewing his cigar, anxiously awaiting the outcome of this clash of styles and philosophies that reflected not just on the game, but on African-Americans everywhere. But in this game, there was no clowning, no playing to the crowd, there was just straight-up basketball. Bigger and more experienced, the Rens pressed their advantage at every opportunity. Said the *Chicago Defender*, "At no time did the Globetrotters get a chance to put on an exhibition of ball handling or passing. They were guarded so close that most of their shots were from a distance." A basket by Tarzan Cooper in the last fifteen seconds clinched the victory for the Rens, 27–23. Play was so intense that both teams received several ovations from the spectators. The next day the Globetrotters took the third-place prize of $400 by defeating Sheboygan, who took home $200.

Meanwhile, in the other bracket, the Oshkosh All-Stars were having no trouble defeating their opponents. The Clarksburgh Oilers fell 40–33 and the Sheboygan Redskins lost 40–23. Now all they had to do was defeat the Rens, whom they had already beaten earlier in the season by a shocking *twenty-two points*! In fact, they had beaten the Rens in seven of ten games played over the last two years. The crowd, the odds, and history itself were in their favor.

This tense March day was the realization of a lifelong dream for Bob Douglas. But his dream had faced many obstacles. In 1926, Douglas's Rens had been denied membership in the American Basketball League because they were black. Then again in 1937, the Rens were rejected by the National Basketball League on the same grounds. Suddenly, here they were, playing the best teams from both those leagues. Now that his team had finally been given the chance they'd been denied for the past sixteen years, they couldn't afford to fail. If they did, who knows when the African-American athlete would be given such a chance again?

African-Americans all around the country waited anxiously for the outcome. If these young black athletes won, would it finally send a signal to the white world that blacks were just as capable as whites in competing, not just in sports, but for jobs, housing, and basic civil rights? If the white Oshkosh team won, that would just confirm what so many whites already believed: blacks just weren't good enough.

Over three thousand fans, most of them cheering for the Oshkosh All-Stars, watched the final game. The *Chicago American* described the game as a "rough and tumble affair with spectacular passwork and close guarding mixed in great profusion." Despite the encouragement of the fans, and the Rens' loss of their two big men, Tarzan Cooper and Wee Willie Smith, due to fouls, Oshkosh never managed to keep pace with the methodical teamwork of the Rens, falling 34–25 to Harlem's finest. Pop Gates led the Rens scoring with twelve points. Puggy Bell was selected the Most Valuable Player. Following the game, Chester Washington Jr. in *Pittsburgh Courier* crowed, "You just can't take it away from them. The Rens still reign supreme as the greatest pro basketball team in the country."

After the game, Bob Douglas threw a banquet for the team at the Hotel Grand. The Rens received championship jackets that said on the backs COLORED WORLD CHAMPIONS. When John Isaacs saw the lettering, he took a razor to it, cutting out the word *colored*. When Douglas saw what he was doing, he protested, saying, "You're ruining the jacket!" Isaacs replied, "No, just making it better."

The next morning, the world champion Rens boarded their bus and headed to Cleveland and their next game. And the next. And the next.

FOOTPRINTS IN THE SIDEWALK: THE LEGACY OF THE RENS

For the Rens, winning the world championship was the pinnacle of their career as a team, a moment of perfection they would never again duplicate. At the 1940 tournament, the Globetrotters again faced the Rens, this time before a crowd of nine thousand expectant fans. The Globetrotters won, 37–36, thanks to a last-second midcourt shot. The Globetrotters went on to win the championship, and thereafter their fortunes increased as the Rens' decreased. (In 1995, the Globetrotters lost an exhibition game 91–85 to Kareem Abdul-Jabbar's All-Star Team in Vienna, Austria, ending a run of 8,829 straight victories in exhibition games going back to 1971.) In 1949, ten years after nurturing them to the world championship, Bob Douglas leased the Rens to his nemesis, Globetrotter owner Abe Saperstein. The Rens played warm-up games for the Globetrotters, and Bob Douglas turned to booking wrestlers at the Renaissance Casino. Two years later, Douglas resumed ownership of the Rens and once again sent them on a barnstorming tour. But their games were rarely reported and their past glory was never to be repeated.

But it was to be remembered.

Joe Lapchick's son, sports historian Richard Lapchick, remembered, "I was raised hearing that the Celtics were the greatest team of all time. My dad's friends would say that and all our neighbors would say that. But he would correct them and say, 'The Rens were every bit as good as we were in the beginning and were better than us in the end.'" In 1963, the Naismith Memorial Basketball Hall of Fame remembered and inducted the entire 1932–33 Rens team. Bob Douglas was inducted in 1972, Charles "Tarzan" Cooper in 1977, and William "Pop" Gates in 1989. Douglas, who had by now picked up the nickname "the Father of Black Basketball," was the first black individual to be inducted. Former Original Celtic Nat Holman had endorsed Douglas's nomination: "His leadership, his integrity, his intelligence, qualifies Bob Douglas for a place in the Hall of Fame. His greatest reward is written in the hearts of his players. His influence in the black community on both amateur and professional players will remain long after he and the rest of us are forgotten."

Bob Douglas and the Rens were to be remembered, even if many of the individual players were forgotten. Some critics claim the Basketball Hall of Fame was prejudiced in electing only two Rens as individual players given that the Rens' white rivals the Original Celtics have twice as many players in the Hall. For the past few years, John Isaacs, the last remaining Rens player alive, has been nominated for inclusion but not inducted. Given the legacy of fame and fortune that they have left for others, the fates of many of the star players seems downright shameful. Tarzan Cooper took to painting houses and in 1980, at the age of seventy-three, lay dead for several days in his Philadelphia apartment before his body was discovered. "Pappy" Ricks's career was cut short by alcoholism. Casey Holt became a police officer for New York City, but was mistaken for a thief by fellow officers and shot to death. Wee Willie Smith was a school janitor and later had to have his leg amputated. Though their educational background was similar to that of the Celtics, the veterans of the white team went on to coaching jobs or careers as successful businessmen.

Beyond the individuals, there was the legacy of how the Rens and other earlier black basketball players changed the style of the game itself. Segregation and racism kept many budding black players from being trained by the popular white coaches, whose approach was more formal and scientific. Black players began to improvise. Like some of the jazz musicians who had been denied formal training or forbidden to perform with whites, they developed a style all their own. The artistic impulse in the black athlete was described by NBA star Julius "Dr. J" Erving: "Basketball was—and is—a very simple game. But what the black athlete did was to enhance the game with an expression all his own, taking the basics to another dimension. Soon the white player began to emulate these thoughts and moves and eventually the game became what it is today—a stage where a unique combination of the team concept and individual expression is presented in pure form."

Eight black men putting a ball through a hoop more often than eight white men doesn't seem that world-shaking. But the world can be a fragile place sometimes. A Great Depression had shattered a lot of people's faith in the conventional wisdom they'd clung to so blindly for so long. Having endured a crucible of hardships, some people were ready to look at the world in a different way, maybe a way that would make it better. The Rens' victory offered one more way to look at the world anew. Whites could look at their black neighbors with greater respect, maybe see what they were capable of rather than where the past had relegated them. Blacks could hope for a better future. Pop Gates summed up their achievement as both athletes and ambassadors: "We loved being with the Renaissance because we thought we were the best, and we were happy and proud to represent the Negro people and give them something they could be proud of and adhere to. And we were happy that a lot of white fans loved us also."

The Rens had left footprints in the sidewalk that the next generation could follow into a future filled with new opportunities. Noted Ed Henderson, who'd spent most of his ninety-three years of life promoting black athletics, "It is our opinion that when the final record is written as to contributing values in the battle of human and civil rights, our Negro athletes should be accorded high esteem."

No, blacks and whites weren't ready to join hands in a giant meadow of daisies and sing "Kumbaya." But they were now ready to play basketball together. And that was a start. A start, after all, was all that the greatest minds of the Harlem Renaissance had been asking for.

And that's exactly what the Rens delivered. In 1939, the year the Rens became the first black team to win a world professional title in any sport, black basketball players in the ABL, the forerunner to the National Basketball Association (NBA), stood at 0 percent. In 2004, the number of black players in the NBA amounted to 77 percent.

The Rens taught the world to see what had before been invisible: the color black.

"Hoping Against Hope"

How the Rens Basketball Team Influenced My Life

BY KAREEM ABDUL-JABBAR

I was supposed to be a baseball player.

Not basketball. Definitely not basketball.

I was only seven years old, but I knew one thing for certain: I loved baseball and sucked at basketball. My passion for baseball originated with my babysitter, Mary Mitchell, a friend of my mother's and a rabid baseball fan. My mom also liked baseball and would often listen to the play-by-play Brooklyn Dodger broadcasts announced by Red Barber. Mary's home was only a short bus ride from Yankee Stadium, and a very short walk from the Grounds, so by the time I was five years old, I had already in 1951 watched Joe DiMaggio play his last season and Willie Mays play his first season. I quickly became a serious Dodger fan and learned to appreciate, and participate in, the hysteria that was New York baseball in the fifties. Baseball was the greatest game in the world. Period.

My love of the game grew at the same rate as my body, and when I was finally old enough, I eagerly joined Little League baseball. Inwood, the neighborhood where I was raised, was just a mile or so north of Harlem, and I played for them during the whole time I was eligible for Little League. I played the outfield, first base, and occasionally pitched. However, I was starting to grow to such a height that basketball was a choice that I couldn't completely ignore. So when I was about seven, I ventured out on the basketball court and tried a few shots. I failed miserably. My father even took me out to the public park to show me a few pointers. "This is how you protect the ball," he said, then elbowed me in the face. After that, I avoided any additional lessons from him and abandoned basketball.

Two things changed my mind about basketball: (1) going to a movie with my mother, and (2) getting the snot beat out of me. The movie, called *Go, Man, Go!* (1954), took place during the Harlem Renaissance and starred Dane Clark as Abe Saperstein, the founder of the Harlem Globetrotters, and Sidney Poitier as his assistant. It tells the story of how one day in 1927, Saperstein sees a group of talented black kids playing basketball and becomes obsessed with making them the greatest team ever. The Globetrotters played themselves. I was only seven years old, but I was transfixed. This was the first time I had seen basketball played by athletes who knew the game at the highest level. Before that day, the best I had seen were the kids that played at the park in my neighborhood. This wasn't even the same game.

One particular scene was especially memorable. Marques Haynes, considered by many at that time to be the world's greatest dribbler, dribbles a basketball past Dane Clark in a narrow hallway with such agility and flair that I knew I had to possess such skill. (Haynes later said that scene actually happened when he met Saperstein.) I started practicing dribbling immediately. Of course, being seven, my dedication was short-lived, mostly because I was still a lousy player. I returned to baseball, my first love, and vowed to remain loyal ever after. But that magical scene stayed with me for many years to come. (I wasn't the only one. I later found out that when *Los Angeles Times* film critic Kenneth Turan was asked to name a "guilty pleasure" movie, he replied, "*Go, Man, Go!*, the Harlem Globetrotters movie, where Marques Haynes dribbles around Abe Saperstein in his tiny hotel corridor.") I couldn't get out of my mind that although Haynes was only six feet tall and 160 pounds, he could make much bigger men look foolish, like lumbering woolly mammoths chasing a darting hummingbird. Though my lack of skill, and my father's lessons, kept me away from basketball for a couple more years, much later, when I was playing professionally, I focused on being the kind of big man who could move like Marques Haynes. Okay, I could never move like Haynes, but that was my goal, and I succeeded better than most men my size. Better to be the quick hummingbird than the extinct mammoth.

The beating that brought me back to basketball took place in 1956. I was nine and my parents had sent me to attend the all-black boarding school Holy Providence in Cornwall Heights just outside Philadelphia. Holy Providence contained forty boys and about three hundred girls; the benefits of such a lopsided gender ratio were completely lost on a shy nine-year-old. Besides, my problem was with the boys. Although I was already a towering five feet eight inches tall, I was mild-mannered and cheerful. I also excelled in my classes. Thanks to my mother's coaching and father's example, I could read several grade levels beyond my fellow fourth-graders and was earning straight A's in all my classes. Naturally, I was hated. This hatred was expressed by the school bullies, Eddie Johnson and Sylvester Curtis, pugnacious seventh-graders who treated me to a series of brutal beatings between the opening of school and spring when my parents came to pick me up. Two weeks before school let out, I was jumped by two boys in a narrow hallway, not unlike the one in which Haynes had moved so gracefully and powerfully. Only I didn't move at all. They pummeled me relentlessly until they tired and ran away. When my parents arrived to pick me up at the end of the semester, they immediately noticed a distinct change in me, complaining that I didn't smile anymore.

It was true, I had changed. I'd learned not to joke around with the other students, to not volunteer answers in class, to isolate myself as much as possible. Smiling just seemed to antagonize the bullies, so, yeah, I'd stopped smiling. Since the nuns were power-less to protect me, I had to find some refuge on my own. I found it on the basketball court. Basketball was one of the few activities at Holy Providence, and despite my lack of ability or interest, being on the team kept me away from Sylvester Curtis and his knuckle-dragging crew. I was a nine-year-old kid imprisoned in a grown man's body and played like a newborn colt running on wobbly legs and waving gangly arms. I must have looked like a puppet being controlled by a drunken puppeteer. If my teammates passed the ball to me, I soon made them regret it. But no matter how badly I played, at least on the court no one was punching me in the face.

In one game, trapped by the other team and having lost the dribble, I was desperate to get rid of the ball. Unable to find an open teammate to rescue me, I glanced over my shoulder at the basket, pivoted, and tossed up my first hook shot. An in-and-out miss. But that feeling—the sense of power and control as I was being swarmed, yet still able to rise above them to do what I had to do—that feeling energized me. In an environment in which I was swarmed daily by bullies and had no control but to become invisi-ble, I found something on that court, and in that shot, that gave me back a little of what I had lost. Pride, self-respect—visibility. I practiced that hook shot all winter, perfecting it as much as I could. For the next thirty-three years, I was always on a basketball team. And the skyhook became my signature shot.

I was never invisible again.

ESCAPING NARROW CORRIDORS: LIFE LESSONS OF THE RENS

The New York Renaissance Big Five, known locally as the Rens, were the first team to win the World Professional Basketball Tour-nament, in 1939. Amazingly, despite being born in Harlem and raised only a mile away, I hadn't heard about the Rens until 1964, when I was seventeen years old. And yet, I'd had connections to

37

The 1939 World Championship Rens: (left to right) William "Wee Willie" Smith, Charles "Tarzan" Cooper, John "Boy Wonder" Isaacs, William "Pop" Gates, Clarence "Puggy" Bell, Eyre "Bruiser" Satch, Zach Clayton, Clarence "Fats" Jenkins. The Rens were the first team—black or white—to win the World Championship Professional Basketball Tournament. They were inducted into the Basketball Hall of Fame in 1964.

Robert "Smilin' Bob" Douglas, 1972. The "Father of Black Professional Basketball." Born in the West Indies, Douglas (1881-1979) fell in love with basketball the first time he saw it played at a New York City gym. Soon after, he founded the New York Renaissance team (The Rens), which became the first black salaried professional basketball team. Under his ownership and management, the Rens amassed an astounding 2,318-381 (.859) record. Douglas was determined to overcome the many obstacles of racism that his teams faced in order to show the world just how good black athletes could be. He was inducted into the Basketball Hall of Fame in 1972.

38

39

The Rens versus the Original Celtics. Original Celtics center Joe Lapchick with Rens center "Tarzan" Cooper in what is considered the first jump ball between a white man and a black man in professional basketball. The friendly rivalry between the Original Celtics and the Rens brought out the best in both teams as they battled back and forth for years. In order to quell the racism among fans, Lapchick would often embrace Cooper before a game. Lapchick would later refer to the Rens as the best team the Original Celtics ever played.

Oshkosh All-Stars, 1939. The All-Stars were Western Division Champions in the National Basketball League, the same league that had refused to allow the Rens to join because they were a black team. Although the All-Stars had defeated the Rens seven out of the last ten games they'd played, once by twenty-two points, the Rens defeated them in the finals to claim the title of first-ever World Champions of Basketball.

Original Celtics, c. 1920s. The Original Celtics were the most dominating team of the 1920s. The professional team was formed in 1918 by promoter James Furey. Like the Rens, they helped build national interest in basketball by enduring an intense 205-game schedule on the road. The friendly rivalry with the Rens lifted both teams' popularity. Fierce competitors on the court, they were respected friends off the court.

Abe Saperstein and the Harlem Globetrotters, 1940. Bought by twenty-four-year-old Abe Saperstein in 1927, the Harlem Globetrotters were from Chicago. Saperstein chose to add "Harlem" to their name so patrons would know they were black. The Rens defeated them at the 1939 World Championship Professional Basketball Tournament, but the Globetrotters came back the next year to defeat the Rens and win the 1940 World Championship Professional Basketball Tournament. In 2002, the team was inducted into the Basketball Hall of Fame.

43

Basketball and Music, 1926. Vivian Marinelli teaching the Charleston to basketball players of Washington, D.C.'s Palace Club in order to improve their footwork. Forty years later, a young Kareem would follow in their dance steps listening to jazz to help improve his game.

Jazz Bandleader Cab Calloway. Before Calloway (1907–94) rose to fame as a jazz performer at the Cotton Club, he played for the Baltimore Athenians in the Negro Professional Basketball League in 1926, while a senior in high school.

Scott Joplin. Joplin (1868–1917) was one of the most important ragtime performers and composers and forerunner to jazz. His composition, "The Entertainer," was featured in the Robert Redford–Paul Newman film *The Sting* (1973), which launched a renewed interest in and popularity of ragtime.

45

Fats Waller, 1943. Waller (1904-43) is credited with being one of the first and most influential jazz pianists and composers. His most famous compositions include "Squeeze Me" (1919), "Ain't Misbehavin'" (1929), "Blue Turning Grey Over You" (1930), "Honeysuckle Rose" (1929), "I've Got a Feeling I'm Falling" (1929), and "Jitterbug Waltz" (1942).

46

Duke Ellington, 1929. Ellington (1899–1974) leads his band behind the chorus line at the whites-only Cotton Club. Girls in the chorus line had to be under twenty-one years old, over 5'6" tall, and of light complexion. Though Ellington didn't like seeing himself confined by the description "jazz musician," he is nevertheless regarded as the most important jazz influence of the twentieth century.

47

Billie Holiday and Louis Armstrong in the 1946 film *New Orleans*. Armstrong (1901–71) and Holiday (1915–59) were two of the most dominant jazz icons of the Harlem Renaissance. More than just internationally admired musicians, they were also outspoken about civil rights. In 1939, the same year the Rens became the first World Champions of Basketball, Holiday recorded "Strange Fruit," a powerful indictment of lynching. In 1957, Armstrong, disgusted by President Eisenhower's lack of action in desegregating Little Rock, Arkansas schools, publicly referred to the president as "gutless" and "two-faced," resulting in many cancelled concert dates.

Gertrude "Ma" Rainey. Billed as "The Mother of Blues," Rainey (1886–1939) was one of the first women to professionally record the blues. She recorded over a hundred of her own songs and worked with the best musicians of her time, including Louis Armstrong and Fletcher Henderson. Because she was outspoken about women's rights and a successful businesswoman who took complete control of her career, she was extremely popular as both a singer and role model.

Miles Davis, 1952. Davis's (1926–91) version of *Porgy and Bess* (1958) inspired eleven-year-old Kareem's interest in jazz. Davis's outward cool provided a role model for an awkward teenage Kareem, while Davis's discipline and passion for music inspired Kareem's own dedication to and passion for basketball.

51

Thelonius Monk at Minton's Playhouse, 1947. (Left to right: Thelonius Monk, piano; Howard McGhee, trumpet; Roy Eldrige, trumpet; Teddy Hill, saxophone & clarinet.) Minton's is known as the birthplace of bop. Kareem's father would often come here to jam with other jazz musicians, sometimes all night long.

52

Kareem's parents in their apartment. Although he was a transit cop by day, Kareem's father, a graduate of Juilliard and an accomplished musician, continued to play at night with various jazz bands.

Kareem in Power Memorial school uniform, 1965. Kareem led the high school team to many championships. But when his white coach used a racial epithet to motivate him during a game, Kareem became motivated to learn more about African-American history.

53

Kareem, 3, holding baseball mitt. Baseball, not basketball, was young Kareem's first sport of choice. But his growth spurt and bullying from other students drove him to both seek refuge and prove himself on the basketball court.

54

Kareem playing for Power Memorial, c.1964. Kareem's ability to leap so high allowed him to perfect the slam dunk. His ability to consistently deliver the slam dunk resulted in the NCAA banning dunking from 1967 to 1976. The ban is popularly known as the "Lew Alcindor Rule," based on Kareem's name when he started playing college ball.

55

Kareem perfects his hook shot while playing for Power Memorial, c. 1964. The shot, later called the "sky hook" because of Kareem's ability to leap so high while launching it, became nearly unstoppable during his amateur and professional career.

56

Kareem's parents watching their son play for Power Memorial.

57

Richard Avedon's famous portrait of Kareem at sixteen, standing in a playground at 61st Street and Amsterdam Avenue, New York City, May 2, 1963. The photo captures the young teenager's mixture of confidence and anxiety as he stands on the brink of an uncertain future. The gray starkness of the street behind him suggests his past conflicts, but the crisp purity of the uniform evokes a hopeful future. One year later, Kareem would begin his in-depth studies of the Harlem Renaissance that would help him choose his path as a basketball player, historian, writer, jazz enthusiast, and community activist.

them I wasn't even aware of. Dolly King, one of the officials at some of my high school games, had played for the Rens in the 1940s. The Harlem Globetrotters, featured in *Go, Man, Go!*, which had first inspired me to try basketball, were perennial rivals of the Rens. They had even faced the Rens, and lost, in that 1939 championship tournament. William "Pop" Gates coached boys' basketball in Harlem. He was one of the first blacks to play in the National Basketball League and the only player to appear in all ten World Professional Basketball Tournaments in Chicago. Many of the guys I knew who were five to ten years older than I had been taught by him, one of the greatest players in basketball history, yet I had no idea of who he was. Joe Lapchick, former Original Celtics great, had given me the MVP for the New York Catholic High School Championship. Not only was his team the main rivals of the Rens, but he had been friends with the Rens and had personally helped them during some intense racist episodes. My high school coach, Jack Donahue, was friends with Joe while Joe was coaching the Knicks and later St. Johns University. St. Johns had a great program and was often highly placed in the national rankings. Coach Lapchick gave Coach Donahue films of St. Johns games that he in turn showed the guys who played for him at the summer camp, including me. Watching those films, I was undoubtedly learning Rens plays and moves without ever having heard of them. Joe's son Ritchie attended Coach Donahue's camp in the summer and ended up sleeping in the bunk next to mine at camp. We became good friends and have maintained this friendship ever since those days. The Rens' history was brushing against me all the time, like strangers bumping while passing on a crowded street.

Historical connections and influences were all around me, but I hadn't noticed. That same year I first heard of them, 1964, I became part of a summer internship in journalism and started earnestly studying the Harlem Renaissance (see the chapter " 'Mad Medley': How Harlem Influenced My Life"). The more I studied the giants of the Renaissance, the more I realized how many influences we have acting on us, whether or not we know it. If a teenager first learning guitar tries to copy Jimi Hendrix, it doesn't matter to him that Hendrix was influenced by Muddy Waters. But how much richer his enjoyment would be, how much better he might play that guitar, if he did know. For me, studying the greats of the Harlem Renaissance was like watching a dozen more Marques Hayneses trapped in a narrow corridor determined to get past an unmovable obstacle. Each found a way around, some using words, some using a musical instrument, some using art, some using their athletic prowess.

The goal of the heavyweights of the Renaissance was to make the black American visible to white America. To have them seen for whom they really were, not some stereotypical cartoon image that whites had been raised on and therefore were comfortable with. Jazz made the black musician visible. Du Bois, Garvey, Locke, and Johnson made the black political agenda visible. Hughes, Hurston, McKay, and Toomer made the black writer visible. The Rens made the black basketball player visible. Now they could all be seen for who they really were, what they were capable of achieving—and contributing.

REWRITING HISTORY: INVESTIGATING MYSELF

American philosopher George Santayana said, "History is always written wrong, and so always needs to be rewritten." That's pretty much why I write history books that focus on the heroic exploits of African-Americans. Many of the people I write about were deliberately left out of the history books that we were forced to read in school. For me, that history was "written wrong" and needed to be corrected. My intention was to make them visible so they could be role models for others. To show how each, in his or her own way, dribbled gracefully around that obstacle in the narrow corridor. Novelist Robert Penn Warren (*All the King's Men*) said, "History cannot give us a program for the future, but it can give us a fuller understanding of ourselves, and of our common humanity, so that we can better face the future." For African-Americans, uncovering that past, which has purposefully been buried or distorted or simply ignored, is especially important. And so I intend to continue rewriting history merely by revealing some truths that have been hidden.

The impact history has on our daily lives is monumental, even if we're unaware of it. Of course, the more we are aware of it, the more we can understand the impact and use it to "better face the future." The person unaware of history is like a rudderless boat just floating out in the middle of the ocean, hostage to the waves and currents. The person who has some awareness of the past knows how to fashion a rudder and which direction land is.

Even though I became aware of the Rens at seventeen, I didn't really find out about all their accomplishments until 1995, the same time I learned that the Harlem Globetrotters hadn't come from Harlem, but from Chicago! I didn't even know that the two teams had been vocal and sometimes bitter rivals for many years, though they played each other for the first time at the World Professional Basketball Tournament in 1939. The more I found out about the Rens, the more I realized how much of my career as a black professional basketball player I owed to these courageous and talented young men who had barnstormed through the country on a bus, sometimes playing two games a day, every day, enduring racist threats and abuse, so that I could step out on the court as a black man and no one would even question it.

You might say that since I didn't fully know about the Rens until after my playing days were over, they had no direct effect on me. Two problems with that. First, as I've shown, we are constantly influenced by forces of which we are unaware. Sometimes it's biological: from male-pattern baldness to a deadly disease that is genetically passed along. Sometimes it's psychological: a traumatic experience as a toddler, now long forgotten, makes you avoid public places or dislike small dogs. The Rens' influence on me as a player was a subtle six-degrees-of-separation kind of thing: learning the Rens' plays and moves by watching Coach Lapchick's films and playing on the playground with older players coached by Pop Gates.

Second, just because I was no longer a professional player, I wasn't dead. Standing in the Basketball Hall of Fame in 1995 during my induction, learning about the glories of the Rens for the first time, made me wonder how great it would have been to me as a kid if I'd known about them then. And that inspired me to make sure their story—and the stories of other "forgotten" African-American heroes—were told. The Rens had directly and powerfully influenced me, if not so much as a basketball player, definitely as a historian and member of my community. At the same time, I couldn't help but wonder whether those two childhood events that brought me to basketball—the movie and the beating—also had some historical connection beyond the moment. According to historian Arnold Toynbee, the word *history* comes from Greek for "investigate." And so I investigated.

One day in 1954, I walked into a dark movie theater with my mother and a couple hours later stepped out into the daylight a changed boy. I had seen what basketball, when played by the greats, could be like. And so, for the first time, I saw it as a possible alternative to baseball. I didn't know or care about how historically accurate the film was. Nothing could change that those guys really knew how to play. That while they were on that court with a basketball in their hands, they were in complete control of their world. That was a Truth beyond facts.

But the facts of how *Go, Man, Go!* made it to that theater also reveal a Truth. The film is one of the few directed by legendary cinematographer James Wong Howe (*The Rose Tattoo*), who received sixteen Academy Award nominations during his career. During World War II, racial animosity against the Japanese forced Howe to wear a button that said, "I am Chinese." In support, his pal actor James Cagney also wore a button. Howe compounded his social problems when he married a white woman. They'd had to wait several years to marry because of the laws against interracial marriage. Even after the laws were repealed, it took them three days to find a judge who would marry them. The accommodating judge's enlightened comment at their marriage was "She looks old enough. If she wants to marry a Chink, that's her business." The House Un-American Activities Committee questioned Howe because of his work with so-called Communists like actor John Garfield.

The name of the writer of *Go, Man, Go!* appeared on the screen as "Arnold Becker." But Becker wasn't the real writer; he was a front for Alfred Palca, who wrote and produced the film, single-handedly raising the $175,000 budget. "I'm an old lefty, and I thought I could do something to help the blacks," he said. "That mattered to me . . . I would do anything I could to help society, and as a Jewish fellow, I was for the underdog. I didn't have to do that story, but I liked that story." Before the film was released, the House Un-American Activities Committee blacklisted him when he refused to give them names of possible Communists (Palca had never been a Communist himself). One additional reason the FBI reportedly investigated him was because he'd hired a relatively unknown, but apparently suspicious, actor who owned a rib joint in Harlem: Sidney Poitier. No studio would release the film with Palca's name, so he removed it himself: he gave producing credit to his brother-in-law and assistant on the film, Anton M. Leader; he gave writing credit to Arnold Becker, his cousin, a Connecticut pediatrician. The film inspired a lot of people beside myself, including Mannie Jackson, who became the first black owner of the Globetrotters. Jackson recalls watching the movie over and over as a boy in Edwardsville, Illinois: "It wasn't so much the basketball that intrigued me, but the story line. It was the first of the *Rocky* films, the achievement films, that I had seen that involved people of color." The film still has such a strong cult following that plans are currently under way for a Broadway version, with Marques Haynes as a consultant. The film also destroyed Palca's Hollywood career; he never made another movie. However, in 1997, the Writers Guild of America had Palca's credits restored.

James Wong Howe and Alfred Palca made a film that reflected their own struggles with prejudice. Had they not suffered those indignities, they might never have been attracted to the story of the Harlem Globetrotters or worked so hard to make sure the movie was made, especially during a time when most white Americans didn't want to go to the movies to see the inspirational story of black athletes succeeding. (The U.S. Supreme Court *Brown v. Board of Education of Topeka* decision outlawing school segregation was issued the same year *Go, Man, Go!* was released.) The various tributaries of history flowed together to create this film that inspired me and many others.

What about my incarceration at Holy Providence? Were the beatings that year merely a typical case of bored dumb kids picking on the nerdy egghead, or was it something more subtle and sinister? I had never claimed any extraordinary intelligence. I knew my academic ability was merely the result of a family tradition of discipline and training that extended back to my grandparents, who had come to the United States from Trinidad in 1917. They were part of the Great Migration, arriving in Harlem just as the Renaissance was starting to stir. But a clear and distinct racial hierarchy existed among blacks in Harlem at that time. Those who were born and raised in New York thought the immigrants from the South were ignorant hicks, and they thought the immigrants from the West Indies, like my grandparents, were snobbish and self-important. The average Harlem resident resented the West Indians, sometimes refusing to shop at their stores. Bob Douglas, the founder of the Rens, was from the Indies, as was William Roach, the real estate entrepreneur who built the Renaissance Casino and Ballroom, which was home court for the Rens. The department store that was initially part of the Renaissance Casino building was owned by another immigrant from the Caribbean, and he quickly went out of business from lack of patronage from local blacks. Harlemites had a derogatory word for those who strove to better themselves:

dicty. (The word, commonly used during the Harlem Renaissance, appears in works by Claude McKay, Countee Cullen, Arna Bontemps, Carl Van Vechten, James Baldwin, Billie Holiday, and Duke Ellington.) Were the beatings that shoved me onto the basketball court given to me with such enthusiasm as a form of trickle-down racism because they thought I was "dicty," even if they'd never heard the word or knew I was of West Indian heritage? After all, it had only been fifteen to twenty years since the end of the Renaissance. In fact, with over half a million West Indians living in the New York City area today, sociologists have recorded similar attitudes toward them from local blacks born in the United States.

But is there a Truth beyond those facts? True, West Indian blacks tended to be better educated than the locals, but that was because many professionals, faced with discrimination and a poor economy in their homelands, decided there would be more opportunities in the United States. Being immigrants and being educated, they would emphasize education in their children. However, even when the educational playing field was level, West Indians were often hired over local blacks, implying that they were indeed smarter and better workers. It's easy to see why Harlemites would resent West Indians: If they both came from the same background of slavery, yet one group is more successful, doesn't that imply that the less successful group has less success, not because of racism, but because they don't work as hard?

Two recent studies by sociologists asked that same question. They wondered why, when the local Brooklyn economy was booming in the 1990s, so many longtime Hispanic and black residents weren't being hired, but newly immigrated Hispanics and blacks were. Interviews revealed that the employers were not discriminating against blacks or Hispanics, but against locals, whom they unconsciously associated with local crime. The farther away an applicant lived, the more likely they were to be hired. The conscious rationale of the employers was that foreign-born blacks and Hispanics were harder workers, even though there was no evidence for that. This unconscious racism justified prejudice under the guise of liking "good" blacks, even though their criteria are based on the same stereotyping as all other racism. Even blacks bought into it. Their disdain of Southern blacks as being slow and lazy was based on judging a different culture. In reality, how could men and women who worked day and night to eke out a living farming, and who had the courage to move their entire families across the country to a strange new world, be anything less than hardworking and brave?

Not all tall men or women become professional basketball players. But chances are good that, with my love of sports as a child, I would probably have become one eventually. Yet, without those two character-shaping events, I might not have become the kind of player I did—nor the man I did. *Go, Man, Go!* inspired me to develop a variety of skills and not just rely on my height. The story of the perseverance of these young black players during the struggles of the Harlem Renaissance invigorated me to persevere in my own struggles. In 1969, the Globetrotters offered me a million dollars to play for them. Though I declined and entered the NBA draft instead, I couldn't help but feel some sense of pride and completion at the offer. Ironically, I faced the team that helped launch my interest in basketball on September 12, 1995, during an exhibition game in Vienna against my All-Star Team. We defeated the Globetrotters 91–85, ending their unbroken run of 8,829 exhibition game victories dating back to 1971. Considering the millions of people they've entertained, and the thousands of kids like me they've inspired, they can never be defeated. That's a Truth beyond the facts.

Although the physical abuse I suffered at Holy Providence drove me to seek refuge on the basketball court, it also drove me to focus on being, not a star, but a team player. My year at Holy Providence had resulted in a basically friendly boy becoming isolated and marginalized. But on the court, I was part of a team. I wasn't a skillful part, but I was still a welcomed part. Yes, without that year at Holy Providence I would still eventually have played basketball, but I might have entered the game like so many other kids do, dreaming of being the Big Star, motivated by the lust for sports cars, flashy jewelry, and a fat wad of cash. Of course those incentives occasionally flitted through my mind (with the addition of gorgeous, shapely women), but I never wanted to achieve that by showboating so I could become a media darling. Let's face it, even when I was a star, I was rarely a media darling. Part of that is because I saw myself more as a team player, not just on the court. On the court, I felt that I was just part of the team, so attention focused on me as an individual made me uncomfortable, almost as if I were betraying the team rather than promoting it. Off the court, I was outspoken about political events that affected the black community, my larger team.

Basketball made me visible, but my rough times at Holy Providence taught me to use that visibility for something more than seeking adulation. I would try to inspire others as I had been inspired: to seek excellence in personal achievement, but to see themselves within the larger context of a team.

POSTGAME WRAP-UP

Dr. Martin Luther King Jr. once said, "To be a Negro in America is to hope against hope." In this statement he was testifying not just to the struggles of black Americans, but also to their indomitable optimism. To me, hope is like some magical telescope that can see into the future, not necessarily the future as it will be, but as it *should* be. When Dr. King told us he had a dream, he was describing what he saw from looking through that telescope. And we were all energized by that dream because we could see it, too. If we can envision that possible future in our minds, then we can create it in real life. The tools we need to create that grand future come from what we learn about our past, from the examples of those, like Dr. King, who tried to create that future. Both during my career as a professional basketball player and since retiring, I have tried to generate that bright hope in younger generations.

I've tried to accomplish that in two ways: (1) by being a role model myself as a way of respecting all the role models that helped guide me, and (2) by providing as many other role models as possible for members of my community.

Believe me, I'm aware of just how self-aggrandizing it can sound to claim role-model status for oneself. In truth, it's not really a position I sought. Such responsibility can feel like a crushing burden. Who wants to have his every move scrutinized and judged by strangers as to whether it's "appropriate," especially appropriate behavior for blacks? The skyhook was meant to lift *me* above the clamoring throng, to push *me* past the obstacle in the narrow corridor. Who was I to tell anyone else what to do; I was too busy figuring it out myself. But as I progressed in my career and matured as a man, I soon saw that—like it or not, ready or not—I was thrust into the bright, burning spotlight as a role model, and that relentless spotlight was never going to dim. Once that realization sank in, I tried to behave accordingly.

I didn't try to please people by fitting into their expectations of who they thought I should be, either as an athlete or a black man. I tried to act according to my principles. I didn't drape myself in gold chains and desperate women, I pursued discipline in my job, my religion, my family, my community. In a lot of ways, I was still that nerdy schoolkid with his nose in a book. In fact, when I first attended UCLA, I saw myself standing in a line behind my own role models: Arthur Ashe, Rafer Johnson, Jackie Robinson, and Dr. Ralph Bunche, all of whom created a legacy of black American athlete-scholars. Like them, I didn't want to just win games, I wanted to win *respect*—for myself, for my community. For all of us who "hope against hope."

I accomplished the "athlete" part of the athlete-scholar equation with great success. I was a team player and my teams tended to win. But I was less successful at the public relations aspect of being a role model. I thought my actions would speak to my character. But actions don't translate that well to sound bites and interviews. My quiet, diffident manner earned me the reputation of being aloof, nonverbal, high-and-mighty. The perception of the time was that the black athlete should at least give the appearance that he was grateful for what benefits society had granted him. What people really wanted was an athlete who would gush and grin and gab. As much as I would like to have been a person who felt comfortable doing those things, I never did. Instead, I was shy, reserved, a little wary. I realized that a white person looking up at a seven-foot-two-inch black man who isn't smiling is going to be intimidated. But plenty of white athletes were quiet, shy, or even hostile, yet no one was afraid of them, no one expected them to pretend to be otherwise. I wanted to be judged for my playing ability, my dedication to teamwork, my loyalty to the fans, not my public persona, which, frankly, I was lousy at projecting. It was like Holy Providence all over again: being on the court was a refuge because I was judged for what I did; off the court was brutal because I was judged by what I didn't do.

Once I retired, those expectations pretty much disappeared, and I have been able to focus on the scholar part of the equation, which has been just as rewarding to me as the athletics. As a writer, I am judged on the content of my chapters rather than the colorfulness of my public image. And the effect I have now can be even more dramatic. Once I was eating in a restaurant when a man approached me. He had read my book *Black Profiles in Courage* and told me how he used the different accounts of black historical figures as bedtime stories for his daughters. He said the profiles of these black role models gave his girls a strong sense of pride as well as a confidence that they belonged in America. I've since heard from many inner-city history teachers who used the book to create lesson plans for their courses. One teacher told me about a student of his who had had numerous run-ins with the police and seemed on a fast track to prison and a hopeless future. The teacher gave him a printout of the chapter about Bass Reeves, a U.S. marshal in Oklahoma from 1875 to 1905. Reading about Reeves's accomplishments and how he overcame his obstacles inspired the boy, who went on to do quite well in high school. He had looked through the telescope and seen an alternative future to becoming just another burnt-out inner-city statistic.

I played basketball for forty years. But basketball never defined me, it provided an opportunity for me to define myself. It still does. I didn't learn all about the Rens until 1995, but since then they have never stopped inspiring me. Recently, I have had the honor to meet the last surviving member of the Rens' world championship team, John Isaacs. At ninety, he still has the energy of men thirty years younger. He jumps rope daily, works out with thirty-pound weights, and volunteers at the Madison Square Boys & Girls Club. Though his shoulders are thinner and a little more fragile than when he was one of the top basketball players in the world, they are still mighty enough to lift many of us to glimpse a future where we might all be a little more like him.

Nearly seventy years ago, a team of brave and dedicated athletes defied all expectations by becoming the first world champions of basketball. Because of them, black players were soon allowed to play on professional white teams. Because of them, I was able to become a successful athlete. Because of them, black Americans could look through that telescope of hope and see a future of limitless opportunities for us and for our children. Their history gave us our future.

"MUSICAL FIREWORKS"

Jazz Lights Up

the Heavens of Harlem

■ Men have died for this music. You can't get more serious than that.

DIZZY GILLESPIE

■ Jazz is music made by and for people who have chosen to feel good in spite of conditions.

JOHNNY GRIFFIN

■ Put it this way: Jazz is a good barometer of freedom. . . . In its beginnings, the United States of America spawned certain ideals of freedom and independence through which, eventually, jazz was evolved, and the music is so free that many people say it is the only unhampered, unhindered expression of complete freedom yet produced in this country.

DUKE ELLINGTON

WHAT'S ALL THIS FUSS ABOUT JAZZ?

For many people unfamiliar with jazz, the word conjures a seedy image of a dark, smoky room, long, spidery fingers banging on a piano in seemingly random notes, a jowly man blowing away on his sax while mopping sweat from his forehead, a hunched bass player wearing sunglasses, behind which are eyes glassy from toking too much weed before the set. Seated in the audience are finger-snapping patrons at small, round tables with the goofy ecstatic expressions of cult followers listening to a fiery sermon. For the well-read historian, the word *jazz* conjures a definite time, place, and people: an original American musical form, sometimes referred to as "America's classical music," originating among the black musicians of New Orleans in the early 1900s. For the trained musicologist, the word *jazz* conjures a more formal definition: a musical form characterized by blue notes, syncopation, swing, call and response, polyrhythms, and improvisation.

But for the jazz lover, the word means much more than the smoky room or its historical context or its technical definition: it is a way of looking at and experiencing life. "What we play is life," jazz great Louis Armstrong explained. "Jazz is played from the heart. You can even live by it."

Nicely said, might even look good on a T-shirt selling at a French Quarter souvenir shop. But what does that actually mean? What exactly is this jazz that brought forth so much vitriolic condemnation from authorities and yet became so popular as to revolutionize, not just music, but popular culture for decades to come?

Trying to define jazz is very much like the old Indonesian fable of the six blind men trying to describe an elephant by only touching one part of it. The guy fondling the trunk thought it looked like a snake; the guy hugging a leg thought it looked like a tree. And so forth. But one thing all six men could agree upon is that when that elephant started charging through the jungle, it changed the shape of that jungle. And so jazz charged through the early twentieth century, changing the shape of the landscape wherever it passed through. When jazz charged into Harlem in the 1920s, it reinvented the place, literally changing the buildings, the economy, the way black people saw themselves—and, eventually, the way white people saw black people. No other musical form would have such a pervasive impact on American society again until the advent of rock 'n' rollers Elvis Presley, Jerry Lee Lewis, Chuck Berry, and Little Richard in the 1950s, and then again in the 1960s with the British Invasion spearheaded by the Beatles and the Rolling Stones—all of whose music was greatly influenced by jazz. Today, that same influence is seen not only in the music of hip-hop but in the culture it inspired. As one observer said, "Hip-hop without jazz is like a man without a soul."

Jazz is still charging through the jungle. Still affecting our souls.

At first, the arrival of jazz in Harlem was met with mixed reactions from the architects of the Harlem Renaissance. Some praised it and some condemned it. Many of the Renaissance's most brilliant and articulate writers and intellectuals—including W. E. B. Du Bois, Alain Locke, and James Weldon Johnson—considered jazz to be nothing more than low-class "entertainment" music that recalled the stereotypical image of the decadent "Old Negro," the very image they were so desperately trying to vanquish. These influential spokespersons that were laying out the guidelines for the sophisticated New Negro preferred the "classier" concert music (though they also appreciated the "Negro spiritual" for its historical context). Jazz musician Benny Carter recalled the attitude of Harlem's black intelligentsia when he played during that time: "Jazz was viewed either ambivalently or with outright hostility by many of the leading figures of the movement. We in music knew there was much going on in literature, for example, but our worlds were far apart. We sensed that the Black cultural as well as moral leaders looked down on our music as undignified."

But that haughty attitude came mostly from the old guard intellectuals; the new generation of writers who were revitalizing the Harlem Renaissance celebrated jazz by incorporating its rhythms in their writing. Benny Carter considered Langston Hughes, who wrote extensively and lovingly about jazz, "the poet laureate of the Renaissance and a man who had much respect for and understanding of [jazz]." Hughes felt that jazz was more than a form of music, it was another crucial note in the composition of the New Negro: "Let the blare of Negro jazz bands and bellowing voice of Bessie Smith singing Blues penetrate the closed ears of colored intellectuals until they listen and perhaps understand."

The battle lines were drawn—and not just in Harlem. The debate swept through the entire country, with public officials and religious leaders condemning jazz as a savage music meant to heighten and unleash people's darkest desires. Some of the public attacks on jazz were thinly disguised racial diatribes against African-Americans themselves. Just as the old guard intellectuals had feared, white critics were associating the sensuality of jazz with the stereotype of the randy African-American, unable to control his basic urges. Yet, many rose to the defense of jazz as not only an expression of the hopefulness of the times, but as a link to the struggles of the past. Rather than characterizing the black stereotype, they argued, jazz actually celebrated the enduring strength of character in the face of oppression and the indomitable spirit that was at the heart and soul of the African-American. Renowned white classical conductor Leopold Stokowski, who directed the classical music for Disney's *Fantasia*, enthused about jazz at the peak of the Harlem Renaissance:

Jazz has come to stay because it is an expression of the times, of the breathless, energetic, superactive times in which we are living, it is useless to fight against it. Already its new vigor, its new vitality is beginning to manifest itself. . . . The Negro musicians of America are playing a great part in this change. They have an open mind, an unbiased outlook. They are not hampered by conventions or traditions, and with their new ideas, their constant experiment, they are causing new blood to flow in the veins of music. The jazz players make their instruments do entirely new things, things finished musicians are taught to avoid. They are pathfinders into new realms.

So, while jazz was creating a new image of blacks as energetic and innovative, the roots of jazz paid homage to the emotional past that helped motivate these changes. Harlem Renaissance writer Joel A. Rogers (of whom W. E. B. Du Bois said, "No man living has revealed as many important facts about the Negro race as has Rogers") described jazz as a sort of Jungian collective unconscious, a tribal music that many diverse cultures unwittingly shared:

In its elementals, jazz has always existed. It is in the Indian wardance, the Highland fling, the Irish jig, the Cossack dance, the Spanish fandango, the Brazilian *maxixe*, the dance of the whirling dervish, the hula hula of the South Seas, the *danse du ventre* of the Orient, the carmagnole of the French Revolution, the strains of Gypsy music, and the ragtime of the Negro. Jazz proper, however, is something more than all these. It is a release of all the suppressed emotions at once, a blowing off of the lid, as it were. It is hilarity expressing itself through pandemonium; musical fireworks.

When these musical fireworks came to Harlem, they lit up the heavens above and cast a new light of communal joy on the streets below. Though the hard-knock life of African-Americans left little to celebrate, jazz music found a new and invigorating way to illuminate their daily struggles and express their complex and conflicting emotions: hope, despair, love, hate, outrage, accomplishment. These emotions were going to be portrayed in new ways because these were new times. And if doing so made these musicians outsiders, then so be it. In fact, it was precisely because they were outsiders to the established way of experiencing music that black musicians were free to break all the rules—rules that never did them any good anyway—and create their own music. And wasn't that New Negro attitude exactly what the intellectual writers of the Harlem Renaissance were encouraging?

Yet, while these literary writers focused on articulating the new artistic and political movement through poetry, fiction, plays, and essays, it was the musicians who expressed the sensuality of the movement through jazz. They proved that the pleasures of the mind are hollow without the corresponding pleasures of the body. Life may be a struggle, but it was also a celebration. As marching band composer John Philip Sousa explained, "Jazz will endure as long as people hear it through their feet instead of their brains."

WHERE JAZZ CAME FROM: LONG AGO AND FAR AWAY

Minerva, the Roman goddess of music, was said to have sprung forth fully armored from the head of her father, Jupiter. Jazz, however, did not spring forth fully orchestrated from the heads of frolicking New Orleans musicians. Instead, jazz stumbled into Louisiana after a long and arduous trek across several continents and hundreds of years, not at all looking like the same music that started out on that trip: Every stop along the way shows up in some characteristic of jazz, making jazz a road map of not only the history of the music, but of the cultures of the people who passed the musical torch from generation to generation.

Naturally, every time one form of music becomes popular, another musical tradition peeks around the corner and claims paternity, saying, "If not for me, kid, you wouldn't exist." If it weren't for the blues, jazz wouldn't exist; if it weren't for work songs, the blues wouldn't exist; if it weren't for slave songs, the work songs wouldn't exist; etc. This question of heredity isn't merely one of bragging rights for who came first and therefore deserves the most credit, it's one of recognizing that jazz is the culmination of a lot of influences that represent the cultural history of a people. By following the lineage of jazz, one can experience the history of Africans and African-Americans in all its joyous, tragic, and inspirational tradition. When Louis Armstrong trumpets a looooong, resounding note, he is echoing the communal voices that date back over a thousand years.

That "thousand years" is not hyperbole. In fact, thirteen hundred years ago the seeds of jazz that would eventually flourish in New Orleans were being planted in Spain under the marching feet of African invaders. In 711 CE, Moorish general Tariq ibn-Ziyad conquered Spain with seven thousand African soldiers and began an occupation that would last seven hundred years. Thanks to these invaders from Africa, Spain received a kick start toward the Age of Enlightenment that the rest of Europe did not. These Muslim occupiers brought with them an advanced concept of civilization that included everything from education to government to science. Hundreds of years before Paris had paved streets or London had streetlamps, Córdoba, with a population of 1 million, had both. The city had hundreds of public baths during a time when Christian Europe decried cleanliness as sinful. While the rest of Europe had no public libraries, Moorish Spain had over seventy. Education was made available to most Spanish citizens, while Christian Europe was almost entirely illiterate. Along with all this scientific and artistic advancement, African music merged with European music, the hybrid of which Spanish explorers would spread to the New World. When these Spanish invaders occupied North and South America, they brought their African-influenced music with them. And when slaves from Africa were unceremoniously dragged onto American soil (having arrived a year before the Pilgrims), they brought little with them except their memories and their music, which gave them some comfort and connection to their heritage. Ironically, these two violent events—the brutal conquering of Spain and the cruel slave trade in America—would help parent jazz, one of the most joyous musical forms ever.

THE RISE OF THE BLACK MUSICIAN: FROM MINSTREL TO MAESTRO

The official end of slavery in 1863 may have brought freedom, but it did not bring much economic opportunity. In the South, the political and social backlash against emancipation resulted in many laws designed to promote racial discrimination that kept blacks from getting well-paying jobs or even voting. As a result, only menial jobs at menial pay were open to blacks, with the exception of the new holy trinity of opportunity: teacher, preacher, or musician. Even during slavery, whites accepted blacks as musicians, but only in what were considered low-class venues such as dances or minstrel shows. A black pianist might be seen in a church or a brothel, but never in a proper concert hall.

The minstrel show, which featured white performers smearing burnt cork on their faces and presenting insulting caricatures of African-American life, was wildly popular in post–Civil War America and continued in spirit right up through the 1950s. Although performers in blackface date back to the 1790s, Thomas "Daddy" Rice is credited with popularizing the tradition in the 1820s when he took to the stage in blackface to perform "Jump Jim Crow," a song he'd heard an old black man sing, supposedly about himself. The sheet music was published in 1823 and sold well throughout the country. "Jim Crow" then became not only a stock character in subsequent minstrel shows, but also the term used for the racially discriminatory laws and customs meant to repress people of color.

The start of the more formal minstrel show was the result of desperation rather than commitment to racist social commentary. In the 1840s, four out-of-work white actors, anxious for employment, saw a popular act called the Tyrolese Minstrel Family, who were touring the United States singing European folk songs. In a parody of the show, the actors created Dan Emmett's Virginia Minstrels, a revue that featured the four of them in blackface performing songs, dances, and comic skits. As the Virginia Minstrels' popularity grew, so did that of some of the songs they introduced, such as "Polly Wolly Doodle" and "Blue Tail Fly." Author Lee Davis, in *Scandals and Follies: The Rise and Fall of the Great Broadway Revue*, describes the appeal of the Virginia Minstrels:

Most of all, there was exuberance and excitement. The minstrels, in their wide-eyed, large-lipped, ragged-costumed absurdity, rolled onto the stage in a thundercloud of energy which hardly ever dissipated. They insulted each other, they baited each other, they made mincemeat of the language, they took the audience into their fun, and, in one night, they added a new form of show business in America—in fact, the world.

Hoping to cash in on this popular new act, other all-white companies quickly formed and began touring both the United States and Europe, even during the Civil War. In fact, the minstrel song "Dixie" was adopted as the unofficial anthem of the Confederacy. Even after the abolition of slavery the popularity of the minstrel show continued to grow, not just in the South, but in the North as well. By the end of the Civil War, New York City alone had twenty full-time resident minstrel companies. It seemed that white America refused to accept any image of African-Americans that wasn't the familiar—and nonthreatening—version of the slow child that needed stern parenting. And even when black musicians refuted this image by demonstrating remarkable skills, those skills were ignored until a white performer made it more palatable.

Because the minstrel show claimed to be an accurate, though exaggerated, portrayal of black culture and values, it helped solidify the way blacks would be viewed by most white Americans for many years to come. The typical minstrel show featured several standard grotesque characters, among them Jim Crow, the carefree slave; Bruder Tambo, who played the tambourine; Bruder Bones, who played rib bones or spoons; and Zip Coon, who was a freed slave putting on high-class airs. Usually, the show was divided into three acts. The first act was the Minstrel Line, in which the actors would sit in a semicircle and perform songs, dances, and jokes. The second act was the Olio, in which songs or variety acts were performed by the actors without blackface makeup so the audience could be assured they really were white. The final part of the Olio was a comic speech given by one of the standard blackface characters (e.g., Jim Crow or Zip Coon), in which contemporary politics and personages were satirized. This last format was the start of what would later be called stand-up comedy. Act 3 was the presentation of a one-act musical that lampooned a well-known novel, play, or political or social issue. This act usually presented the characters of slow-witted doofus Jim Crow and "uppity" social striver Zip Coon.

After the Civil War, blacks began to join some of the minstrel shows. Some even formed their own all-black minstrel companies, which toured both the United States and Great Britain. Ironically, these black performers still had to wear blackface makeup to make their skin darker to fit in with the audience's expectations. They were now in the strange position of being black men imitating white men imitating a twisted version of black culture. And although the format required that they degrade their own people, the minstrel show gave African-Americans their first opportunity to perform on a professional stage.

The next barrier to be broken was that of gender. For a long time, minstrel shows had been all-male. Then in 1890, *The Creole Show* featured several women in the cast. The show became so successful that women became common in minstrel shows, thereby launching the acceptance of black women performers that would later reach its greatest success in the many popular female blues and jazz singers. Their break came just in time, for the minstrel show would quickly lose popularity, nearly disappearing after the 1920s, as jazz began to rise.

Dismissing the minstrel shows as merely another ugly episode in American racial history would be easy, but that would ignore their significant contribution. They provided the first stage for black actors. They originated stand-up comedy that leads directly to Redd Foxx, Richard Pryor, Eddie Murphy, and Chris Rock. Black women performers got their start in minstrel shows, presaging Bessie Smith, Ma Rainey, and Billie Holiday. Even though renowned abolitionist and ex-slave Frederick Douglass condemned minstrelsy for its overt racism, he also grudgingly acknowledged some benefit: "It is something to be gained when the colored man in any form can appear before white audiences."

By being the first to commission songs for their acts, minstrelsy promoted the widespread growth of popular music in the nineteenth century. White composer Stephen Foster's hit songs—"Camptown Races," "My Old Kentucky Home," "O Susanna," and "Old Folks at Home"—were written for and became famous because of the minstrel shows. James Bland, America's first black composer of popular songs, wrote "Carry Me Back to Old Virginny" for the minstrel shows. Both Bland and Foster, two of the most famous chroniclers of Southern life, were raised in the North. Even if the songs weren't anywhere close to authentic depictions of African-American lives or sentiments, they did create a white audience receptive to what they thought was black music. This made it easier for the more authentic music such as ragtime, the blues, and jazz to later reach such popularity.

Minstrelsy reached its height, and its most famous (though erroneous) connection with jazz, through the talents of Al Jolson (1886–1950), the son of Jewish Lithuanian immigrants. Jolson's popularity was extraordinary, even by today's standards. His Broadway career lasted nearly thirty years (1911–40); he recorded the equivalent of twenty-three number one hit records, the fourth-highest total between 1890 and 1954; and he starred in several popular, though not especially good, films. His most popular movie was *The Jazz Singer* (1927), credited with being the first commercially successful "talkie" (a movie that included sound with the images). The title was more a tribute to the popularity of jazz than the actual music Jolson performed. In the film, Jolson sang minstrel classics like "Mammy" while wearing blackface. Although Jolson has become something of a poster boy for the evils of minstrelsy, Jolson himself was a friend to many black performers during a time when it could have hurt his career. Once he heard that the noted black songwriting team of Eubie Blake and Noble Sissle had been turned away from a restaurant. The following night he provided both of them with not only dinner, but a private performance.

Even as the minstrel shows were dying out, the two stereotypes of Jim Crow and Zip Coon continued in popularity. The radio show *Amos 'n' Andy* debuted in 1928, featuring the same basic Jim Crow and Zip Coon characters. And as in the minstrel shows, two white actors portrayed the two main black characters. The show became the longest-running radio show in history. When the show was brought to television in 1951, black actors played the parts. The TV show lasted only two years, in part due to rising protest from the black community. However, not all members of the black community condemned the show. The *Pittsburgh Courier*, a highly influential black newspaper that led the outrage against the movie *Gone With the Wind* for its use of black stereotypes, printed an article defending the show. Despite this contentious history, *Amos 'n' Andy* was the first TV show with an all-black cast, a landmark that wouldn't be equaled for another twenty years.

Blackface itself continued to appear in popular movies. In *Babes on Broadway* (1941), Judy Garland and Mickey Rooney perform a musical number in blackface. And the beloved Christmas movie *Holiday Inn* (1942) features Bing Crosby in blackface, making the movie not so beloved by African-Americans. Blackface entertainment was satirized in Spike Lee's film *Bamboozled* (2000), in which a black television executive introduces blackface minstrelsy to contemporary TV audiences, only to be shocked by its success.

The apparent lesson of the wide success of minstrelsy is that if Americans couldn't see blacks in their traditional subservient roles, they wouldn't see them at all. It was this myopic vision and entrenched attitude—as well as the images of Jim Crow and Zip Coon burned into the white collective retina—that the Harlem Renaissance fought so hard to dispel by parading before white America the boundless talents of black writers, intellectuals, actors, athletes, and artists. And leading the parade right down Main Street, USA, and into the homes of white America were the black musicians. They created the white audience that would be receptive to all other talented African-Americans who followed.

THE PIANO PLAYS A NEW TUNE
FOR AFRICAN-AMERICANS

That magnificent parade might never have traveled out of Harlem if it wasn't for one unexpected vehicle: the piano. For African-Americans, the piano was more than a musical instrument; it became a speedy getaway car to escape the black stereotypes that blocked them from opportunity—artistic, educational, and economic.

Like that giant meteor that supposedly was responsible for wiping out all dinosaurs, the piano hit post–Civil War African-Americans with an impact that would destroy and bury the popular image among white Americans of the dumb and lazy Negro, too slow-witted and undisciplined to learn the complex piano. To white America, African-Americans could only handle the most primitive of instruments, such as the drums or banjo. True, few blacks at the time played the piano, but that was because during slavery they had little access to pianos. However, after emancipation, many African-American families bought small organs or harmoniums (pianos were too expensive) as a means both to proudly display their independence by owning what had before been denied them, and to promote cultural assimilation for their children. Raising children who could play the piano not only dispelled the derogatory myths, but also boosted the children's chances for rising up out of their class, even within the black community. And the cost for this opportunity was only fifty cents down and fifty cents a week for the rest of their lives. In his autobiography, *Up from Slavery*, Booker T. Washington recounts a dinner visit with one such hopeful family in their Alabama cabin: "When I sat down to the table for a meal with the four members of the family, I noticed that, while there were five of us at the table, there was but one fork for the five of us to use. . . . In the opposite corner of that same cabin was an organ for which the people told me they were paying sixty dollars in monthly installments. One fork, and a sixty-dollar organ!" Fingers could substitute for forks, but the organ was the hope for the future.

At this same time, a new musical phenomenon was sending feet everywhere into wild spasms of dancing: ragtime. Whether the popularity of the piano spawned the popularity of ragtime, or the other way around, both benefited from the relationship. Those who wanted to learn to play the newest ragtime piece could do so on the standard piano, while those who liked the sound but found the compositions too challenging could just crank up the player piano. The spread of these two instruments throughout the United States helped create a market and made ragtime in great demand. And it was ragtime that would launch the nationwide, and even international, popularity of the black musician.

THE RAGTIME RAGE

When the Paul Newman–Robert Redford movie *The Sting* was released in 1973, the world rediscovered a musical form that had once dominated American society: ragtime. Scott Joplin's songs, particularly "The Entertainer," were prominently featured on the film's sound track, which became a huge hit. Suddenly ragtime was heard on major radio stations, on TV, and in other movies. As popular as ragtime was in the early 1970s, that was nothing compared to the enormity of its popularity in the early twentieth century. So great was its fame that in 1900, Scott Joplin's "Maple Leaf Rag" (named after the Maple Leaf Club in Sedalia, Missouri, where he sometimes played) became the first sheet music to sell more than a million copies—at a time when there were only 76 million people in the entire United States.

Art critic Russell Lynes once said, "Ragtime was a fanfare for the twentieth century," meaning that ragtime's lively beat and celebratory attitude made it the perfect music to herald the arrival of a century filled with hope that we would right the wrongs of the last century and prove ourselves more worthy this time around. People felt more empowered in this "modern era," demanding more rights—rights for minorities, rights for women, rights for labor. And through it all, energetic ragtime music wafted from homes, bars, and brothels like an encouraging friend. This optimistic energy and independent attitude spilled over into jazz. Ragtime's influence on jazz was so great that the terms *jazz* and *ragtime* were sometimes used interchangeably, even by the musicians who played them.

Ragtime's independent attitude partially came as a result of musicians not being trained in traditional musical theory. While a number of black pianists were formally trained in the classic European approach to the piano (Scott Joplin among them), most were self-taught and could not read music. For many of the early ragtime pianists, as well as those who played blues and jazz, this lack of traditional training made them less rigid in their musical tastes and more willing to experiment with different sounds and techniques. While European-inspired music emphasized counterpoint and harmonies, the ragtime musicians were working on "ragging" popular songs that employed the European techniques. *Ragging* meant to alter the rhythm to make it syncopated, which involved shifting the accent to the weak beat of the bar. This ragging technique did not appear out of nowhere, but was a major part of West African music, which slaves brought with them to their new homes. The origin of the term *ragtime* isn't definitively known. Some historians claim it was the result of the ragged rhythm described above, which even ragtime musicians such as Scott Joplin halfheartedly accepted ("It suggests something like that"). Yet others believe it came from the nineteenth-century African-American tradition of handkerchief-flaunting. By the end of the nineteenth century, the terms *rag* and *dance* were interchangeably used because it was as much about the way the music made your body want to move as any specific structure of playing.

Eventually, ragtime became more formalized, typically structured around a four-theme form and a sixteen-bar melody. In the novel *The Autobiography of an Ex–Colored Man*, Harlem Renaissance writer James Weldon Johnson offers a less technical explanation of ragtime by re-creating his personal experience of watching ragtime pianists in Harlem:

After the singer had responded to a rousing encore, the stout man at the piano began to run his fingers up and down the keyboard. . . . Then he began to play; and such playing! . . . It was music of a kind I had never heard before. It was music that demanded physical response, patting of the feet, drumming of the fingers, or nodding of the head in time with the beat. The barbaric harmonies, the audacious resolutions, often consisting of an abrupt jump from one key to another, the intricate rhythms in which the accents fell in the most unexpected places, but in which the beat was never lost, produced a most curious effect.

However they did it, they did it right, and ragtime became a national rage.

There is some disagreement about what constitutes the "official" beginning of ragtime. The first published song to include the word *rag* is thought to be white bandleader William Krell's "Mississippi Rag," which appeared in 1897. Several months later, Tom Turpin's "Harlem Rag" was published, the first ragtime work published by a black composer. While these two works are acknowledged as the "official" beginning of ragtime, the genre actually got its start through another musical genre called coon songs, the word *coon* being a racial slur toward blacks because whites thought that raccoons were a preferred source of meat for plantation slaves. However, the coon song bridged minstrelsy and ragtime because it employed syncopation. In fact, in 1896, a year before the two aforementioned works were published, black composer Ernest Hogan's "All Coons Look Alike to Me" featured the caption "Choice Chorus, with Negro 'Rag' Accompaniment." This song became so popular that during the Ragtime Championship of the World Competition in New York in 1900, each of the three semifinalists were required to play it for two minutes. Despite the song's success, Hogan was hurt by the many musicians who refused to play his work because the title was offensive, even though the lyrics portray a black woman who rejects her boyfriend in favor of another man by declaring that "All coons look alike to me." Certainly by those same standards, many current hit rap and hip-hop songs would never be played by black performers. Still, the coon songs' popularity made it easier for ragtime to take hold.

With popularity there is always the backlash. Some music critics dismissed ragtime as a mere fad, the way rock 'n' roll was similarly dismissed in the 1950s. *Metronome* magazine described it as "a popular wave in the wrong direction." The American Federation of Musicians told its members to refuse to play ragtime, explaining that "the musicians know what is good, and if the people don't, we shall have to teach them." Ragtime would go on to introduce white America to something it wasn't used to: a large group of piano-playing, music-composing African-Americans. One of the most prominent among them was Scott Joplin.

SCOTT JOPLIN: MORE THAN THE ENTERTAINER

Scott Joplin (1868–1917), sometimes known as the King of Ragtime, provided some broad shoulders for future generations to climb aboard. Although other composers may have produced more complex works, Joplin's ambitions for ragtime were far beyond anyone else's. In his efforts to raise ragtime above its perceived pop music status, he composed not only some of the most famous ragtime songs, but also two ragtime operas and a ragtime ballet. Just as the Who, with their rock opera *Tommy*, attempted to expand the limited boundaries of how the world viewed rock 'n' roll, so did Joplin want the world to see that ragtime could be more than just peppy saloon music. In direct opposition to the perception of ragtime music as fingers blazing across piano keys, he added this notation to his published compositions: "NOTE: Do not play this piece fast. It is never right to play Ragtime fast."

Born in Texas in 1868, Joplin received much of his musical background from his parents. Scott's father, Jiles Joplin, before the Emancipation Proclamation freed him, played the violin at slave owners' parties. Scott's mother, Florence Givens Joplin, sang and played the banjo. When Jiles Joplin left his family, Florence relied on domestic work to support her six children. Sometimes Scott would go with his mother to the homes where she worked, playing on the homeowners' pianos while his mother cleaned. By the time he was a teenager, he was performing as a professional pianist as well as teaching music.

In the mid-1880s he moved to St. Louis, making a living as a pianist in nightclubs. In the mid-1890s he moved to Sedalia, Missouri, and began attending the George R. Smith College for Negroes to study harmony and composition. Then in 1897, with the publication of "Maple Leaf Rag," his career took off. But rather than exploiting his success by writing the same song over and over, he began pushing the limits of the form. Each new song took ragtime in a new direction, cross-pollinating with other musical genres. His canon of work reveals a man driven to ride ragtime not just through the foot-stomping party of the average music lover, but also into the thin atmosphere of critical appreciation. One particular area he pioneered was the use of more sophisticated lyrics to go with the ragtime music. Commenting on the typical ragtime lyrics, Joplin said, "I have often sat in theaters and listened to beautiful ragtime melodies set to almost vulgar words . . . and have wondered why some composers will continue to make people hate ragtime because the melodies are set to such bad words." If the lyrics improved, Joplin reasoned, not only would ragtime be more appreciated, but so would African-Americans, who originated it. Why wouldn't whites see blacks as degenerate, he argued, if this was the kind of message we promoted through our songs (an accusation also made more recently against the lyrics in rap and hip-hop songs)?

These new directions were often grandly visionary, but financially unsuccessful. Joplin's folk ballet, *The Ragtime Dance* (1899), received one performance. He staged one performance of his rag opera, *A Guest of Honor* (1903), with his own Scott Joplin Drama Company. Although he never found a publisher for the score of that opera, he immediately began work on his second opera,

Treemonisha, which he finished in 1905. Despite his mounting success, no one was interested in publishing his new opera, so he published the 230-page work himself in 1911. Two years later he was able to stage a bare-cupboard production himself in Harlem. But the lack of costumes, scenery, lighting, or orchestra (only Joplin playing the score on the piano) left the audience underwhelmed and the show closed immediately. Joplin's opera, which explored the folk roots of black American music, didn't inspire a black audience that was trying to create a new image of the African-American, not celebrate ties to the old image that white America held on to with both fists.

A year after the failure of *Treemonisha*, Joplin was committed to the Manhattan State Hospital, where he died several months later from complications brought on by syphilis. By now the ragtime craze had already passed, and many of Joplin's unpublished compositions were destroyed when his publisher moved in 1935. Joplin, once the foremost ragtime celebrity, died in near obscurity. Then came *The Sting*, and Joplin, as well as ragtime, was hot again. Even his most prized and nurtured work, *Treemonisha*, was revived. When the Houston Grand Opera performed it in 1976, Joplin, though dead nearly sixty years, was posthumously awarded a Pulitzer Prize.

Though Harlem rejected Joplin's more groundbreaking efforts, ironically he embodied many of the qualities that the Harlem Renaissance promoted. He celebrated the past accomplishments of African-Americans, yet he pushed the boundaries of traditional music composition to create new forms. In doing so, he became one more shining black face that white Americans had to acknowledge did not fit their stereotypical image. And, he charged through the musical landscape to create a clear path for jazz. "Joplin's single-minded determination to merge vernacular African-American music with the mainstream traditions of Western composition prefigured, in many regards, the later development of jazz," wrote music historian Ted Gioia (*The History of Jazz*). "By straddling the borders of highbrow and lowbrow culture, art music and popular music, African polyrhythm and European formalism, Joplin anticipated the fecund efforts of later artists such as Duke Ellington, James P. Johnson, Benny Goodman, Charles Mingus, Stan Kenton, and Art Tatum, among others."

Ragtime had proven to be such a commercial success that American sheet music publishers were hungry for the next "new thing" that would catch America's fancy. And their eyes were watching the blues.

BIRTH OF THE BLUES: A DISTURBANCE IN THE SOUL

Blues and jazz seemed to come of age at the same time, like fraternal twins who share the same parents and bone structure but don't look alike. Yet, most people use the words *jazz* and *blues* interchangeably. That's an easy mistake to make since some of the most famous musicians from the Harlem Renaissance played both. But, while the two styles are inexorably intertwined, they are in no way interchangeable. Novelist and music critic Albert Murray offers a succinct description of their difference in attitude: "The blues is a device for transcending, or at least coping with, adversity," while jazz is a device for "stomping away the blues." Comedienne Carol Burnett's famous definition of comedy as being "tragedy—plus time" can be adapted here as "Jazz is the blues—plus time." In other words, blues is the ailment; jazz is the treatment. Blues mourns the hardships of daily life and love—hardships made worse by the restrictions of a harshly racist society—while jazz embodies the Harlem Renaissance's optimistic vision of the future.

The term *blues* seems to have come from the phrase *the blue devils*, which dates back to at least the eighteenth century. One theory of its origin is that indigo dyers who worked in textile mills dying cloth were physically affected by the blue dye seeping into their skin, causing symptoms of depression. But the blues as we've come to know it in music had much more emotional origins, evolving from the slave songs, spirituals, field hollers, and other forms of music that slaves and dirt-poor laborers sang to express the hopelessness and darkness of spirit they sometimes felt. Blues and jazz singer Alberta Hunter (1895–1984) captured the essence of those emotional origins with her own description of the blues: "Blues means what milk does to a baby. Blues is what the spirit is to the minister. We sing the blues because our hearts have been hurt, our souls have been disturbed."

The hurt heart and disturbed soul can express themselves in various ways, and the blues attempted to embrace that entire emotional spectrum. While the musical structure of the song was fairly standard—twelve bars in $\frac{2}{4}$ or $\frac{4}{4}$ time—the lyrics ran the gamut of emotions. Blues lyrics often were a personal narrative expressing the hardships of love and life. And while those lyrics certainly evoked the mournful blues we're all so familiar with, the blues could also be humorous, playfully bawdy, or even downright graphic. "Down in the Alley" by Memphis Millie, for example, describes a prostitute having sex with johns in an alley. This kind of explicit blues song was known as gut-bucket blues because the bucket used to fashion a makeshift bass to accompany the blues was also used to clean pig intestines for chitterlings, a familiar African-American dish. The gut-bucket blues helped make the blues popular among some, but also caused a backlash among the more "upstanding," churchgoing members of the black communities. But, as we've seen so far in the history of jazz, every musical innovation—whether ragtime, blues, or jazz itself—provoked a moral backlash. In some cases, the indignation was based on an affront to prevailing morality; but some of the rejection of the music was based on blacks not wanting to be associated with the sensuality and earthiness that they felt played into the negative stereotypes whites already had of them. How, they wondered, would African-Americans be taken seriously as artists, thinkers, and businesspeople if the image white America constantly saw was a black face singing about sex, cheating, and runaway fathers? However, the blues was so much more than gut-bucket songs, much more than revealing the emotional dirty laundry of blacks; it was also a cry of outrage that exposed the dirty laundry of American history.

The soul of the blues comes from somewhere deep inside the murky heart, but the technique of the blues has a clear musical lineage. Some historians have traced it back to the Islamic music of West and Central Africa, where slaves played stringed instruments, sometimes pressing a knife against the strings similar to the slide-guitar technique later used by blues guitarists. In the United States, the blues evolved out of the same repressed environment. Conventional wisdom dates the beginning of the blues as a musical form between 1870 and 1900, the period following emancipation during which former slaves had to adjust to the economic pressures and personal expectations—and bitter disappointments—of freedom. Especially when that "freedom" was under constant attack by Jim Crow laws and brutal lynch mobs. Fighting to survive in the face of all these onslaughts took a heavy emotional toll on blacks, and the blues helped express their mounting frustration. Harlem Renaissance writer W. E. B. Du Bois described this frustration when he noted that "sorrow songs," the slave spirituals that were the forerunners of the blues, were "the music of an unhappy people, of the children of disappointment; they tell of death and suffering and unvoiced longing toward a truer world, of misty wanderings and hidden ways."

In part, the blues was about economics. Being poor is an enormous rock to try to shoulder up a steep hill, day after day, especially when so many are trying to kick your feet out from under you. Being poor was something many Southern whites had in common with blacks during the post–Civil War years. As a result, they developed their own form of the blues: country music. Today when we talk about the blues and country music, it's as if we're discussing two different planets. But both kinds of music developed at the same time in the same place, both expressing some of the same emotional content. In the 1920s, record companies made the distinction between the two kinds of music based solely on the color of the performer. If the performer was white, it was marketed as "hillbilly music"; if the performer was black, it was sold as "race music." Sometimes the music was so similar that record companies miscategorized the records. Certainly, when it comes to human beings reflecting on the passions of love, loss, and disappointment, there is an overlapping that is indistinguishable. Yet, as both evolved, the blues articulated the nuances of the black experience more precisely, while country music revealed that of the white experience. True, emotional urges may be universal, but how we express them, how we react to them, what options we have to do something about them—they are the result of our cultural surroundings.

African-American writer Richard Wright, author of the seminal novel *Native Son*, thought that the sadness in blues songs had a deeper, more sinister origin: "The most striking feature of these songs is that a submerged theme of guilt, psychological in nature, seems to run through them. Could this guilt have stemmed from the burden of renounced rebellious impulses?" He goes on to wonder if the sexual nature of many of the songs isn't in fact more about the impotence of black people in failing to act on their own behalf in the face of the racism that was at the root of much of their "blues." Weren't the blues just redirected self-loathing, the result of an oppressed people believing the oppressor's propaganda that they are not worthy? Still, Wright admired the blues for nurturing an indomitable spirit that still lurked within: "Yet the most astonishing aspect of the blues is that, though replete with a sense of defeat and down-heartedness, they are not intrinsically pessimistic; their burden of woe and melancholy is dialectically redeemed through sheer force of sensuality, into an almost exultant affirmation of life, of love, of sex, of movement."

W. C. HANDY: FATHER OF THE BLUES
The blues as a separate musical form received its "official" launch in 1912 with the publication of W. C. Handy's (1873–1958) "Memphis Blues." Though Arthur Seals's "Baby Seals' Blues" and

Hart Wand's "Dallas Blues" were published that same year, W. C. Handy became the most famous—and took the most credit—mostly because his skill as a musician was matched by his ability as a businessman. He promoted himself as the Father of the Blues and eventually the tag stuck. Handy's legendary story of how he discovered the blues, recounted in his 1941 autobiography, *Father of the Blues*, only adds to the music's giddy mythology. In 1903, thirty-year-old Handy, the son of an ex-slave turned minister, was waiting at a train stop in Tutwiler, Mississippi. Handy was already an accomplished musician, the leader of the Mahara Minstrels, a small orchestra that played operatic overtures and popular songs. As he waited for the late train, trying to sleep, a raggedly dressed black man sat beside him and began playing the guitar, sometimes pressing a knife blade against the strings for a more mournful sound meant to imitate the voice of the singer (a signature technique in the blues). He began singing, "Goin' where the Southern cross' the Dog." Confused by the words, Handy asked him what they meant. The man explained that he was going to where the Southern railroad crossed the Yazoo Delta railroad, which black sharecroppers had nicknamed Yellow Dog. Said Handy, "This was not unusual. Southern Negroes sang about everything. Trains, steamboats, steam whistles, sledge hammers, fast women, mean bosses, stubborn mules. . . . They accompany themselves on anything from which they can extract a musical sound or rhythmical effect, anything from a harmonica to a washboard." From this, Handy realized that the power in a song could be generated by the most mundane experiences.

That encounter awakened Handy's musical curiosity, but another event awakened his business acumen. While he was leading his orchestra at a dance in Cleveland, Mississippi, he received a note from a spectator requesting that he play some "native" music. Admittedly, he was baffled, but led his orchestra in an old-time Southern medley. Immediately afterward, he received a second note, this one asking if it would be okay if a few local musicians played for a while. Happy to take what amounted to a paid break,

Handy agreed. Three scraggly black musicians took the stage; their only instruments were a battered guitar, a mandolin, and a shabby bass. Handy described their music "as pretty well in keeping with their looks. They struck up one of those over-and-over strains that seem to have no clear beginning and certainly no ending at all. The strumming attained a disturbing monotony, but on and on it went, a kind of stuff that has long been associated with cane rows and levee camps."

Classically trained Handy could only shake his head at the noise and enjoy his paid break. Until something unusual happened. The patrons began to throw money at the upstart band. Recalled Handy, "A rain of silver dollars began to fall around the outlandish, stomping feet. The dancers went wild. Dollars, quarters, halves—the shower grew heavier and continued so long I strained my neck to get a better look. There before the boys lay more money than my nine musicians were being paid for the entire engagement. Then I saw the beauty of primitive music. They had the stuff people wanted. It touched the spot."

THE BLUES LOOKS FOR THE GREEN: THE JUMP TO MAKING RECORDS

Indeed the people wanted it, but getting it to them was not that easy. Records were the best way to spread the music. In the 1920s, the United States was riding a wave of unparalleled prosperity. Homes were quickly filling with the latest products: 12 million homes had radios and 30 million automobiles roamed the streets. Record players were also flying off the shelves, creating a demand for more records. In 1927 alone, 100 million records were sold. Some of this prosperity even trickled down to the poorest homes. Much of the rural South did without electricity, yet by 1930, as many as a third of the families in these poor, remote areas owned a phonograph player, for which electricity was not needed. What *was* needed, however, was more records.

Black composer and bandleader Perry Bradford (1893–1970) saw the need and did everything he could to meet it. Bradford tried to convince white executives from phonograph recording companies to let him record one of his own songs—using a black singer. His pitch to the executives was not based on racial indignation or a plea for artistic innovation, just pure marketing sense. "There's fourteen million Negroes in our great country," he told them, "and they will buy records if recorded by one of their own, because we are the only folks that can sing and interpret hot jazz songs just off the griddle correctly." Record companies continued to be skeptical, rejecting his appeal. In his autobiography, *Born with the Blues*, Bradford recounts the combination of wile and humility required: "I had greased my neck with goose grease every morning, so it would become easy to bow and scrape to some recording managers. But none of them would listen to my tale o' woe, even though I displayed my teeth to them with a perpetual-lasting watermelon grin." Finally, Bradford convinced Fred Hagar of Okeh Records to take a chance. Despite the threats from disgruntled whites of a boycott of both Okeh records and phonograph machines, on February 14, 1920, Mamie Smith recorded Bradford's "That Thing Called Love" and "You Can't Keep a Good Man Down." Though the songs were more pop tunes than blues, though the studio musicians were all white, this was the first time a blues singer was recorded.

The record was a hit, prompting Okeh to return Mamie Smith to the studio to record Bradford's composition "Crazy Blues." This time the musicians, the Jazz Hounds, were black, and this time the song was authentic blues. The record surpassed expectations, selling an amazing seventy-five thousand copies in its first month of release. Bradford and Smith's success started a stampede of record companies anxious to capitalize on this latest trend. The public was hungry for race music, and Northern recording studios were the only restaurant that served it. But the demand was so great that by 1923 the competition decided to do "field recordings." Recording companies hauled their equipment down to the South, hobbled together makeshift studios in hotels, schools, and hired halls. Like some Andy Hardy version of *American Idol*, long lines of black performers waited to audition, and executives obliged by recording nearly any musician who had a woeful song.

The blues has few rigid musical characteristics. Rather, its impact comes from the style of the performer. As the blues grew in popularity, the many variations of style came to light, providing a clearer demarcation between blues and jazz. Country blues usually featured a singer accompanied only by a banjo or guitar, or sometimes without any instrument. The most notable figures in country blues included Robert Johnson (whose guitar playing was so magnificent that he claimed his skill was the result of making a deal with the devil), Charlie Patton, Leadbelly, Blind Lemon Jefferson, and Blind Blake. Often these musicians had little formal training and were unable to play with other musicians in a group setting. But that quality was more a strength than a detriment, because it allowed them to focus on their music as a personal testament. Indeed, Alberta Hunter declared, "The musicians that didn't know music could play the best blues. I know that I don't want no musicians who know all about music playin' for me."

The Memphis blues style offered a more funky orchestration, including unusual instruments such as jugs, washboards, fiddles, kazoos, and mandolins. Notable artists included Memphis Minnie, John Estes, Robert Wilkins, and Joe McCoy. Memphis blues style is credited by some experts as being the first to separate lead and rhythm guitar into clearly defined roles, the precursor to rock 'n' roll and pop music.

Probably the most famous style was the city blues, which was more elaborate and featured many female singers such as Mamie Smith, Bessie Smith, and Victoria Spivey. In fact, it was the female singers who popularized the blues, while men desperately tried to play catch-up. At the forefront of these influential women was Gertrude "Ma" Rainey, known as the Mother of Blues. A stout woman with a mouthful of gold teeth, Ma Rainey was as beloved for her kindness as she was admired for her voice. She performed many of her own compositions as well as those of other writers. Working her way up through various minstrel shows, Rainey became, by the 1920s, Paramount Records' biggest-selling star. (Owned by the Wisconsin Chair Company, Paramount Records, after failing to profit from white popular music, turned to "race music," becoming one of the most influential recording companies in the field until its demise in 1932.) Ma Rainey retired in 1935, settling down to run her two theaters in Georgia and immerse herself with the Congregation of Friendship Baptist Church, of which her brother was deacon. When she died in 1939, her death certificate named her occupation as "housekeeper."

The influence of the blues has been traced through some of the greatest icons in American musical history. Louis Armstrong, Duke Ellington, Miles Davis, Bob Dylan, Tracy Chapman, and the Red Hot Chili Peppers have all recorded blues songs. Modern variations of the blues, such as the West Side blues, the Chicago style, the Texas style, American rock-blues fusion, and the British rock-blues produced blues-inspired music from musicians such as Taj Mahal, Ry Cooder, the Paul Butterfield Blues Band, Fleetwood Mac, the Rolling Stones, the Yardbirds, Cream, Janis Joplin, Jimi Hendrix, Led Zeppelin, Canned Heat, ZZ Top, and many others.

In describing the unrelenting racism that produced a social and economic environment that spawned the blues, Richard Wright lamented, "The American environment which produced the blues is still with us, though we all labor to render it progressively smaller. The total elimination of that area might take longer than we now suspect, hence it is well that we examine the meaning of the blues while they are still falling upon us." Although he said that in 1959, some argue that the edgier and more aggressive rap and hip-hop music of today merely continues in this same tradition. Even more important, perhaps the continuing appeal of blues is a testament to its artistry beyond its origins. Not a static monument to historical racism, the blues has become accepted as a universal language for expressing certain emotions, regardless of one's cultural background. Its lasting value lies not only in the injustice it exposes about American history, but in the depths it reveals about the human heart.

WHEN JAZZ WAS YOUNG: NEW ORLEANS

Despite the blues' popularity, the 1920s and 1930s are referred to as the Jazz Age, not the Blues Age. And though the blues strutted and fretted its hour upon the stage of the Harlem Renaissance, jazz was the showstopping main attraction. Jazz orchestrated the sophisticated yet playful attitude of the Renaissance. Blues and jazz musician B. B. King (b. 1925), who was inducted into the Blues Foundation Hall of Fame in 1984, acknowledged this difference when he said, "Jazz is the big brother of the blues. If a guy's playing blues like we play, he's in high school. When he starts playing jazz, it's like going on to college, to a school of higher learning."

Jazz would school the country about the principles of the Harlem Renaissance.

The New Orleans of the late nineteenth century where jazz was born was the perfect place for a new musical form that combined the music of various cultures. After all, since the city's founding in 1718, New Orleans had been owned by the French, then the Spanish, then back to the French, then to the United States. Even the black population was diverse: some came from Africa, some from the Caribbean, and some were native born. All these cultural influences blended together to provide a fertile and receptive site. "You got something to offer," the city seemed to say, "then toss it into the gumbo and we'll see how it tastes." That gumbo received its most flavorful spice from the culture of the American slaves. The eventual dish was jazz. Ted Gioia (*The History of Jazz*) describes the result: "Anthropologists call this process 'syncretism'— the blending together of cultural elements that previously existed separately. This dynamic, so essential to the history of jazz, remains powerful even in the present day, when African-American styles of performance blend seamlessly with other musics of other cultures, European, Asian, Latin, and, coming full circle, African." Of course, this tumultuous syncretism also defines the creation of the United States itself: the blending together of various cultures and nationalities that previously existed separately. This is why jazz is seen as symbolic of something greater than the sounds of the notes, why it is called America's classical music.

Although the musical ingredients to make jazz were already in place—the slave songs, work songs, call-and-response songs, gospel songs—these elements came together in New Orleans because that was the only open kitchen door. In most other states, which were dominated by Christianity, African music was considered pagan and therefore not allowed. Various states banned drums (which they feared would be used to signal slave uprisings), horns, or any loud instruments. However, Louisiana, with its confluence of so many cultures, permitted them. In fact, New Orleans featured Congo Square (today appropriately called Louis Armstrong Park), where slave dances were routinely held. These slave dances, called ring shouts, involved hundreds of dancers swaying, stomping, and chanting. The form of this ritual dance, which continued to take place well into the twentieth century, reveals the initial bridge of African music to American culture. As bandleader Paul Whiteman (1890–1967), known as the King of Jazz, said, "Jazz came to America three hundred years ago in chains." But in New Orleans, the rattle of those chains became the rhythm of a new age.

New Orleans gave jazz not only its unique sound, but also its name. The word *jazz* is a derivative of *jass*, a slang term for sexual intercourse. *Jass* itself is thought to be a derivative of either *jism* (semen) or *jasmine*, the favored scent of perfume among local prostitutes in the brothels where some early jazz players performed. Because the audience at brothels seemed to be preoccupied with other matters than listening to music, these musicians overcame their own boredom by playing for each other, messing with the prescribed notes, bending them, slurring them, changing the emphasis, altering the rhythm—what they called "jassing it up." In some way, their relationship with the music was similar to that of the brothels' clients with the female employees. A joyful, playful intimacy resulting in a burst of inspired sound.

African-American writer James Baldwin wrote, "It is only in his music, which Americans are able to admire because a protective sentimentality limits their understanding of it, that the Negro in America has been able to tell his story." Certainly it's true that the history of jazz is also the history of African-Americans. Yet, while no one doubts the essential African influences that went into the creation of jazz, it is also clear that many other cultural influences contributed to shaping its personality. Many of the standard instruments used to play jazz—the trumpet, saxophone, trombone, and double bass, for example—came from Europe, as did some of the music theory that jazz musicians used as a jumping-off point. Jazz musicians used these elements the way master origami artists use a plain sheet of paper, folding it again and again, transforming it into an intricate shape that no longer resembles the original form, though that form still determines the structure. Nor can the influence of Spanish music be ignored. Famed New Orleans jazz musician Ferdinand "Jelly Roll" Morton claimed that "if you can't manage to put tinges of Spanish in your tunes, you will never be able to get the right seasoning . . . for jazz."

Clearly the creation of jazz required a lot of influences from a lot of different cultures. Although many white musicians are key figures in the development of jazz—including Paul Whiteman, Benny Goodman, Stan Getz, Dave Brubeck, etc.—there has always been some controversy about the role of non-African-Americans in jazz. Famed jazz trumpeter Roy "Little Jazz" Eldridge often claimed he could easily tell the difference between white and black musicians playing jazz. In 1951, British jazz critic Leonard Feather accepted this as a challenge and arranged a blindfold test in which Eldridge would listen to jazz recordings and determine which musicians were black and which were white. In the end, Eldridge was wrong most of the time, finally admitting,

"Couldn't tell who was colored and who was white. They could be Eskimos for all I know."

Rather than indicting Eldridge, the results underscore what jazz scholar Jurgen E. Grandt refers to as "the apparent paradox that jazz music is at once a distinctly black American art form as well as a cultural hybrid." Although the artists may express their own insights, pains, and joys born from their own unique experiences, once they send the art out into the world, it belongs to everyone. Sylvia Plath's poem "Daddy" may reveal her own oppressive relationship with her father, but once it is published, it becomes the articulation of anyone who identifies with it. One can claim paternity, but once the child is grown and on its own, the parent no longer controls the child. With an art form, no one gets to claim stewardship. In fact, the true mark of success may be when the art form can stand apart from the parent, when it bleeds into the collective unconscious of all society. Maybe this is what historian Carter G. Woodson (1875–1950), known as the Father of Black History, hoped for when he commented, "What we need is not a history of selected races or nations, but the history of the world void of national bias, race hate, and religious prejudice." A lofty utopian ideal that might just have become realized in jazz.

WHEN JAZZ WAS HIP: HARLEM

As jazz music evolved, the meaning of the word *jazz* also evolved from its origins as a crude reference to sexual intercourse; used as a verb, *jazz* now meant "to make enthusiastic, lively." And when jazz came to Harlem, it "jazzed" the whole town. Harlem was remade in jazz's image, transforming it into a bustling epicenter of entertainment. Though jazz was not born in Harlem, jazz was treated here like a favorite son. And jazz returned the favor by boosting the local economy. Most of the greats played Harlem, in every venue possible, from high-class nightclubs to smoky jazz joints to neighborhood rent parties. On any given night, one could enjoy the musical stylings of Bessie Smith, Duke Ellington, Billie Holiday, Fats Waller, Fletcher Henderson, Cab Calloway, Chick Webb, Louis Armstrong, Eubie Blake, James P. Johnson, William Grant Still, and many others. In Harlem, jazz developed into the jubilant, sassy, hopeful music that the rest of the country—including white America—would come to embrace as the sound track of not just a race, but an entire age. The Jazz Age.

The Jazz Age in Harlem "officially" began on April 6, 1917, the same day the United States declared war on Germany and entered World War I. While American naval forces steamed toward Europe to engage the enemy, the Harlem Renaissance was engaging the enemy of racial stereotypes. Ironically, the first salvo fired by jazz in New York came from a white band: the Original Dixieland Jass Band. The band's leader, Nick La Rocca, described their style: "Jazz is the assassination of the melody and the slap of syncopation." Playing at the Paradise Room of Reisenweber's Café on Columbus Circle, they introduced this New Orleans–style jazz and started a chain reaction that created the Jazz Age, changing the way whites perceived blacks—and the way blacks perceived themselves.

This chain reaction didn't just happen; it was fueled in part by booze. Or lack thereof. Between 1920 and 1933, the Eighteenth Amendment outlawed alcohol. Prohibition wasn't just the dour reaction of a few constipated party poopers, it was a reflection of the national mood of a lot of Americans. Individual states were already banning alcohol at an increasing rate: in 1905 alcohol was illegal in only three states, but by 1916 it was illegal in twenty-six of the forty-eight states. A lot of people wanted America to clean up its act. But there were two Americas: the one attempting to curtail the excesses of an increasingly indulgent society; and a society that was looking to increasingly indulge itself. One preached the practice of restraint; the other practiced the particulars of celebration. This latter group continued to indulge in alcohol, either homemade or purchased in "speakeasies" (so called because the patrons had to "speak easy" to convince the guard at the door to allow them entrance). The speakeasies that populated Harlem at the time offered illegal alcohol and unrepentant jazz, generating a partylike atmosphere that guaranteed the popularity of both.

The Prohibition Era was the perfect dance partner for the Jazz Age because it created an irresistible Forbidden Fruit Syndrome. By wagging a stern parental finger, Prohibition made the booze all the tastier to the "hipsters," who saw themselves as the fun, carpe diem half of society. While the 1960s declared itself the era of "sex, drugs, and rock 'n' roll," the 1920s was more like "sex, booze, and jazz." Although history has rightly elevated the jazz greats to the firmament where they belong, these musical movers and shakers weren't saints. They were musicians playing music for people in the mood to party. And they didn't mind partying themselves. When jazzman Tommy Dorsey (1905–56) was told his band had to arrive on a film set at 8 a.m., he replied, "Jesus Christ, my boys don't even start vomiting until eleven."

Harlem became the place where any desire might be fulfilled, an adult Disneyland whose motto could have been "the hippest place on earth." Within a few years of that first Original Dixieland Jass Band performance, Harlem developed a thriving nightlife of such legendary proportions that downtown Harlem became a must-see on the itinerary of nearly every white celebrity and well-to-do traveler visiting New York. In Harlem, jazz's newly adopted home, the music took on its own international celebrity and notoriety. Naturally, anything that popular sends off alarm bells to the guardians of social standards, and the attacks on jazz came with a ferocity rarely seen in the music world. In part, the intensity of the attacks was because jazz was viewed as the smirking crony to intemperance and unbridled sexual behavior. The general tone of the attacks is reflected in the 1921 comments of Fenton T. Bott, head of the National Association of Masters of Dancing: "Those moaning saxophones and the rest of the instruments with their broken, jerky rhythm make a purely sensual appeal. They call out the low and rowdy instincts. All of us dancing teachers know this to be a fact. . . . Jazz is the very foundation and essence of salacious dancing."

Embedded within the criticism was a measured fear of sensuality, and a conventional attitude about anything associated with African roots. Harlem Renaissance intellect James Weldon Johnson argued that the only way to dispel white people's preconceived notions about black people would be by dispelling their bias toward Africa itself: "Popular opinion has it that the Negro in Africa has been from time immemorial a savage. This is far from the truth. Such an opinion is possible only because there has been and still is an historical conspiracy against Africa which has successfully stripped the Negro race of all credit for what it contributed in past ages to the birth and growth of civilization." Despite the barrage of condemnation, jazz continued to thrive and spread its influence. As usual, the forbidden fruit was winning out over the "healthy" diet.

However, those feasting on jazz tended not to be the middle- and upper-class blacks, many of whom were deliberately distancing themselves from their African-American heritage because they saw it as a barrier to acceptance among whites. "The average Negro family did not allow the blues or even raggedly music played in their homes," recalled Harlem jazz pianist Willie "the Lion" Smith (1897–1973). "Among those who disliked this form of entertainment the most were the Negroes who had recently come up from the South to seek a better life." Their dislike wasn't just a matter of musical taste, it was a matter of practical adaptation. As Smith observed, "Native or longtime Harlemites looked down on Southern blacks." To gain acceptance from their fellow blacks, these transplanted Southerners discarded anything that identified them as such, including clothes, food, the way they talked, or the music. Harlem Renaissance intellectuals fought against this racial hierarchy as well as the jettisoning of their cultural past. W. E. B. Du Bois argued that the past had to be embraced if African-Americans were going to be accepted for who they were rather than how much they could become like whites: "In this merging, he wishes neither of the older selves to be lost." While that was fine in theory, in reality, whether from the upper class, middle class, or Deep South, each group was trying to reinvent itself to be accepted by others, and to accomplish that, they disavowed jazz. Ironically, over the next few years, jazz would help them be accepted for who they really were—their "older selves."

While jazz changed the face of Harlem, Harlem reciprocated by changing the sound of jazz. Four factors contributed to this change: the size of the venues in Harlem; the popularity of Latin music; musicians commuting outside of Harlem; and the proliferation of rent parties. Because the ballrooms where musicians played in Harlem were larger, holding more people, the jazz bands became larger so they could produce louder music. More brass instruments and saxophones, recalling jazz's origins from marching bands, produced the fuller sound that helped make it so popular. At this time, jazz wasn't about sitting around swooning over the skill of the musicians, it was all about the dancing. Though times were tough for Harlemites, they adhered to the old saying "We are fools whether we dance or not, so we might as well just dance." And jazz adapted to both the venues and the customer expectations. When Duke Ellington moved his band to the Cotton Club in Harlem, he had to nearly double his band size from six to eleven. Jazz bandleader Paul Whiteman's dance bands were so popular that he had sixty-eight bands using his name, eleven of them in New York City.

The influence of Latin music became more pronounced in Harlem. In 1910, jazz bandleader James Reese Europe (1881–1919) founded the Clef Club, part fraternal organization and part union for African-Americans in the music industry. More than half of the Clef Club's roster of 180 musicians were listed as Puerto Ricans. In part, this was because they had a higher level of musical training and were able to sight-read as well as play in different styles. This Latin influence was manifested in both the music and the Harlem lifestyle. W. C. Handy's "Saint Louis Blues" and "Memphis Blues" revealed a Cuban influence. Puerto Rican valve trombonist Juan Tizol joined Duke Ellington's band in 1929; together they penned the jazz classic "Caravan." "Tango teas," which featured dancing to both ragtime and tangos, became popular in Harlem. In fact, the ritzier of the nightclubs often hosted three bands: one for dancing, one for shows, and one to play Latin music, especially tangos.

Many prominent musicians who lived in Harlem commuted to their work in downtown recording studios, shows, and clubs. By the time they returned home late at night, most clubs would have been closed. Duke Ellington and Billy Strayhorn's famous "Take the 'A' Train" ("the quickest way to get to Harlem") reveals this pattern of travel. In their honor, the "after-hours" clubs arose. In these clubs, musicians gathered to play their music, not just for patrons, but for each other. And here, learning from each other, they developed their individual styles that would be incorporated into the body of jazz. These clubs weren't in it to promote musical history—they made money. In his autobiography, *Music Is My Mistress*, Duke Ellington recounted how he would earn $100 to $200 in tips from playing downtown, only to spend it all the same night at after-hours clubs. These clubs provided an alcohol-soaked petri dish for the jazz culture to thrive. Because part of the jazz musician ethos was combat by instrument, jazz musicians honed their skills by playing against each other in musical showdowns. This tradition is still plain in the infamous "duels" among rap and hip-hop artists today, including Kool Moe Dee vs. LL Cool J, KRS-One vs. MC Shan, Jay-Z vs. Nas, Tupac vs. Biggie, Ja Rule vs. 50 Cent, and Eminem vs. Benzino.

Nowhere was this combat more pronounced than among the pianists in Harlem. "Anybody who had a reputation as a piano player," said Duke Ellington, "had to prove it right there and then by sitting down to the piano and displaying his artistic wares." These jam sessions in which jazz musicians tried to outplay each other were called "cutting" contests, because each player tried to "cut" the other with his talent. This trial by musical fire became the rite of passage for the ambitious jazz musician wanting to make it in Harlem. Willie "the Lion" Smith, whom Ellington referred to as "a gladiator at heart," crushed many a newbie player in these cutting contests. Count Basie himself lost a cutting contest to pianist Seminole, who "had a left hand like everybody else has a right hand. . . . And he dethroned me. Took my crown!"

Here in Harlem, in this intensely competitive atmosphere, a new style of piano playing was born: the "Harlem stride." In this style, the left hand played a bass note on the downbeat, then a higher-octave chord on the offbeat. Meanwhile, the right hand pounded out syncopated melodies. The Harlem stride was perfected at the usual clubs as well as at the many rent parties that occurred almost nightly throughout Harlem. Because the rents were high ($12 to $30 a month more than in the rest of Manhattan) and the incomes low, rent parties became something of a necessity for people struggling to make their monthly rents. Harlem residents spent 40 percent of their income on rent, and because more migrants were always arriving daily, failure to pay rent on time meant your possessions were on the street the following day. Although such parties offered booze, food, dancing—and sometimes even more illicit amusements—the most compelling attractions were the musicians who came to play into the small hours of the morning. Jazz greats such as Fats Waller, James P. Johnson, and Willie "the Lion" Smith entertained at many rent parties. In fact, Fats Waller's music "video" of him playing his jazz hit "Ain't Misbehavin'" is set at such a rent party.

When Giants Roamed the Earth: Three Jazz Greats

The number of Harlem Renaissance jazz giants who stood as models for future generations is too large to cover here. Any list that tries to reduce the number to the most important names does an injustice to those not mentioned. But three names stand out because their influence was unique in defining and promoting jazz, and for embodying the qualities of the New Negro that the Harlem Renaissance cultivated: Fats Waller, Duke Ellington, and Louis Armstrong.

Thomas "Fats" Waller (1904–43) was born in Harlem to a Baptist minister father. Though Waller became famous for his boisterous improvisational style of piano playing that he learned from stride master James P. Johnson, he was also classically trained in music at Juilliard. These two sometimes conflicting sides of his personality defined him as both a man and a musician. On one hand, he refined his roguish persona, seeming to embody the care-free, hard-drinking party lifestyle, a lifestyle that bloated his weight to nearly three hundred pounds and may have hastened his death. Yet, he was also an ambitious, well-trained musician who wrote many popular jazz standards such as "Squeeze Me" (1919), "Ain't Misbehavin'" (1929), "Honeysuckle Rose" (1929), "Blue Turning Grey Over You" (1930), and "Jitterbug Waltz" (1942). During a twenty-year period, Waller released six hundred record-ings.

Never satisfied to just thump a piano, he conducted a success-ful tour of Europe in 1938, wrote the music for the stage show *Early to Bed* in 1943, and later that year costarred with Lena Horne and Cab Calloway in the landmark film *Stormy Weather.* So popu-lar was Waller that when he was performing in Chicago in 1926, he was kidnapped by four men and driven to a party. He was forced to a piano at gunpoint and ordered to play. He quickly dis-covered that he was the "surprise guest" at a birthday party for gangster Al Capone. Waller allegedly continued playing for the three-day duration of the party, finally being released with thou-sands of dollars he'd earned in tips from Capone and the other guests. Waller died of pneumonia at the height of his popularity at age thirty-nine.

"Music is my mistress," Edward Kennedy "Duke" Ellington (1899–1974) once said, "and she plays second fiddle to no one." The unbending determination in that statement is why, in terms of sheer range of influence, Duke Ellington towers over most other jazz artists of his, or any other, age. His father, the son of a slave, was a butler in a wealthy Washington, D.C., physician's household; from him, Ellington learned the niceties of proper dress and society manners that he adopted as a performer. His mother, the daughter of a police captain, taught him the moral and social values that guided his private life. Though raised in the servants' quarters, Ellington had access to two pianos in the main home. Both his parents could play passably well, and so their son was given lessons from the time he was six years old. As a musician, he was less than dedicated and soon abandoned playing. But a few years later he saw a young boy play the piano and was inspired to try again. He described the epiphany in his autobiography, *Music Is My Mistress:* "I hadn't been able to get off the ground before, but after hearing him, I said to myself, 'Man, you're just going to *have* to do it.'" As a result of that encounter, he composed his first song, "Soda Fountain Rag," recalling his teenage job as a soda jerk. His parents were pleased that he was playing again, though not so pleased with his music of choice: ragtime and blues.

Despite his renewed commitment, Ellington's career as a musician did not suddenly rocket him to fame and fortune. Instead, he married when he was eighteen and became a father the next year. His new responsibilities as husband and father set him on a more cautious road. He still played the piano for money, but he also pursued a career as a commercial artist, even opening a sign-painting business. Finally, he got up his nerve to give being a full-time musician another shot and, together with drummer Sonny Greer and saxophonist Otto Hardwick, moved to New York to join a band. The move was far from successful, and Ellington and his pals were forced to return to D.C., where Ellington resumed his old job of painting signs. Despite the setback, he was determined to become a professional musician. So, after a few months, back to New York he went, this time burrowing himself into the jazz community with more tenacity and business savvy than he had shown the first time. The hard work paid off: he and his band, the Washingtonians, finally got a steady job playing at the Club Kentucky.

In 1924, Ellington recorded his first song, "Choo Choo."

From that year forward, the recordings continued at a tremendous pace; in 1927 alone he made over thirty recordings. That same year, Ellington's biggest break came when his band was selected as the house orchestra for Harlem's premier nightclub, the whites-only Cotton Club (see the chapter " 'Some Technicolor Bazaar': How Harlem Became the Center of the Universe"). The Cotton Club, owned by mobster and convicted murderer Owney Madden, catered to celebrities and high society. The illegal booze flowed freely while the scantily dressed young black girls danced seductively. Ellington was well aware of the bitter irony that his music was attracting many patrons to the club, yet he would not be welcome as a patron himself. Nevertheless, for the next four years he used the Cotton Club as a launching pad for his own career, performing six nights a week while continuing to record prodigiously. He became so popular that his music was regularly broadcast live on the radio. In 1930, Ellington had his first national introduction to white audiences when he and his orchestra appeared as themselves in the Amos 'n' Andy movie *Check and Double Check*. The following year he was invited to the White House to meet President Herbert Hoover.

After that, Duke Ellington ascended to the heights of popularity that few entertainers—white or black—have ever achieved. And he achieved it during the depths of the Great Depression, when many other entertainers were scratching to make a living. Critics were comparing his music with that of Mozart, Schubert, and Bach. Some of his finest works were written during this time, including "Mood Indigo," "It Don't Mean a Thing (If It Ain't Got That Swing)," "Sophisticated Lady," "Solitude," "In a Sentimental Mood," and "Echoes of Harlem." Just as Scott Joplin pushed the boundaries of ragtime, Ellington tried to prove that jazz could be much more than what was accepted. Toward that end, he composed ever-longer works that defied the limitations of the typical three-to-four minute 78 rpm recordings: "Creole Rhapsody" (1931) was eight minutes; "Symphony in Black" (1934) was nine minutes; "Reminiscing Tempo" (1935) was thirteen minutes. Also like Joplin, Ellington was awarded the Pulitzer Prize in music long after his death (in 1999).

The Harlem Renaissance preached that talent would lead the way out of the bondage of racism. Duke Ellington's talent and intelligence provided a model for those who would try. In Ellington's achievements, white America was exposed to just what a black man was capable of. In this case, he was capable of winning many Grammy Awards; of being nominated for an Academy Award for *Paris Blues* (1961); of receiving top awards from *DownBeat, Esquire,* and *Playboy* magazines as well as the highest ranking from the Jazz Critics Polls; of appearing in and writing music for many films, including the Marx Brothers classic *A Day at the Races;* of receiving the Presidential Medal of Freedom in 1969 and the Legion of Honor from France in 1973, each country's highest civilian honor; of receiving honorary degrees from sixteen colleges and universities; of having postage stamps issued with his image in the African nations of Togo and Chad, as well as in the United States (1986); of receiving a special papal blessing from Pope Paul VI in 1969. Those are mighty shoulders from which great vistas of possibilities could be seen—and have since been achieved.

Louis "Satchmo" Armstrong (1901–71) was as popular for his exuberant personality as he was for his magnificent music. His generous and kind persona earned him the unofficial title of Ambassador of Jazz, while his energetic and innovative trumpet playing earned him the accolade of Mr. Jazz. "If anybody was Mr. Jazz, it was Louis Armstrong," said Duke Ellington. "He was the epitome of jazz and always will be." Jazz musician Miles Davis marveled, "You can't play anything on a horn that Louis hasn't played." And *Jazz* documentary producer Ken Burns noted, "Armstrong is to music what Einstein is to physics and the Wright brothers are to travel." Hard to believe they are talking about the same boy whose high jinks resulted in his being continually sent to the New Orleans Home for Colored Waifs, the final time for a year when he was twelve or thirteen after firing his stepfather's gun into the air to celebrate the New Year.

Armstrong's birthplace of New Orleans gave him exposure to jazz, the means to choose his lifestyle, while his birth into a poor family gave him the motivation to want more from his own life. He wasted no time in combining the two. He formed his own six-man orchestra when he was seventeen, quickly coming to the attention of Joe "King" Oliver, one of the most prominent jazz bandleaders of the time. In 1922, at the age of twenty-one, Armstrong moved to Chicago as a cornet player in Oliver's band. The following year, he made some of his first recordings while playing with Oliver. Oliver was a surrogate father to Armstrong, and it is a measure of Armstrong's ambition that he left Oliver to move to New York to play with the Fletcher Henderson Orchestra, the top African-American band of the time. For Armstrong to fit in better with the rest of the band, Henderson suggested he play the trumpet. Armstrong did so, becoming, some critics say, the best trumpet player ever. In addition, his unusual singing voice and performing style earned him a dedicated following. The voice—half-growl, half-laugh—was only part of the formula; he also popularized (some say invented) the "scat" style of singing, in which words are replaced by nonsensical syllables that can be lengthened or shortened to sound just like a musical instrument. This was full circle in the evolution of jazz: the instruments followed the African tradition of trying to emulate the human voice; now the human voice emulated the musical instruments. Despite his increasing influence as the Ambassador of Jazz, Armstrong was less concerned about defining jazz than just playing it. When asked to define jazz, he responded with a smile, "Man, if you gotta ask, you'll never know."

Armstrong's popularity increased as a result of his thousands of recordings, his playing three hundred gigs a year while touring Africa, Europe, and America, as well as his appearances in over sixty movies—including *Pennies from Heaven* (1936) and *Hello, Dolly!* (1969)—and dozens of television shows. Some of his hit recordings included "Stardust," "What a Wonderful World,"

"When the Saints Go Marching In," "Dream a Little Dream of Me," "Ain't Misbehavin'," and "We Have All the Time in the World." His recording of "Hello, Dolly" in 1964 achieved two landmarks: it knocked the Beatles out of the number one slot on the Billboard Top 100, and it made the then sixty-three-year-old Armstrong the oldest singer to have a number one hit. In 1990, he was inducted into the Rock and Roll Hall of Fame as an "early influence."

Some of the same criticism that a few African-American activists leveled against the Harlem Renaissance was also aimed at Armstrong. He was accused of playing a modern version of the blackface minstrel in a desperate effort to appeal to white audiences. He was also criticized for not being more openly vocal during the Civil Rights Movement. Although Armstrong preferred to stay quietly out of the political spotlight—whether because of his personality or because he feared repercussions to his career—he did support civil rights through his major financial contributions to Dr. Martin Luther King Jr. and other civil rights activists. One exception he made was in his very public 1957 criticism of President Dwight D. Eisenhower, whom he referred to as "gutless" and "two-faced" for refraining from action in the desegregation conflict in Little Rock, Arkansas. As a result, he canceled his State Department–sponsored goodwill tour of the Soviet Union, declaring, "The way they're treating my people in the South, the government can go to hell." In a Larry King interview in 1967, Armstrong discussed his civil rights stance: "As time went on and I made a reputation, I had it put in my contracts that I wouldn't play no place I couldn't stay. I was the first Negro in the business to crack them big white hotels—oh, yeah! I pioneered, Pops!"

Louis Armstrong died in his sleep of a heart attack in Queens, New York, on July 6, 1971, at age sixty-nine.

FINAL NOTES THAT LINGER:
THE LEGACY OF JAZZ

Musicologist Samuel Floyd remarked, "The Harlem Renaissance has been treated primarily as a literary movement, with occasional asides, contributed as musical spice, about the jazz age and performances of concert artists. But music's role was much more basic and important to the movement." While it's true that the great works of literature and art affected many people, reshaping how whites saw the African-American, and providing successful artists as role models for black children to emulate, that number was relatively small. It was music, specifically jazz, that reached out to the general population of America and made them reconsider the type of people who could produce such lovely sounds. As such, jazz became the most influential black-created art form in America. Miles Davis once said, "Jazz is the big brother of Revolution. Revolution follows it around." That was certainly the case here: jazz revolutionized the role of African-Americans in society.

Writer F. Scott Fitzgerald, who is credited with popularizing the phrase *Jazz Age*, observed, "The word *jazz* in its progress toward respectability has meant first sex, then dancing, then music." True, at the beginning jazz was merely the accompanying music to a larger parade of attitudes and behavior. But in the end, it was the music that endured, that outlived the Jazz Age—and every other age that has followed. The New Negro of the Harlem Renaissance was supposed to change America, and that's exactly what these extraordinary musicians did. They gave Harlem life its own sound track—and America its own musical identity. The music may have evolved over time, but its heart is still in Harlem.

Any celebration of an art form lends itself to overstatement. Let's be clear: Jazz didn't cure cancer. Jazz didn't stop world hunger. Jazz didn't even eliminate racism. But it is not an exaggeration to state that what jazz did do was provide a subtle and entertaining means to communicate to white America that black America was a lively, innovative, creative, and talented contributor to the culture. Once jazz, and all the types of music that jazz influenced, became an acknowledged part of American culture, biases began to fade. When some of a person's most treasured memories include the music of men and women of color, those musicians are seen with the same fondness as the memory. Jazz— and its progeny of rock 'n' roll, rhythm 'n' blues, soul, rap, and hip-hop, to name a few—raised generation after generation on the notes and words that articulated their teen angst, provided the lush background to falling in love, gave them the rhythm to dance at their weddings, and blared from the radio on all those long family car trips. And each of those generations has shed one more skin of racism. The Harlem Renaissance wanted America to take notice of the greatness African-Americans were capable of. Jazz accomplished just that.

"EVERYTHING WAS MOSTLY FUN"

How Jazz Influenced My Life

BY KAREEM ABDUL-JABBAR

Jazz's impact on me has been monumental. First, jazz stands as a series of mileposts that chronicle my maturation from childhood to manhood. There's a jazz song attached to the memory of every major event in my life. Miles Davis taught me how to be cool, or at least to *think* I was cool, as a gawky, towering teen. Thelonious Monk's exuberant piano playing infused me with the same exuberance on the basketball court. Certainly it didn't hurt my chances to have Sarah Vaughan and Billy Eckstine harmonizing behind the sofa when I first kissed a girl. And it wasn't just the music, but also the musicians, many of whom I met at various points in my life and whose wisdom guided me. For example, Thelonious Monk was fiercely independent and encouraged others to have faith in their own vision. He once said, "I say, play your own way. Don't play what the public wants. You play what you want and let the public pick up on what you're doing—even if it does take them fifteen, twenty years." He was talking about playing jazz, but he could just as easily been talking about playing professional basketball. That kind of confidence inspired me to be more independent, more confident of my decisions, even if others didn't agree.

Second, jazz connects me to African-American history. Because its origins date all the way back to Africa, it's like a musical slide show of four hundred years of everything that black people have had to endure and overcome and celebrate. I can't listen to certain songs without thinking about our collective history. Billie Holiday's mournful and haunting "Strange Fruit" conjures horrific images of the lynchings, mutilations, and burnings of hundreds of black people:

Southern trees bear strange fruit,
Blood on the leaves and blood at the root,
Black bodies swinging in the southern breeze,
Strange fruit hanging from the poplar trees.

Jazz reminds us never to forget just how precarious any group's place in a society can be. If we never forget their suffering, especially the causes of it, we are less likely to have to endure it again.

The third way that jazz influenced me is best summed up in Count Basie's assessment about his life as a jazz musician: "Everything was mostly fun, the whole thing!" All those generations of jazz greats who shimmied and gyrated and played their hearts out would be sadly disappointed if all we came away with was a dry, passionless historical perspective. "Not to deny that [jazz] is a thinking people's music," said jazz drummer Brian Blade, "but when I listen to music, if I ever catch myself thinking, I'm in trouble—I know something is wrong." The best of art evokes strong emotions—emotions that can later be examined as to what they mean in the larger scheme of the universe. But at the time I'm listening to the music, I just want to feel it swimming around inside my body and animating my limbs as if I were a puppet with each string tugged by a different instrument. And when the song is over, I want to feel my heart beating faster in my chest, as if something I really cared about had just happened.

Raised on Jazz

Jazz's influence on me probably started while I was still in the womb. In those prenatal months my parents sang with the famous Hall Johnson Choir, who performed some of the era's most notable choir singing onstage and on-screen. They did the choral music for the all-black movie *Cabin in the Sky* (1943), which starred jazz legends Ethel Waters, Lena Horne, and Louis Armstrong. The choir also performed in classic Disney movies, such as *Dumbo* (1941) and *Song of the South* (1946).

When I was a baby, my dad was playing his trombone at various places with other musicians whenever possible. He would often play jam sessions at Minton's Playhouse on 118th Street in Manhattan. Minton's jam sessions were famous for including jazz legends such as Thelonious Monk, Dizzy Gillespie, and Charlie Parker. Sometimes these after-hours sessions would last until after sunrise, and my mom would just put me in the stroller at seven o'clock on Sunday morning and walk up to Minton's to collect my dad for Sunday breakfast, which was an important family meal in my household.

As I got older, my dad would sometimes take me with him to rehearsal. This is where I met such jazz greats as Dizzy Gillespie, Yosef Lateef, Cecil Payne, Kenny Dorham, Randy Weston, and Max Roach. Sometimes I would be out walking with my dad and he would point out members of famous bands to me, people like Ben Webster or Jimmy Rushing or Johnny Hodges. They'd be strolling by, a bag of groceries in their arms or an unfiltered cigarette dangling from their lips, just like everyone else. They seemed a little like superheroes walking around in their secret identities.

Living in northern Manhattan meant that you would encounter jazz greats at many different places. Some of my friends went to school with Johnny Hodges's daughter. Johnny played alto for Duke Ellington's band as a principal soloist. My friend Woody Owens lived in the same building as George Duvivier, a superb bass player. Woody took lessons from George with other kids from the neighborhood. For George, it was his way of giving back to the community and keeping the tradition alive. My friend Tyrone Leonard lived across the street from Jimmy Cobb, who was Miles Davis's drummer in the later fifties. Tyrone introduced me to Jimmy when I was fifteen years old. There would often be other guys who played with Miles at Jimmy's house, which is how I got to meet bass players Paul Chambers and Ron Carter. Ben Riley, Thelonious Monk's drummer, also lived in Tyrone's building. Sometimes Tyrone would babysit for Ben and his wife, Inez. One day Tyrone had a hot date and I took over his babysitting duties. From then on Ben would leave my name at the door of the Village Vanguard Jazz Club whenever Thelonious was performing. I was there so often that I got to know the band members pretty well, and I have considered them friends ever since. I've been told that Thelonious watched the NBA finals in 1980 because he knew "that kid" from the Vanguard. It is an honor to have brought some joy to his life as he has in mine.

To us kids in the neighborhood, jazz musicians were like today's rock stars, but more humble and more connected to the people. Sure, they wanted to be successful, make lots of records, and make even more money. But for most that was more wishful thinking than a real possibility. After all, they'd chosen to dedicate their lives to a type of music in which the odds of achieving all that were slim. Even some of the more famous jazz musicians were still anxious about their next paycheck. Like wealthy athletes who stay in the game well past their prime, they were in it for love of the game. They couldn't have quit jazz even if they'd wanted to. Like my father, who, despite his prestigious Juilliard education and natural musical talent, couldn't support his family as a musician. So he became a transit cop. But that didn't stop him from jamming at Minton's or anyplace else he could find a couple of jazz musicians anxious to play. They couldn't *not* play. It was a calling.

That's what we admired about them. That's what I admired about him.

Recorded jazz was on the turntable at my home every day of

the week. Walk into our home and you'd likely hear Count Basie, Nat "King" Cole, Louis Armstrong, Billy Eckstien, Duke Ellington, and Sarah Vaughan. When my dad started attending the Juilliard School of Music, classical music was added to the mix. Still, jazz dominated and wafted through the house the same way the smells from my mother's cooking did, seeping into the walls and furniture as if it were another member of the family. It wasn't just the music that made my parents such intense jazz fans. They also felt that jazz, with its roots firmly planted in African-American history, was a dignified and enjoyable aspect of black culture and that the prominent musicians were appropriate heroes and role models for young blacks. Like most kids, I was looking for role models and mentors. I was searching for black faces who had a passion for what they did, but also knew how to project cool and confidence, the two most important tools for surviving childhood, especially at my awkward height. Duke Ellington said, "By and large, jazz has always been like the kind of a man you wouldn't want your daughter to associate with." I may not have known exactly what that meant, but I knew it was cool and confident. I knew I wanted to have those qualities.

Exposure to jazz celebrities through my dad made me feel special and also made me appreciate my dad as a musician. Once when I was five or six years old, my dad took me backstage at the Apollo Theater to meet Sarah Vaughan. A few of Dad's friends had been hired to play backup for her performance. We arrived earlier than curtain time and he took me to Sarah's dressing room. Even at my young age I knew that Sarah was a major star, and so I was afraid to approach her. She was sitting in front of one of those multibulbed makeup mirrors smoking a cigarette in her dressing robe. With a little prompting from my dad, I walked up to her and said, "Hi, Sarah," and she said, "How you doin', boy?" After saying "Fine" I was at a loss for words. She just chuckled and made some small talk with my dad. Some thirty-five years later, in 1986, I was doing some master-of-ceremonies work for the Los Angeles Playboy Jazz Festival and had the chance to meet Sarah again. She didn't remember our first meeting but she still had her easygoing regal presence. And she was still at the pinnacle of female vocalists.

Louis Armstrong was a favorite of mine at an early age, just as he had been a favorite of my dad's from his childhood. I vividly remember when I was nine years old going to the movie theater with my mom to watch *High Society* (1956), a remake of the classic film *The Philadelphia Story* (1940), starring Cary Grant, James Stewart, and Katharine Hepburn. Only this was a musical version starring popular jazz singers Bing Crosby, Frank Sinatra, and the incomparable Louis "Satchmo" Armstrong. His nickname was short for "satchel mouth," due to his saddlebag cheeks. His charisma, lively sense of humor, and charm—the way he seemed always to be thoroughly enjoying himself—made jazz more than just music, it made jazz an attitude.

I also learned early that jazz could be used as a yardstick to measure who was and was not a worthy role model. For example, when I was attending Power Memorial Academy, an all-boys Catholic high school, there was only one black faculty member, the French teacher, Brother Watson. I remember how excited I was when he told us he was also a drummer. The perfect role model. In fact, I was so impressed that I brought an Art Blakey record to school to show him. Blakey, also known as Abdullah Ibn Buhaina, was famous as the inventor of the modern bebop style of drumming, and one of the most influential jazz musicians ever. But when I excitedly showed the album to Brother Watson, he just stared blankly and said he'd never heard of him. That would be like telling a kid today that he'd never heard of Tupac or Cypress Hill. I knew right then that, despite his being the only black teacher (and some kind of drummer), he probably wasn't someone I wanted to emulate.

MILES DAVIS: THE KING OF COOL

Someone I definitely *did* want to emulate was the King of Cool, Miles Davis.

Anyone who's ever met him, seen him, or heard his music knows you only need one word to describe Miles: smoldering. The way his glaring black eyes were framed by his shining dark skin gave his face the blazing intensity of someone who just *had* to blow that damn horn in the next two seconds or explode. The way he gripped his trumpet like a weapon, a sniper horn that in his trained hands could fire a spinning jazz note straight through your heart and out the back of your head before you even knew what the name of the song was. This was a serious man of unmistakable passion, who got up every day burning to do the one thing he loved to do.

I wanted that kind of passion in my life, too.

Everyone knew he was the best jazz musician around. Unquestionably he was the best jazz trumpeter since Louis Armstrong and Dizzy Gillespie and played with all the greats of his time, including Thelonious Monk, Herbie Hancock, Wayne Shorter, and Charlie Parker. He was the touchstone at the center of nearly every movement in modern jazz: bebop, "cool" jazz, hard bop, orchestral jazz, fusion, and on and on. As one critic said, Miles was "probably the single artist who best represents the turbulent course jazz has taken." He influenced almost every other jazz musician of his time, and most who came after. (In proof of the breadth of his influence, he was inducted into the Rock and Roll Hall of Fame, the St. Louis Walk of Fame, and the Big Band and Jazz Hall of Fame.) But I wasn't a musician. I was a kid, a kid who towered over others but still needed someone to look up to. Miles was the epitome of everything I hoped to be: stylish, physically fit, and the best at his chosen profession. And look up to him I did. Still do.

My first exposure to Miles was in 1959, when I was about twelve. My dad brought home the Miles Davis–Gil Evans album of *Porgy and Bess*. (Three of my dad's friends play in the orchestral ensemble.) Originally, *Porgy and Bess* was an opera written and performed in 1935, during the Harlem Renaissance, with music by George Gershwin and libretto by his brother Ira Gershwin and DuBose Heyward, the author of the novel *Porgy*. All three white.

Now, opera is definitely not something I would have wanted to listen to then (or, to be honest, now). Nor am I especially sympathetic to the idea of three middle-class white men writing about what it was like to be living in a poor black community in Charleston, South Carolina, in the 1930s. But Miles Davis must have liked it, and my dad must have liked it, so I thought I'd give it a fair chance. (Not until much later did I find out that Harlem Renaissance poet Langston Hughes had described Heyward as a man who saw "with his white eyes, wonderful, poetic qualities in the inhabitants of Catfish Row.") I am so glad I didn't let those cocky adolescent biases stop me from listening, because that dynamic album became a milepost for me, marking my entry into puberty and young manhood.

Recently, jazz critic Robert Gilbert wrote about the power the album still generates, almost fifty years after its release: "In jazz, only a handful of albums never lose their lustre. Each listening is a magical experience, no matter how familiar the material has become. . . . *Porgy and Bess* is one such distinctive recording. . . . It reaches a higher plateau than most, though, in its way that it can reach the listener on both a musical and emotional level." Of course, back then, just barely a teenager, I wouldn't have been able to describe its effect on me so eloquently. I just knew that the music moved me in ways I hadn't experienced before—and that Miles Davis was the coolest, most dignified man I'd ever seen. That elegant personal style he exuded was as influential on me as the music.

I first saw Miles in person while he was training at the Harlem YMCA on 135th Street and Seventh Avenue, the same place where Harlem Renaissance poets Countee Cullen and Langston Hughes used to read their poetry and where writers Hughes, Ralph Ellison, Claude McKay, and James Baldwin all lived at one time or another. At the time, I was in high school and sometimes hanging with Wilt Chamberlain, who also worked out at the Y. Wilt's nightclub, Small's Paradise, was nearby. Small's Paradise had been one of the most prestigious black-owned clubs during the height of the

Harlem Renaissance, featuring roller-skating waiters who would dance the Charleston while carrying trays. This was a favorite club for important Harlem Renaissance figures, including Alain Locke and Countee Cullen. Wilt and I entered the gym and I saw Miles deeply focused on his boxing routine, his white T-shirt soaked with sweat, his sinewy muscles sharply defined. I was immediately impressed by how dedicated and disciplined he was in his workout, as dedicated and disciplined as he was with his music. It made me admire him even more.

I didn't meet him then; that honor wouldn't take place for a few more years. In the spring of 1966, we met for the first time at the Orange County Jazz Festival in California. He didn't know anything about me and was rather brusque, saying only that a guy my size would probably have to pay $500 to have a necktie made. Not exactly the deep bonding moment I'd hoped for. But when we met again two years later, it was a very different experience. I ran into him on the corner of 135th Street in Harlem, just as he was coming out of the YMCA. By now I had achieved some acclaim as part of the UCLA program and he knew who I was. We talked on that busy corner like old acquaintances happy to see each other after a long separation. We spoke about the NCAA tourney and he said he liked the way I played the game. "You're not like Wilt, dunking everything!" He admired my dedication, discipline, and elegance—all of which I'd learned from him.

After our talk, he invited me to his town house in the West Seventies to watch fight films of his favorite boxer, Johnny Bratton, a welterweight champ in the early fifties. Johnny was seen as a smaller version of the incomparable Sugar Ray Robinson. Sitting there in Miles Davis's living room, watching his intense eyes follow the fighters around the ring, I could feel his respect for me, which gave me a sense of accomplishment that I'd never experienced before.

Miles Davis playing *Porgy and Bess*. Still one of my favorites. Two other of my favorite albums are Miles and Gil collaborating on *Miles Ahead* and *Sketches of Spain*. Miles's powerful trumpet blaring out mournful notes something like a lone wolf howling on a moonless night. A sound not easily forgotten.

JOHN COLTRANE:
A MUSIC FROM WITHIN

The autumn of 1965 was a rough time for me. I was an eighteen-year-old kid just starting my freshman year at UCLA. Everyone was expecting great things from me, but my usual support system of friends and family were three thousand miles away. Worse, Los Angeles was nothing like New York City. The buildings were short and squat, like a theme-park, kiddie-size version of New York. And what was up with all those frilly-topped palm trees sticking up in rows like parking meters. Where was the noisy subway always pulsing just under the surface of the streets, keeping everyone knocking against each other as they moved about the city? How did people out here interact if they were always locked up in their climate-controlled cars?

One aspect of Los Angeles that helped me adjust was the thriving jazz scene. Listening to jazz made me feel connected to my family, to my friends, to my old neighborhood. I started frequenting the local jazz clubs to plug into that feeling of being back home, to wash away the loneliness. Clubs such as Shelly's Manne-Hole, The Lighthouse, and Marty's on the Hill consistently featured top jazz performers. One day I saw an advertisement for the It Club announcing that John Coltrane would be appearing for a weekend engagement. I was excited because, although I had most of his records, I'd never seen him perform live. I had a slight connection with his drummer, Elvin Jones, who'd gone to high school with my uncle, Steven Alcindor, and I hoped that would be enough to get to meet "Trane." It was. Elvin was happy to see me and hear news about my uncle Steven. Then he introduced me to John Coltrane.

At this time, John Coltrane was already considered one of the best saxophonists and composers in jazz. He'd played with Miles Davis, Dizzy Gillespie, and Johnny Hodges and was making sounds with his sax that nobody had heard before. But what most impressed me when I met him was his quiet, spiritual presence. I knew he'd gone through some personal changes in the past few years after he'd married Naima, a Muslim convert (as I would one day be). His submission to Islam helped him kick his problems with heroin and alcohol. His spiritual quest didn't stop there; he'd studied Hinduism, the kabbalah (made popular today by such practitioners as Madonna, Mick Jagger, and Britney Spears), yoga, African history, and even the Greek philosophers. "During the year 1957, I experienced, by the grace of God, a spiritual awakening," he once explained, "which was to lead me to a richer, fuller, more productive life. At that time, in gratitude, I humbly asked to be given the means and privilege to make others happy through music." That year I'd met him, he'd released an album called *Meditations*, which he'd said was designed to uplift people: "To inspire them to realize more and more of their capacities for living meaningful lives. Because there certainly is meaning to life." This selfless ambition brought him to study music from all over the world, searching for specific sounds that he hoped would even cure illness. He described his quest: "I would like to bring to people something like happiness. I would like to discover a method so that if I want it to rain, it will start right away to rain. If one of my friends is ill, I'd like to play a certain song and he will be cured; when he'd be broke, I'd bring out a different song and immediately he'd receive all the money he needed." (Louis Armstrong had a similar belief in the healing powers of music: he would send records—a variety of sounds, not just his own—to mental institutions and the labor rooms in hospitals, believing the music would nurture people's spirits.)

As I stood before Coltrane that night, shaking his hand, I could feel a warmth in his grip that seemed to come from some glowing source within him. He was humble and patient enough to listen to me babble about all his records I owned. Between sets I got into a conversation with Jimmy Garrison, Coltrane's bassist. He gave me an impromptu bass lesson in the dressing room. I also exchanged a few words with McCoy Tyner, the group's piano player. But it was those few moments with John Coltrane that most impressed me. Often it's best not to meet one's heroes, because the experience can be disappointing, but this was the exception. The evening was even more special than I had hoped for.

If Miles Davis taught me something about dedication, passion, and personal style, John Coltrane taught me about having purpose. For him, it wasn't enough to just play music to entertain; he wanted his notes to reshape the world, to make it a happier, more fulfilling place for everyone. Okay, that might have been too much for an eighteen-year-old kid to take on, but it made me realize that maybe basketball wasn't just a game. Maybe, like jazz, it was an art form that also had the power to transform the audience. Maybe when they saw one of us make a difficult shot, they were inspired to try to do something that had before seemed impossible, but now seemed within reach. Maybe when they sat shoulder to shoulder, screaming in unison for their team, they felt like a team themselves, no longer isolated in climate-controlled cars, but like a church choir belting out a gospel song. And maybe they left the building a little happier with themselves and with their world.

Thanks to John Coltrane, I now felt part of all that.

SATCHMO'S WONDERFUL WORLD

I never met Louis "Satchmo" Armstrong, but he also had a major impact on shaping an aspect of my personality. Earlier in this chapter I mentioned listening to him as a child, enjoying not just his lively style, but also his joyful attitude. But as I became older, I came to appreciate another less-known but courageous aspect of Satchmo: civil rights advocate.

To most people, even fans of his, that aspect of his life may come as a surprise. It's certainly not what he's known for. Instead, he's known as the man who popularized jazz in America and abroad, among blacks and whites, from the time of the Harlem Renaissance until his death in 1971. Jazz critic Nat Hentoff describes his legacy: "The one undisputed fact of jazz history is that Louis was the first, stunningly original jazz soloist to set timeless standards for imagination, daring, virtuosity, rhythmic assurance and unconquerable spirit." Billie Holiday put it in more sensual terms: "He didn't say words, but somehow it just moved me so. It sounded like he was making love to me. That's how I wanted to sing." His smiling face and endearingly croaky voice were familiar all over the world. Yet, many people in the black community had a problem with his style. That huge toothy smile seemed to play up to the old stereotype of a shufflin'-grinnin' Negro from a minstrel show. Was that happy-go-lucky trumpeter grinning onstage who he really was, or was that just a character he was playing to make himself more popular among whites? For many blacks, the jury was out as to where his heart was on the subject of black equality. Even my mom and dad, who were big fans of his music, would wonder from time to time about Louis's civil rights position.

Then on September 18, 1957, the world learned his true feelings. In Little Rock, Arkansas, Governor Orval Faubus defied federal orders to desegregate the schools by bringing in the National Guard to prevent African-American children from attending Little Rock Central High School. At the time, Louis Armstrong was so popular worldwide that the U.S. State Department had asked him to conduct a goodwill tour of the Soviet Union. Upon hearing what was going on in Little Rock, and disgusted at President Eisenhower's lack of action in either stopping Governor Faubus or protecting the children, Louis stunned the world with his response. He canceled his trip to the Soviet Union, saying, "The way they are treating my people in the South, the government can go to hell." Then he accused President Eisenhower of being "two-faced" and of having "no guts," and Governor Faubus of being an "uneducated plowboy." The State Department accused Louis of providing propaganda to use against the United States, not realizing that what was going on in Little Rock gave the Soviets a lot more propaganda material than anything Louis had to say. When selecting Louis as one of the Top 100 Most Important People of the Century, *Time* magazine commented on the incident, stating that when the Little Rock standoff occurred, only Louis condemned it: "There was not a peep heard from anyone else in the jazz world. His heroism remained singular."

The backlash was immediate. Recording sessions and concert dates were suddenly being canceled. But Satchmo wouldn't back down. He took the barrage of criticism from some of the public and press without flinching. In my home—as in many other homes of African-Americans—my mom was pleasantly surprised by Louis's determined stand. She'd always been a fan of Louis the musician, but from that day on she became a permanent fan of Satchmo the man. Louis's civil rights stance never diminished. In 1965, when Dr. Martin Luther King Jr. was marching on Selma, Alabama, Louis watched the bloody attacks on the marchers by police while on tour in Copenhagen. Disgusted, he commented, "They would beat Jesus if he was black and marched."

For me, Louis's courage in standing up to President Eisenhower despite the consequences taught me something about the responsibility that someone in the public eye has to use their celebrity to make the world better. That's been a goal of mine ever since. I've tried to take vocal and public stances whenever I thought a wrong was being committed, regardless of who was committing it, regardless of the public backlash. I think it would be a betrayal of Louis to do any less. Also, I hope the work I've done with various charities, just as Louis was so generous with charities, and the books I write about African-American history, will have some positive effect on the world. In other words, what he taught me was simply this: it's not enough to be a good trumpet player or basketball player, you have to be a good member of your community. Louis's outrage at racial injustice never diminished his cheerful hopefulness. He summed up his attitude in a letter he wrote to jazz critic Leonard Feather: "I'd like to recall one of my most inspiring moments, I was playing a concert date in a Miami auditorium. I walked on stage and there I saw something I'd never seen. I saw thousands of people, colored and white, on the main floor. Not segregated in one row of whites and another row of Negroes. Just all together—naturally. I thought I was in the wrong state. When you see things like that, you know you're going forward."

JAZZ AND BASKETBALL

From everything you've read so far, there can be no doubt that jazz has made me a better person than I would have been without it. The music inspires my passion to participate fully and richly in life. And the jazz greats I've known, from Miles Davis to John Coltrane to Louis Armstrong to my dad, have inspired me to be disciplined, ambitious, caring, and dedicated to my community.

But jazz has also made me a better basketball player.

Now, if that statement motivates a bunch of young basketball hopefuls to rush to their computers and download classic jazz tracks onto their iPods, then I'm pleased. Because the values I learned from jazz to apply to basketball are values that apply off the court as well.

Many people unfamiliar with jazz think the music is all about the solo riffs. A single player suddenly jumping to the front of the stage, the spotlight shining brightly on him, while he plays whatever jumble of notes that pop into his head. But really, jazz is just the opposite. True, there are magnificent solos, but those moments aren't the point of jazz, they are all part of the larger musical piece. Each person is playing as part of the team of musicians; they listen to each other and respond accordingly. When the time is right, one player will be featured, then another, and so on, depending upon the piece. Indeed there is improvisation, but always within a musical structure of a common goal.

Same with basketball. When you play basketball, everything is timing, just as with a song. You must be able to instantly react to the choices your teammates make. You must be able to coordinate your actions with your teammates' and you must understand when you need to take over the action—when to solo—and when to back off. The timing of group activity is a major part of basketball, as it is with jazz. A team of basketball soloists, without the structure of a common goal, may get TV endorsements for pimple cream, but it doesn't win championships.

Many athletes listen to music while they train, whether it's jogging, lifting weights, or just stretching. The type of music depends upon what motivates that individual. For me, jazz not only motivated me, but also helped me perfect my footwork on the court. Unlike some other types of music, jazz has a unique combination of being explosive yet controlled, measured yet unpredictable. The exact virtues necessary for effective footwork while in high school. Before every Saturday practice, I would listen to Sonny Rollins for a little motivation. Then I'd hit the gym floor with his music in my head and in my feet.

Jazz has also provided a valued source of camaraderie with other players. During my career with the NBA, some of the loneliness of those long road trips was eased by sharing my love of jazz with other players that were jazz enthusiasts, including Walt Hazzard, Spencer Haywood, and Wayman Tisdale. Wayman was also a bass player and released a few records himself. Most of the other guys also enjoyed pop, rhythm 'n' blues, and reggae, but I stayed pretty faithful to jazz, listening to other genres only if jazz wasn't available.

I was also excited on those occasions when a jazz great sang the national anthem before one of our games. Cab Calloway, a major jazz star from the Harlem Renaissance, sang the national anthem several times at Warrior games in Oakland. Grover Washington Jr. performed it, and Earth, Wind, and Fire have played it both at the Forum and the Staples Center. My favorite jazz instrumental version of the national anthem is Wynton Marsalis's performance at the 1986 Super Bowl XX. My favorite vocal version by a jazz singer was sung by Al Jarreau. I don't know if hearing a jazz artist perform the national anthem made me play any better, but I like to think so.

It Don't Mean a Thing If It Ain't Got That Swing

"The memory of things gone is important to a jazz musician," said Louis Armstrong. "Things like old folks singing in the moonlight in the backyard on a hot night or something said long ago." The memory of things gone is important to all of us, because the more we know about the past—our personal past as well as that of the rest of humanity—the better we can choose which direction to go in the future.

In the large scope of things, that Kareem Abdul-Jabbar likes jazz is pretty insignificant. But what isn't insignificant is the impact jazz has had on African-American history as well as American history. The men and women who created and refined the jazz sound during the Harlem Renaissance had America dancing and moving to a sound it had never heard before. And they had white Americans appreciating black artists as they never had before.

Certainly we are not obligated to listen to jazz just because it has historical significance. All the jazz greats from the Harlem Renaissance such as Duke Ellington, Count Basie, and Louis Armstrong would be horrified if they saw children being spoon-fed jazz as if it were some bitter-but-good-for-you medicine. I feel the same way. I hope that through your exposure to the history of jazz and through my history with jazz, you'll be curious enough to play a few of the tunes discussed. But if you don't, jazz will endure. Because, in the end, jazz isn't about musical theory or historical significance or even personal memories.

It's about toe-tapping.

It's about head-bobbing.

It's about wanting to get up out of your chair and move your body just because you're alive and the world is fat with possibilities—and because it just feels so good to swing.

PHOTO CREDITS

BIBLIOGRAPHY

Anderson, Jervis. *This Was Harlem: 1900–1950*. New York: Farrar Straus Giroux, 1982.

Anderson, Paul Allen. *Deep River: Music and Memory in Harlem Renaissance Thought*. Durham: Duke University Press, 2001.

Ashe, Jr., Arthur. *A Hard Road to Glory: The African-American Athlete in Basketball*. New York: Amistad, 1988.

Baker, Jr., Houston A. *Modernism and the Harlem Renaissance*. Chicago: University of Chicago Press, 1987.

Banks, Jr., William H., ed. *Beloved Harlem: A Literary Tribute to Black America's Most Famous Neighborhood, from the Classics to the Contemporary*. New York: Harlem Moon, 2005.

Bontemps, Arna. *The Harlem Renaissance Remembered: Essays Edited with a Memoir*. New York: Dodd, Mead & Co., 1972.

Davis, Francis. *The History of the Blues*. New York: Hyperion, 1995.

Feather, Leonard. *From Satchmo to Miles*. New York: Stein and Day, 1972.

Floyd, Samuel A., ed. *Black Music in the Harlem Renaissance*. Knoxville: University of Tennessee Press, 1990.

Floyd, Samuel A. *The Power of Black Music: Interpreting Its History from Africa to the United States*. New York: Oxford University Press, 1995.

George, Nelson. *Elevating the Game: Black Men and Basketball*. Lincoln: University of Nebraska Press, 1992.

Gioia, Ted. *The History of Jazz*. New York: Oxford University Press, 1997.

Greenberg, Cheryl Lynn. *Or Does It Explode? Black Harlem in the Great Depression*. New York: Oxford University Press, 1991.

Haskins, Jim, et al. *Black Stars of the Harlem Renaissance*. New York: John Wiley & Sons, Inc., 1992.

Hill, Laban Carrick. *Harlem Stomp! A Cultural History of the Harlem Renaissance*. New York: Little, Brown and Company, 2003.

Huggins, Nathan Irvin. *Harlem Renaissance*. New York: Oxford University Press, 1971.

Jones, LeRoi. *Black Music*. New York: William Morrow, 1967.

Kitwana, Bakari. *The Hip Hop Generation: Young Blacks and the Crisis in African American Culture*. BasicCivitas Books, 2002.

Kuska, Bob. *Hot Potato: How Washington and New York Gave Birth to Black Basketball and Changed America's Game Forever*. Charlottesville: University of Virginia Press, 2004.

Lapchick, Richard E. *Smashing Barriers: Race and Sport in the New Millennium*. New York: Madison Books, 2001.

Lewis, David Levering. *The Portable Harlem Renaissance Reader*. New York: Penguin Books, 1994.

Locke, Alain, ed. *The New Negro: Voices of the Harlem Renaissance*. New York: Touchstone, 1992.

Margolies, Edward. *Native Sons: A Critical Study of Twentieth-century Negro American Authors*. New York: J. B. Lippincott Company, 1968.

Oakley, Giles. *The Devil's Music: A History of the Blues*. New York: Taplinger, 1976.

Oliver, Paul. *Blues Fell This Morning: Meaning in the Blues*, 2nd edition. Cambridge: Cambridge University Press, 1990.

Osofsky, Gilbert. *Harlem: The Making of a Ghetto, Negro New York, 1890–1930*. New York: Harper & Row, 1964.

Peterson, Robert W. *Cages to Jump Shots: Pro Basketball's Early Years*. Lincoln: University of Nebraska Press, 1990.

Ramsey, Jr., Guthrie P. *Race Music: Black Cultures from BeBop to Hip-Hop*. Berkeley: University of California Press, 2003.

Rayl, Susan J. *The New York Renaissance Professional Black Basketball Team, 1923–1950*. Diss. Pennsylvania State University, 1996. Ann Arbor: UMI, 1996. 9702370.

Southern, Eileen. *The Music of Black Americans*, 3rd edition. New York: W. W. Norton, 1997.

Spencer, Jon Michael. *The New Negroes and Their Music: The Success of the Harlem Renaissance*. Knoxville: University of Tennessee Press, 1997.

Thomas, Ron. *They Cleared the Lane: The NBA's Black Pioneers*. Lincoln: University of Nebraska Press, 2002.

Vincent, Theodore G., ed. *Voices of a Black Nation: Political Journalism in the Harlem Renaissance*. San Francisco: Ramparts Press, 1973.

Wall, Cheryl A. *Women of the Harlem Renaissance*. Bloomington: Indiana University Press, 1995.

Watson, Steve. *The Harlem Renaissance: Hub of African-American Culture, 1920–1930*. New York: Pantheon Books, 1995.

Wintz, Cary and Paul Finkelman, eds. *Encyclopedia of the Harlem Renaissance*. New York: Routledge, 2004.

ACKNOWLEDGMENTS

I wish to thank all who helped get this project up and running—a list that must begin with the late Dr. John Clarke, who conceived the Harlem Youth Action Project. It was during my participation in HARYOU-ACT that I first learned of the enormous contribution black Americans have made to the United States and world culture. I must also acknowledge Mr. Arthur Schomburg, whose Harlem museum is a treasure trove of history that encompasses so many particulars of black achievement. I would also be remiss if I didn't give heartfelt thanks to my cowriter, Raymond Obstfeld, whose talent and dedication permeates every chapter of this book; and to my financial guru, Deborah Morales, whose day-to-day contribution and unerring energy greatly helped to lighten my load as we saw this sometimes daunting project to completion.

To my good friend Rafee Kamaal for sharing my dream and encouraging me to put in written form the story line that ended up as this book. I'm also grateful to the film's investors, who were willing to risk loss, so convinced were they that this vital piece of heritage be preserved. They include the Dreier family, Ozzie Silna, Michelle Brown, Michael Carabini, Grant Hill, Chris Webber,

Erika Bjork, Stephon Marbury, Etan Thomas, Jerry Reinsdorf on behalf of the Chicago Bulls, Allison Weiss-Brady and Chip Brady, and Rodney Hunt. Thank you one and all for your friendship and support. A special thanks to Chad Dreier, the first to step up and offer me his hand in friendship, not to mention his business acumen. It has also been my good fortune to have the backing of Bob Costas and Dennis Gilbert, two dear friends who saw me through a difficult period of transition. To Herbie Hancock for his insightful musical genius and Spike Lee for his gracious guidance that helped make this dream a reality. To will.i.am for embracing our cultural heritage by integrating these musical insights into today's hip-hop culture. My art team, Dustin Tanalin and Jeremy Castro were invaluable for their creative and artistic contributions. Many thanks to my editor, Kerri Kolen, for helping put all the pieces together. And finally, I extend my gratitude to the NBA, the Basketball Hall of Fame, the NBA Players Association, the Chicago Bulls, and the Los Angeles Lakers for helping to spread the word throughout the basketball community that we are, all of us, truly standing on the shoulders of giants.

INDEX

Hodges, Johnny, 241, 249
Hoffman, Abbie, 66
Holiday, Billie, 34, 41, 62, 187, 225, 240, 251
Holiday Inn (film), 121, 204
Holman, Nat, 157, 174
Holy Providence School (Cornwall Heights), 179–80, 186, 188–89, 191
homosexuality, 84, 103–4
Horne, Lena, 34, 231, 241
House Un-American Activities Committee (HUAC), 113–14, 185
housing, 11, 12–14, 30–31, 32, 42, 44–45, 49, 157–58, 230
Howard University, 81, 94
Howe, James Wong, 184–85, 186
Huggins, Nathan I., 82
Hughes, Langston, 109–15; art views of, 113; autobiography of, 113; Baldwin compared with, 133; black reactions to works of, 112; and blues, 112, 114; as *Chicago Defender* columnist, 21; contributions and influence of, 4, 54, 90, 109–10; and Cullen, 84, 108, 111–12; death/funeral of, 114, 115; and Du Bois, 70, 71, 111, 132; Fauset's support for, 91; and *Fire!!* magazine, 84, 104; first visit to Harlem of, 111; and Garvey, 111; Harlem homes of, 39, 105, 246; Harlem of youth of, 48; on Heyward, 246; and Hurston, 113; influence on KA-J of, 4, 53, 131–32; and jazz, 112, 114, 133, 195–96; and Johnson, 73, 132; KA-J's research on, 53; late years of, 114; and legacy of Harlem, 46; and Locke, 83, 84, 113, 132; and McKay's *Home to Harlem*, 94; Mason's support for, 85–86, 112–13; and NAACP, 111; and New Negro, 83, 84, 112; on ordinary Negroes in Harlem, 42; personal and professional background of, 110–11; and politics, 113–14; and race issues, 112, 113, 133, 182; as representive of Talented Tenth, 91; sexual orientation of, 103; and Thurman, 102, 104; travels of, 111, 113; and

Van Vechten's work, 88; and white influx into Harlem, 35; and writers as activists, 134; writings/publications of, 46, 55, 84, 85, 104, 110–15, 133; and YMCA, 40, 246. *See also specific work or magazine*
Hunter, Alberta, 104, 213, 219
Hurston, Zora Neale, 94–99; age of, 96; attitude about life of, 98–99; audience for, 94–95; awards and honors for, 95–96; black reactions to writings of, 96–97, 132; and civil rights, 98; death of, 98, 106; education of, 95, 96; on fear, 57; and feminism, 94–95; and *Fire!!* magazine, 84; and folktales, 96, 97, 132; and Great Migration, 27; Harlem homes of, 39, 105; and Hughes, 113; influence on KA-J of, 4, 53, 59, 132; influence of, 106; and Johnson (Charles S.), 73, 94; late life of, 97–98; literary debut of, 94; and Locke, 83, 94; Mason's support for, 86, 96; and New Negro, 83; Niggerati of, 88, 105; personal and professional background of, 95–96; and race issues, 98, 132, 182; rediscovery of, 98; themes in works of, 96–97; and white audience, 132; and working-class blacks, 132; writings of, 86, 94–95, 97, 104, 132

"If We Must Die" (McKay), 24–25, 92–93
Illidge, Eric, 160, 163, 167
Isaacs, John "Boy Wonder," 159, 160, 161, 163, 167, 169, 173, 174, 192
Islam, 54, 79, 128, 249

jazz: as America's classical music, 222; and basketball, 253–55; black reactions to, 195–96, 197, 213, 226–28; and blues, 196, 198, 212, 219, 221; call-and-response in, 5; as change agent, 9, 194–95, 237; and Conventional White Wisdom, 130; cultural influences on, 221–24; definition of, 194, 212, 235; Ellington's comment about, 193; and *Fire!!* magazine, 84; greats of, 230–36, 255; in Harlem,

weapon against old racial, 74; and basketball, 4, 166, 167; and blues, 213; and copying white ideals of beauty, 35–36; in film and radio/TV, 203–4; and foreign-born blacks, 188; and Harlem Renaissance, 182, 204, 225; and images of Harlem, 8; and jazz, 195, 196; and Joplin, 211; and minstrel shows, 121; and piano, 205; and science, 122; and whites as nightclub patrons, 33, 35

The Sting (film), 206, 211

Strivers' Row, 38–39, 103

Student Nonviolent Coordinating Committee (SNCC), 128

Sugar Hill, 39

Supreme Court, U.S., 16, 132, 186

Survey Graphic magazine, 81, 82, 86

syncopation, 208, 225, 230

"Take the 'A' Train" (song), 39, 229

Talented Tenth, 5, 71–72, 73, 74, 75, 79, 80, 84, 107–8. *See also specific person*

Tatum, Art, 212

Taylor, John G., 14

Tenderloin, 10–12, 14, 15

Their Eyes Were Watching God (Hurston), 94–95, 97

Their Eyes Were Watching God (TV movie), 98

Thurman, Wallace, 102–6; black criticisms of, 112; contributions and influence of, 53, 102, 105, 106; death of, 106; descriptions of Harlem by, 29–30, 31, 38–39, 48, 49, 105; and Du Bois, 103, 104; and *Fire!!* magazine, 84–85, 104–5; and Harlem Renaissance, 61–62, 102, 103, 106; health of, 105–6; as homosexual, 103–4, 105; and Hughes, 102, 104; influence on KA-J of, 53; and leadership of blacks, 65; and Locke, 104; and New Negro, 104, 105; personal and professional background of, 104; and politics, 102; and race issues, 102–3, 106; and rent parties, 44–45; as representive of Talented Tenth, 91–92; reputation

of, 105; on Striver's Row, 38–39; and Van Vechten's work, 88; writings/publications of, 104–5, 106

Tizol, Juan, 228

Toomer, Jean (Nathan Eugene), 61–62, 70, 83, 84, 91, 99–102, 112, 130, 182

Tubman, Harriet, 2

Tucker, Earl "Snakehips," 34

Turan, Kenneth, 178

Turpin, Tom, 208

Tuskegee Institute, 67, 92

Tyner, McCoy, 250

UCLA, KA-J at, 58, 132, 190, 247, 248

Universal Negro Improvement Association (UNIA), 29, 75, 76, 77, 78–79, 128

Van Vechten, Carl, 88, 97, 187

Vaughan, Sarah, 239, 243–44

Village Vanguard Jazz Club, 242

Virginia Minstrels, 200–201

Walker, A'Leila, 36, 39

Walker, Alice, 36, 98

Walker, "Fleet," 140

Walker, Madame C. J., 36

Waller, Thomas "Fats," 29, 45, 63, 225, 230, 231

Washington, Booker T., 18, 67–68, 69, 75, 89, 129, 205

Washington, Chester Jr., 173

Washington, Dinah, 62

Washington, Grover Jr., 254

Washington, Kenny, 141

Washingtonians, 232

Waters, Ethel, 34, 41, 104, 241

Watson, Brother, 244

Webb, Chick, 225

West Indians/West Indies, 27, 42, 43–44, 48, 77, 186–87

Whirty, Ryan, 166–67

White, George Henry, 18–19

"White House" (McKay), 84, 94

White Mountain Apache basketball team, 118

White, Walter, 17–18, 39, 83, 109

Whiteman, Paul, 222, 223, 228

whites: at Apollo Theater, 41; and art as propaganda, 131; backlash in 1960s by, 54; as benefactors of Harlem Renaissance, 61; blacks as imitators of, 35–36, 202, 227–28; and blacks as musicians, 200, 203; boll weevils as divine retribution on, 20; and challenges facing Harlem writers, 121–22, 123; and Civic Club dinner (1924), 81; and Cullen, 108; flight from Harlem of, 38; and goals/mission of Harlem Renaissance, 3, 5, 9–10, 19, 35, 42, 52, 89–90, 129–30, 182, 237, 238; Harlem as enclave of, 10, 12, 13–14; and Hughes writings, 114–15; and Hurston's writings, 97, 132; idealization of Harlem by, 8–9; images of blacks held by, 33, 35, 121–22, 123, 129–30, 166, 182, 201, 205, 227; and impact of jazz, 195; intimidation by black athletes of, 191; and Johnson's support for other writers, 89; Joplin's views about, 210; and KA-J's name change, 123; as landlords in Harlem, 13–14; as Lenox Avenue tourists, 30, 32; and Locke's *The New Negro*, 82–83; in minstrel shows, 200–201; as nightclub patrons, 8, 29, 32, 33–35, 233; and ragtime, 209, 210; superiority of, 122; as targets of black writers, 88; and Thurman's works, 103; and Washington's leadership, 67–68. *See also* Ku Klux Klan; race issues; stereotypes
Wideman, John Edgar, 137
Wilkins, Roy, 39
Wilson, Edith, 34
Winfrey, Oprah, 98
Within Our Gates (film), 135
women: as blues and jazz singers, 202, 219–20; in minstrel shows, 202
Wooden, John, 132, 161–62
Woodson, Carter G., 2, 224
words, importance of, 60–61, 123–24, 125, 131

work songs, 198, 222
working-class blacks: adversity of, 13, 42–45; and Baldwin's writings, 133; and Black Bohemia, 10–11; and blues, 213; and Garvey, 75–76, 77, 125–27; and Great Migration, 20–21, 42; Hughes's writings about, 112, 133; Hurston's writings about, 96–97, 132; and images of Harlem, 28; and jazz, 197; on Lenox Avenue, 30–33; and overcrowding, 42–43; as part of "Daily" Harlem, 9; racial hierarchy among, 43–44; rent parties of, 44–45; wages of, 10–11, 20–21, 30, 42, 44, 199–200
World Professional Basketball Tournament, 137–38, 139, 167, 169, 170–73, 177, 180, 181, 183, 192
World War I, 15, 20–23, 24, 76, 225
Wright, Richard, 21, 62, 215, 220
writer(s): as activists, 134; and art as propaganda, 131; challenges facing Harlem, 121–22, 123; Civic Club dinner (1924) for, 81; Du Bois's support for black, 71; as embodiment of Harlem Renaissance, 5, 62–63; and end of Harlem Renaissance, 61; Great Eight, 86–115; as heroes, 115–16, 123; influence on KA-J of Harlem, 119–36; and jazz, 197; Johnson's views about, 73; KA-J as, 117–18, 134–35, 191–92; as leaders of black movement, 73; legacy of, 115–16; major literary themes of Renaissance, 87; and 135th Street, 40; and race issues, 182; restraints on, 131. *See also* art/artists; *specific person*

YMCA, Harlem, 40, 53, 109, 246, 247

Zulu Cannibal Giants, 166

About the Authors

Recognized by *Sports Illustrated* and *Time* magazine as history's greatest basketball player (he is the NBA's all-time leading scorer), KAREEM ABDUL-JABBAR is also the author of several New York Times best sellers. His previous books include *Giant Steps*, *Kareem*, *Black Profiles in Courage*, *A Season on the Reservation*, and *Brothers in Arms*. Since his retirement as a player for the NBA, Kareem has worked as a special assistant coach for the Los Angeles Lakers and acted as a volunteer coach for children on the White Mountain Apache reservation in Whiteriver, Arizona. *On the Shoulders of Giants* is currently in production as a documentary film.

An associate professor of English at Orange Coast College, RAYMOND OBSTFELD is also the author of over forty books of fiction, poetry, and nonfiction, including studies of the Italian Renaissance, Napoléon Bonaparte, and *Moby-Dick*.